Daily Guideposts, 1982

Daily Guideposts, 1982

GUIDEPOSTS

Carmel, New York 10512

Unless otherwise noted, Scripture references herein are from the King James version of the Bible. Verses marked RSV are taken from the *Revised Standard Version* of the Bible, copyrighted 1946, 1952 © 1971, 1973. Verses marked LB are taken from *The Living Bible*, copyright 1971 by Tyndale House Publishers, Wheaton, Illinois. Used by permission. Verses marked ML are taken from the *Modern Language Bible, The New Berkeley Version in Modern English*. Copyright © 1959, 1969 by Zondervan Publishing House. Used by permission.

CREDITS: "A Gift of the Heart" by Norman Vincent Peale is reprinted with permission from the January 1968 *Reader's Digest*. Copyright © 1968 by The Reader's Digest Assn., Inc.

Designed by Elizabeth Woll

Foreword

How did King David compose the Psalms? An old legend has it that one mysterious night a wind came through a window, breathed on David's harp, and made the strings quiver with a haunting melody. The music wakened David, and the wonder of it inspired him to sing. For the rest of the night, until dawn broke in the east, David "wedded words to the strains" of the harp. And the words he sang are what we now know as the Psalms.

Psalms: songs of praise. Praise to God, celebrations of His power and love.

The book you hold in your hands can't be called a book of psalms, but we do believe it is a book full of praises. And though the stories in *Daily Guideposts, 1982* were not composed to the strains of a harp, still they were created out of wonder and inspiration.

All of us, in our daily lives, encounter moments that renew our strength and inspire us to devotion, just as that midnight awakening did for David. The 365 devotionals within this book tell of times such as these in the lives of many members of our Guideposts family.

We offer them to you as daily reminders of God's lasting love. Through them we hope that you yourself will be drawn closer to Him.

NORMAN VINCENT PEALE

S	M	T	W	T	F	S
					1	2
3	4	5	6	7	8	9
10	11	12	13	14	15	16
17	18	19	20	21	22	23
24	25	26	27	28	29	30
31						

The First Commandment

Thou shalt have no other gods before Me.

—EXODUS 20:3

ALMIGHTY God,
In my mind's eye I see
Your hard and fast Commandments
as a mighty arch
spanning a firmament.
It is a marvel of masonry,
this arch: ten stones,
ingeniously placed
So that the strength of each
communicates to all.
And there, in the center,
topmost,
lies the keystone
Without which all the rest
would
tumble
into
chaos.
That central stone?
The unmistakable decree
That You take precedence with me.

Almighty God,
Architect of life,
Deep in my heart
I see Your clear Commandments
As a master plan for me,
With You the center,
The solid keystone of my years.

1

O GOD, our help in ages past,
Our hope for years to come . . .

—ISAAC WATTS, HYMN

Henry Ruegg, my husband's great-great-grandfather, kept a daily journal that is a combination weather report, farm record, and family history. Some entries are amusing: Mr. Ruegg listed the birth of his seventh daughter as a postscript to the day's important news, arrival of a new herd bull from Sweden! Often, the news is poignant: "Today we buried Jacob's only son, age three. Fourth death already from summer complaint. Pray God this heat breaks soon." Always, the diary is a testimony to forward-looking faith and perseverance.

The year 1874 in Kansas was especially difficult for the Rueggs and their neighbors. On July 29, a horde of grasshoppers swarmed onto the farm, methodically and monstrously devouring every green, growing thing. The effects of the devastation were recorded in the final entry of the year:

December 31, 1874

I harvested this year:
from 8 acres of corn, nothing
from 36 acres of wheat, 350 bushels
from 6 acres of oats, feed only
from 2 acres vegetables and potatoes, seed only, scarce, and poor quality.

He could have quit. Many others did, moving back east or looking for work in budding towns. But he didn't. Later that same night, Mr. Ruegg turned the page and wrote in his firm, bold hand: "January 1, 1875. A fresh new year, Thanks be to God!"

When I'm tempted to quit, or grumble, or feel sorry for myself, I take out that old diary and read.

Thanks be to God for this fresh new year! —P.V.S.

2

. . . AND after the fire a still small voice. —I KINGS 19:12

I couldn't sleep so I slipped out of bed, pulled on my goose-down robe and stepped out onto the porch of the vacation chalet. Snowflakes fell through the darkness, molding the world into a whitened silence. Despite this wintry beauty, my mind soon returned to the reason for my sleeplessness.

For days I'd been plagued with doubts about my faith. "Oh, God, answer these painful questions. If you are real, if you are here, show me."

My plea drifted up into the night and seemed to vanish. A moment passed. Then something truly wondrous occurred.

As a gentle breeze stirred, I heard music. It seemed to float and twinkle on the air. It was distant, yet near.

Though I saw no one, I knew I was not alone. God was present, filling the night. My doubts evaporated into the freezing air. The wind died and with it the strange heavenly sound.

Sunlight cascaded down the mountains the next morning. I tramped in the snow feeling newly alive, when the wind kicked up and that same haunting music pierced the air. Hanging from a nearby tree was a small and graceful wind chime.

And it is surely true. God moves through our lives like a gentle breeze. And just when we think He is not there at all, if we will only be still and listen carefully, somehow, some way, we will know that He is there.

Hush! I am listening for You, Lord. —S.M.K.

3 *CLOSER is He than breathing, and nearer than hands and feet.* —TENNYSON

Floor-length plate-glass windows can be dangerous if they are so clean that they are invisible. Six-year-old Kevin Adache of East Lansing, Michigan, found this out when he crashed into one and fell bleeding amid pieces of shattered glass.

Rushing to the child, a bystander named George Fomin found that a piece of glass had penetrated Kevin's throat, piercing the jugular vein. It was clear that unless something was done immediately, the boy would bleed to death.

George Fomin had no medical knowledge or training. Frantic and helpless, he prayed an agonized prayer: "Dear Jesus, tell me what to do!"

Instantly, there flashed into his mind the vivid recollection of a page in a first-aid manual he had studied years before as a Boy Scout. As if on a television screen, he could see the diagram that indicated how various pressure points could be used to stop bleeding in different parts of the body. Encircling Kevin's neck with his hands, he pressed with his thumbs just as this extraordinary mental flashback told him to do. The bleeding stopped, and George Fomin continued to control it until paramedics arrived and took over. The child's life was saved.

What is the significance of this extraordinary episode? To me it is clear proof that the Living Christ is with us always, that when we call upon Jesus in times of crisis, He is there and He will answer. We cannot see Him, we cannot touch Him, but still He is "closer than breathing, nearer than hands and feet."

We're so grateful, Lord, for Your constant caring, concern and companionship. —N.V.P.

4

THOU shalt have no other gods before Me.

—EXODUS 20:3

A great many people like to discuss their horoscopes. Their favorite question is: "What's your sign?" Each of us, they tell me, has been born under a sign of the zodiac and thus has acquired certain characteristics attributable to that sign. Aquarians are supposed to be artistically inclined. Tauruses have a stubborn streak. Leos are born leaders. And so on.

I myself have no interest in these things. Recently a man at a party put my feelings into words.

"What's your sign?" this man was asked.

And he replied, "The Cross."

Lord, I do not put my trust in stars or planets. You are all I need.

—G.K.

5

JESUS Christ the same yesterday, and today, and for ever.

—HEBREWS 13:8

A few years ago an English newspaper, the *London Daily Sketch*, asked its readers what they thought it would be like "If Christ Came Back Today."

The answers published in the following weeks were fascinating and varied. "He would be invited to speak on television," one letter read. "Many who call themselves Christians would find themselves classed with the Pharisees of two thousand years ago."

"People would fail to recognize Him just as the people of Jerusalem failed to recognize Him two thousand years ago," said another. "We would probably not break His heart by nailing Him upon a tree. There are more polite ways of crucifixion now."

And still another letter said that "Jesus would find more to applaud than to condemn. For man improves."

Perhaps you are beginning to wonder how you yourself would have replied. So while you're pondering that, let me tell you my own favorite reply that came to the *Daily Sketch*. It came from a Roman Catholic priest who said: "The question is interesting but academic. Our Lord is still here. His church is a city set on a hill. It is we who miss the many-splendored thing. His invitation is still given to those who will take it. 'Come unto Me, all ye that labour and are heavy laden, and I will give you rest.'"

Yes, Lord, You are here — and very near — always. —V.V.

---

6 *...WE have seen His star in the east, and are come to worship Him.* —MATTHEW 2:2

Tonight, because it's Epiphany, I put on my warmest coat and sit out on the porch for a while, leaning back in the lounge chair and looking up into the January sky. The night is clear, quiet, star-graced, but there is no special star in the East this night, no bright light pointing the way to the Christ Child. If wise men from the East were studying the stars right now, there would be nothing there to lead them to the Saviour. "How would they find You?" I ask my Saviour, as I sit all snuggled in my porch chair. And I seem to hear Him reply: "They'd find me through you. You... and all my children are my shining stars."

"But I have no light," I argue.

"You have *My* light," He replies, "the light of the inner Christ."

"But I'm just an average person," I protest. "How could I lead anyone to Jesus?"

The answer comes on a breath of breeze: "The same way the Star of Bethlehem led people — by moving *yourself* closer and ever closer to Me."

Well, it's just a fantasy. Still, I think I'm going to try it — this being a star for Jesus. I'm glad it doesn't mean I have to argue with the wise or shake a shaming finger at my neighbor. Most of all, it seems, I have to move *myself* closer to Him...and then shine there. Will you be His star in the East, too?

Dear God, help me to shine, pointing the way to the Christ Child. —M.M.H.

---

7 *PRAY without ceasing.* —I THESSALONIANS 5:17

Our family has always been very close, but lately geography is beginning to separate us, as our younger members leave East Texas to pursue careers. So we've hit on the idea of a family prayer calendar in which we assign each member a specific day on which the others remember him.

My brother, being the eldest, has the first day of each month. His wife has the second, and so it goes, on down the line. My day is the seventh day of every month, and, believe me, on this day I feel an extra special glow because I know that I am being remembered by countless dear ones across the land. Since there are 60 in our family, I share my day with a cousin.

For the months with 31 days, we all use the extra day to pray for relatives we feel to be in greatest need. On February 28th we include those whose days are regularly the 29th and 30th. We've distributed calendars to each family member with names noted on each date. Your family, of course, can work out its own system.

Since today is my day, I'm using it to pray for each and every one of you across the land who are reading this book. God knows who you are. May He richly bless you.

Amen.

—F.F.

8 *...FOLLOW me, and I will make you fishers of men.*

—MATTHEW 4:19

On the island of Maui in the Hawaiian Islands, 10,000 feet above the blue Pacific, is a dormant volcanic crater. Frequently tourists make the long climb to the summit to see the spectacular sunrise, the golden rays shooting across the blackened lava-flows in awesome grandeur.

Legend has it that Maui, the folk-hero after whom the island is named, once lay in wait for the sun here. The sun's passage across the sky was too swift, crops did not have time to grow, and so Maui lassoed each of the life-giving rays as they appeared over the rim of the crater and held the sun prisoner until it promised to go more slowly across the heavens. Hence the name of the mountain: Haleakala, the House of the Sun.

A charming legend, but if you look a little deeper you will also see that it points up the difference between paganism and Christianity. In the former, the indifferent deity cares nothing for man: it has to be caught and held and tamed, whereas in Christianity it is just the opposite. There it is the patient and caring God Who waits and calls and yearns for indifferent man, trying to catch and hold him in his selfish flight across the years.

Dear Lord, You promised Your disciples that they would become "fishers of men." I pray You, spread Your gentle net under me.

—A.G.

9 *...AND having ears, hear ye not?...* —MARK 8:18

I come from a demonstrative family of huggers, and I like to be told I'm loved. But my husband is the opposite, quiet and reserved.

I'll admit I'm guilty now and then of complaining that I wish Everett would tell me he loved me once in a while. "Maybe he does," my best friend told me one morning over coffee, "and you're just not listening."

"Oh, no," I answered, "I'm a good listener."

"Then try listening between the lines," she said with a smile.

That confused me a little until recently when I was telling Everett about my plans to spend some time with my parents in their new apartment at a retirement center in another city. "There are so many loose ends," I said, "I think it might take me a week or so."

His face fell. "I'm all for your helping your folks, but I didn't know you'd have to be away for a whole week."

Suddenly I knew what my friend was trying to tell me about listening. Everett had just told me he loved me, as he probably had countless times before. But I'd never listened well enough to notice.

Are *you* listening?

Dear Lord, keep my ears open and my heart finely tuned to love's delicate whispers. —M.J.M.

10

THEN said Jesus unto His disciples, If any man will come after Me, let him deny himself, and take up his cross, and follow Me. —MATTHEW 16:24

At certain intersections in the village of Oak Park, Illinois, red-and-white signs warn drivers: "Cross traffic does not stop." I know the signs mean cars in the busy crossing streets don't stop, but each morning as I pass one of those signs I'm reminded of another way in which "Cross traffic does not stop."

As a Christian I've elected to follow the first One Who carried a cross, and to take up my own cross in His wake. But there are days when as a crossbearer I get weary. Weary of household bickerings. Weary of last-minute calls from needy community groups. Weary of doing humdrum tasks instead of glorious deeds. Those are days when I am tempted to put down my cross for a while.

But there is a huge world out there, full of people who are never free to put down their sickness, hunger or loneliness for a while. They need me. Cross traffic should never stop!

Let me run and not be weary, Lord. —P. H. S.

11

THEY have ears, but they hear not... —PSALM 115:6

It was the Monday following the holidays, and I had ahead of me a full day of cleaning, sorting, discarding, rearranging. Then the phone rang. "Hi! How about going up to the shopping mall, maybe staying for lunch?" asked my friend Marian.

Marian and I had done this several times before Christmas, and it'd been fun. But now I had so much drudgery I wanted to get out of the way. "I'm not in the mood today; I've got a lot to do," I said to her.

"Okay," she said. "Sorry I bothered you."

"Maybe another time," I said, but she had already hung up.

Engrossed in my chores I didn't give Marian any further thought. Until that night. Reviewing my day in prayer, it struck me: What Marian had wanted was not just to go shopping, or go out to lunch. What she had really been saying was, *It's hard for me to be alone today.*

Marian had been widowed less than a year ago, and though the holiday season had been difficult, her children coming home from college had helped a lot. Now, on the first day after their departure, she had asked to be with me, and I had said no.

That evening I said a prayer I often say now:

Lord, when someone speaks to me, help me not only to listen, but to hear.

—A.F.

12

IN the cross of Christ I glory,
Towering o'er the wrecks of time. —JOHN BOWRING, HYMN

Today, when I started to take down our Christmas tree, the same thought came to me that I have each year at this time. What a waste! No telling how long our tree took to grow in the forest, yet it graced our living room for only a few days. True enough, it was beautiful, crowned with a shining star that shed its light on a manger scene, and decorated by caring hands. But today, stripped of ornaments and tinsel, it was dry and brittle, and as I carried it out to the porch, it shed its needles like tears. It made me sad that this tree, like the One Whose birth it commemorates, was born to die an untimely death.

This year, however, I was struck by an idea. As my son John helped me saw off the tree's branches, the large branch at the bottom, stripped of its greenery, was just the right size to form a crosspiece. So John and I roped it on the trunk, a third of the way from the top of the tree. Then we carried it to the basement where it will stay until next spring. On Good Friday at noon, we'll bring it up again to remind us of the death of the Child Whose birth we celebrated in December. Then, on Easter Sunday, we'll place a fragrant, white lily at its base, and maybe, as we stand in front of our little tree-turned-cross, we'll hear a voice in our hearts, saying, "He is risen!" And our hearts will reply, "Alleluia!"

Birth, death, resurrection — all part of Your plan, Lord. Praise You! —M.M.H.

13 When the Bible Speaks to Me

MATTHEW 2:1-11

My middle name is Balthazar. It was my grandfather's name, but, most famously, it was the name of one of the three kings of the Epiphany. I have to admit that, as a child, I used to think the journey of the Magi was just a good story — that Balthazar was a colorful character bearing exotic things. As I've grown older, though, the second chapter of Matthew has become deeply important to me. The verses about the coming of the Wise Men are no longer make-believe.

What was Balthazar feeling as he was led by a mysterious light on his way to Bethlehem? Bewildered? Enthralled? And when he came upon this nativity of mysterious peace and power, surely Balthazar knew he was in the presence of God. He fell to his knees, then offered his treasures. True, this was just a Child, but a Child more radiant than any man Balthazar had ever known.

Epiphany was a miracle for Balthazar, and the verses describing it have become a small miracle for me, too. They have become a door for me, my first true entrance into the life of Christ. You see, I'm a young man just out of college, and I can't pretend to know fully the mature Christ of the 40 days in the desert, or the Christ of Gethsemane. I simply haven't lived enough days. The wonders of life are still often bewildering. Many trials still await me. But I can be like my namesake by making the journey to the Holy Child and offering Him what treasures I have. And in this way I am growing as He grows. — EDWARD B. PITONIAK

---

14 *BE still, and know that I am God...* —PSALM 46:10

A few years ago, while living in Venezuela, I was attending a bridge luncheon on the 16th floor of a twin-tower apartment building. Suddenly, one of the women smelled smoke. When our hostess Inez opened the entrance door, clouds of thick black stuff billowed into the living room. She screamed and slammed it shut.

As smoke began to fill the apartment, causing us to cough and our eyes to burn, we all panicked because we knew that the building did not have a fire escape. That door was the only way out of the apartment!

Soon everyone was racing around, shouting and bumping into one another. "God, help us!" one lady whispered.

As if on cue, we quieted down. "Yes, the Lord will save us," Inez said. "Now, let's pray." We all four bowed our heads. After a few moments of silence, Inez said, "I think there is a way out. We'll go out on the balcony and climb up to the flat roof just above us that connects this building to the other tower. If we can walk across the roof, I think we can get down from there." We followed her, and soon we were down on the street in safety.

Our prayers didn't stop the fire, or lessen the danger, but being in touch with God did calm all four of us enough so that we were able to think rationally. Ever since, the Scripture verse quoted above has taken on a new meaning for me. God always stands ready to help us. But to hear His voice, we first have to be *still.*

Teach me, Lord, always to think of You first in moments of stress or danger. —B.R.G.

---

15 *IF we love one another, God dwelleth in us, and His love is perfected in us.* —I JOHN 4:12

For quite a while Jessica was our only cat. She hardly ever went outdoors. She slept in the kitchen chairs, whatever bed she chose and in her favorite open window. There was always food and water at her feeding place in the kitchen. There was also affection and praise for her. Jessica had it made, and she knew it.

Then one day we brought home a new kitty, a tiny Persian whom we named Joshua. When Jessica saw him, she instantly hissed and ran out the door. She began to live in one of our cars that we seldom drive. She wouldn't come in for meals, so I fed her on the carport. She lost weight and didn't groom herself. She didn't purr anymore. Once in a while she'd venture back into the house, and, instantly, Joshua would spring forth, ready to get acquainted. Jessica would hiss and run back outdoors.

Joshua never seemed to give up on becoming friends. Whenever he got a chance he would sit inches from Jessica and regard her in a hopeful way as she glared at him, growling.

Finally Jessica relented and moved back inside, but she still growled a lot. Joshua was excited nevertheless and watched her every move, careful not to get too close. Jessica would look back at him with eyes narrowed, her tail switching back and forth in a leave-me-alone warning.

But very slowly Jessica began to let Joshua come closer. She would shut her eyes and pretend to be asleep, so she wouldn't have to growl so much, I guess. One day I caught them eating together. Another day they both slept in the same favorite chair. Jessica's growling stopped and she began to purr again.

Too often I'm like Jessica, pouting when I think another is getting love and affection that *I* deserve! How much better to be like Joshua, who never worries about how much love he deserves, but, instead, concerns himself with how much love he can give.

Gentle Jesus, help me to find a friend by being one.—M.B.W.

16

PRAYER doesn't necessarily change things for you, but it changes you for things. —ANONYMOUS

Not long ago on the radio I heard an expert on houseplants suggest that they be given names. He said he'd named his and made a habit of addressing them regularly each day with something like: "Good morning, Mary (his begonia). Looks like you're about to get a few nice new blossoms." He claimed that no sooner had he named his favorite plants than they began to flourish.

Nonsense, I thought, but then, just for fun, went ahead anyway and named my poor struggling fern Henry. I began calling out, "Hey, Henry, how'sa boy?" to him each day. Many times, as I greeted him, I remembered that he might be a little thirsty. Or could probably be turned to catch the light better. And, sure enough, Henry began to flourish. Not because *he* had changed. Because I had!

Somehow this made me think about my prayer life. Too often I pray for things to change because they don't suit me. Maybe if my prayers were directed at changing *me* I'd get better results!

Give me the vision, Lord, to see the adjustments I need to make in myself before I demand them from others. —J. McD.

---

17 *FOR man looketh on the outward appearance, but the Lord looketh on the heart.* —I SAMUEL 16:7

No getting around it, our friend Brenda's buckteeth made her very homely. But she was such a really great person that you soon forgot how homely she was. The first time four-year-old Fred met her, he stared at her teeth and exclaimed, "I hope you won't bite me!"

We were horrified. But not Brenda. "Don't worry, honey. You look good enough to eat, but I'm not going to."

Then everybody, including Freddy, burst out laughing. What a wonderful knack Brenda had for taking herself lightly. She never let a personal flaw get the better of her. No wonder we all loved Brenda so.

Lord, we all have personal flaws. Keep me from burdening others with mine. —G.N.

18

WE are not divided,
All one body we,
One in hope and doctrine,
One in charity.

—SABINE BARING-GOULD, HYMN

On this, the first day of World Week of Prayer, a day on which people everywhere bind themselves together spiritually, I think of an inscription that someone scratched on a wall in the Warsaw ghetto during World War II. It reminds me that, even when the world is at its darkest, you and I can pray — with blessed assurance — that we will see a brighter world.

This is the inscription:

I believe in the sun, even though I don't see it.
I believe in love, even though I don't feel it.
I believe in God, even though I don't see Him.

Thank You, Lord, for the gift of faith, the gift that makes prayer the mighty force it is.

—C.C.

19

BUT I say unto you, Love your enemies...

—MATTHEW 5:44

This is the birthday of Robert E. Lee, the great Confederate general beloved by his friends and admired and respected by his foes. In victory and in defeat he was a man of strength, a man who took his Christianity seriously.

I heard a story about him recently that gives the measure of the man. Someone asked him what he thought of a mutual acquaintance. "I think he's a very fine gentleman," Lee answered.

"He goes around saying some very uncomplimentary things

about you," the troublemaker said. "What's your opinion now?"

"You didn't ask what he thought of me," Lee replied with a faint smile. "You asked what I thought of him. I think he's a very fine gentleman."

"Bless them that curse you," the Master told us. It's hard, isn't it? But if you can do it, people will know you're a Christian.

Lord, help me understand that the hard things Jesus taught us can be the ones that help us most. —N.V.P.

20

...YOUR Father knoweth what things ye have need of, before ye ask Him. —MATTHEW 6:8

Once I prayed for more patience. The next day my washing machine broke down, leaving me with three dozen dirty diapers. And then, so help me, the dryer quit working five minutes after a monsoon started!

That day I was reminded of something that C.R. Findley once observed: God doesn't always answer prayer as we expect. Sometimes when we pray for a certain virtue — like patience — God does not necessarily send it to us in a package ready for instant use. He's much more likely to put us in a situation where, with His help, we are given the opportunity to *develop* that virtue.

I know I am more patient today than I was before I washed 36 diapers by hand in a bathtub and hung them to dry from the chandeliers. As usual, God's answers are best, even the unexpected ones.

Lord, help me not to narrow down my expectations of You so much that I miss your wonderful surprise answers. —S.M.K.

21 *THOU hast made us for Thyself, and restless are our hearts until they rest in Thee.* —ST. AUGUSTINE

The Scriptures speak frequently of Heaven, yet, in spite of desperately longing to believe, I had always possessed a measure of doubt in my practical mind that such a place could possibly exist.

Then several years ago, I did extensive research on Sojourner Truth, the remarkable black woman, born in slavery, who, because she could neither read nor write, memorized the Bible. Sojourner devoted the last 20 years of her life to traveling the roads of America, often on foot, preaching God's truth. A devout Christian, her faith never wavered despite poverty, cruel treatment, great sorrow or serious illness.

She died in Battle Creek, Michigan, my hometown, in 1883. Just before she died, a friend asked, "Sojourner, how can you be so sure there's a Heaven?"

Sojourner had appeared to be sleeping. Now she looked up with her dark eyes shining. "Because I've got such a hankering for it here," she replied softly and placed her hand over her heart.

That one sentence will always be with me. Like Sojourner, I have a longing in my heart. And surely God wouldn't have put that longing in human hearts unless Heaven was a reality.

I pray, Father, that You let me live a full, productive life on earth; and I thank You for the assurance of a life beyond.

—A.J.L.

22 *AND went to him, and bound up his wounds...*

—LUKE 10:34

When my children were growing up I often took them with me to see the paintings in the National Gallery in Washington, D.C. One day Melanie, then seven years old, insisted on wearing a new pair of patent-leather pumps. And before long, as we walked among the masterpieces, I discovered she was limping.

"Mommy, I've got to sit down," she admitted, heading for a marble bench. "I think I've got a blister." And sure enough, when she took off her shoe and peeled back her stocking, her poor little heel was rubbed raw.

To our surprise, a gracious-looking older woman approached us, smiling. "Here, honey, maybe I can help," she said, rummaging in her purse. "I've got a Band-Aid right here, if I can find it, and some first-aid cream too, I think." She knelt down, this sympathetic stranger, and doctored the foot of my little girl.

All around us hung the great religious art works of the ages. The Raphaels, the Rembrandts, the El Grecos and Da Vincis and countless more. While in the marble hallways were the sculpture. A great many of them depicting saints and angels. But for a long time afterward the picture etched most vividly in my memory was the radiant sight of that woman so ready and happy to help a child.

The angels we see these days are not confined to canvas or stone. They're all around us. For that matter, sometimes I'm reminded that even *I* can be one!

To all Your beauties, Lord, let me add another one today — the beauty of a good deed. —M.H.

23 *THE Lord shall preserve thy going out and thy coming in from this time forth, and even for evermore.*

—PSALM 121:8

When I called an old friend to invite her to a writing class I was teaching, she suddenly confessed that she seemed to be developing agoraphobia — the fear of open spaces.

"I can barely even shop for food," she told me. "It's become almost impossible to take that first step through the door."

She said she knew she needed counseling, but meanwhile she had to find a way to force herself through the doorway.

After hanging up, I prayed, "Lord, please show me how to help my friend."

At once there appeared in my mind the words: *Psalm 121.*

I checked the verses in my Bible. Then I took a sheet of poster board and lettered the whole psalm in india ink. I drove to my friend's house and gave the poster to her with a suggestion. "Why not try putting this by your front door and read it each time you have to leave the house? Then ask Jesus to take you by the hand and walk with you through that doorway."

A few days later I ran into her at a meeting. "That psalm helped me," she said. "I'm still a little shaky, but I'm trying — I can get out the door."

Her case was an extreme one, of course. But the message of that psalm — especially verse 8 — was right for her — and for me, too. Now, whenever I go out, I take a moment to ask the Lord to go with me. This reminder of His constant presence helps me to step out confidently.

Take my hand, Jesus. I want to walk with You. —M.F.H.

24

...SEEK ye first the kingdom of God, and His righteousness; and all these things shall be added unto you. —MATTHEW 6:33

One night, at our congregation's business meeting, a member spoke out. Too much time and worry, Emma Barling said, was being spent on how to pay the church bills and fix the roof.

"Leaking roof or not, we've got to be doing the Lord's work. If we're serving Him fully, He'll take care of the roof.

"Christmas is coming," Emma continued. "Instead of worrying about money, why don't we get food baskets together? I know of several families who can use them."

When Emma was finished, I thought she'd been awfully naive to think that "the Lord will take care of the roof." But her idea was received enthusiastically.

The congregation came through. By Christmas we had a dozen baskets, each complete with a turkey.

And after Christmas I noticed that our congregation had grown. Word of our baskets had got around; people wanted to join a caring church. As our church grew, so did our collections. The roof was fixed.

Emma Barling was right. The Lord shelters those who earnestly serve Him.

When I put You first, Lord, everything else falls into place. Keep me ever mindful of this, please. —W.D.

25

OUT of the depths have I cried unto Thee . . .

—PSALM 130:1

Cave explorers are a special breed, courageous and curious. Not long ago Ben Jones, an experienced spelunker from Colorado, discovered one of the largest chambers yet found in the famous Carlsbad Caverns of New Mexico.

In a three-day expedition there, Ben took a side trip through a narrow opening he had been meaning to explore for years. After he had crawled on hands and knees for some time, his light seemed to malfunction. When he pointed it up, there was total darkness. But when he pointed it back down to the floor of the passage, it shone brightly.

Just my luck, he thought. *I'm in unfamiliar territory and my light is failing.*

Then he noticed that if he held his hand above his head and pointed the beam of his light at it, he could see it clearly. Finally he realized that his light hadn't failed. The beam was simply disappearing into the vastness of the cavern he'd discovered.

Do you ever fret because you think when you send up a little beam of hope in the form of a prayer it is lost in the vastness of God's universe? Don't worry. Maybe your human mind can't follow it as it wings its way any more than Ben Jones' human eyes could follow his little beam of light as it ascended into the enormous vault above him. But God's all-knowing mind is sensitive enough to pick up the tiniest spiritual spark, as the Psalmist assures us.

So don't ever think your prayer light is failing. Just point it upward and let it go!

Father, guide even my most hesistant prayer until it finds its home with You.

—G.J.R.

26 *...THAT we may be able to comfort them which are in any trouble, by the comfort wherewith we ourselves are comforted of God.* —II CORINTHIANS 1:4

A few years ago, our oldest son was in a terrible car accident that left him critically injured. For weeks, I walked around with what felt like an open wound in my heart. I prayed and worried and prayed and worried until I was almost sick.

Then the Lord healed me of my pain in a most revealing way. I received a letter from an old friend who hadn't heard about the accident. She told me of her worries about her own son, who had just been admitted to a treatment center for alcoholism. How could I answer the letter? What could I say? I started praying for my friend and her son. Immediately, just-right Scripture passages for coping with her aching mother's heart came to my mind: "The prayer of faith shall save the sick" (James 5:15); "Wait on the Lord: be of good courage, and He shall strengthen thine heart" (Psalm 27:14). And in comforting my friend, I was comforted!

If your heart aches today, if you're lonely or grieving or worried, why not imagine you are called upon to comfort a friend with a similar problem? What words might you use? What Scripture passages would you offer? In searching for helpful words, you will find yourself looking at your problem in a new and overturning way. It will separate you from your trouble enough to allow God's healing grace to take over. Try it!

I draw on Your comfort, Lord, by comforting others.—M.M.H.

27 *. . . I WILL trust, and not be afraid . . .* —ISAIAH 12:2

I learned a lot more than our boxer Bronkov when we attended obedience school!

"If you want your animal to trust you," the instructor said, "you must show that you trust him."

That was the night I was to say to Bronkov, "Stay!" and then walk away from him. Without looking back! That's hard to do, of course, when you've got a dog like Bronkov who never sits still.

He's probably right behind me, I thought, as I walked away.

I looked over my shoulder and Bronkov, taking my glance as a summons, sprang forward. It took a lot of hard work for me to undo that backward glance. But when I did, Bronkov "stayed."

I've used the lesson I learned that day a good many times since. If I ask my son to do something, I no longer check on him over and over. And when I pray to God, I try to follow the same good principle. I know He's heard me. I don't have to keep nagging Him.

St. Paul tells us that "Love bears all things, believes all things. . . . " He does not say, "Better take a backward glance just to make sure."

Lord, bless me with an unquestioning faith. —J. M. B.

28 *IN Him was life; and the life was the light of men.*

—JOHN 1:4

"I'd like this set in a ring for my daughter's twenty-first birthday," I told the jeweler, holding out the rather large, square red stone I'd come across in a dusty old jewel case I'd found in our attic.

He examined it carefully through his eye glass, then said, "I think you'd better check first and see if this is a real ruby. It sure looks like it."

I felt the stirrings of excitement, as he continued, "If it is a ruby, it's worth many thousands of dollars."

I went to other jewelers — they gave the same opinion. But still they used the word, "I *think* it's real."

Then I took it to a certified gemologist who told me it was synthetic, but one of the best synthetic rubies he had ever seen.

"How can you tell?" I asked, still hoping he could be wrong.

"By the light. In synthetics the light goes straight through the stone. In real rubies the light stays inside, giving it fire and life."

There are Christians like that stone of mine — synthetic. They go to church on Sunday, but by Monday the light has passed through them. I want to be a real Christian. I want the light and fire of Jesus Christ glowing within me throughout the week.

Oh, Lord, I want my faith to be so true that it doesn't require an expert to recognize it. —A.C.

29

ONWARD, Christian soldiers . . .

—SABINE BARING-GOULD, HYMN

A young couple I know, Midge and Mark Candee, recently faced a severe family crisis, but came out of it stronger than ever. One day when I marveled at how well they had survived their difficulties, Mark said, "We did it by putting on the whole armor of God."

I thought he was speaking symbolically, but he wasn't.

Then he explained how every morning he and Midge actually went through the motions of putting on God's armor, piece by piece, as outlined in Ephesians 6:14-17.

"First, standing beside our bed, we each buckled on the belt of

Truth, saying out loud what we were doing. Then we strapped on the breastplate of Righteousness, and reached down to get the shoes of Peace for our feet. Then we picked up the shield of Faith to protect us against evil, and donned the helmet of Salvation. Last of all we grasped the sword of the Spirit.

"It might sound silly," he added, "but we were in deadly earnest. We truly believed that we had God's protection all day long. The glory of it is, we did!"

Silly? Maybe.

And maybe not.

Father, Your Holy Book is an arsenal for Christian soldiers. Show me how to use it.

—R.S.

30

EVERY good gift and every perfect gift is from above, and cometh down from the Father . . . —JAMES 1:17

"Thank goodness we made it!" I said as our plane touched down after a particularly bumpy flight.

"What did goodness have to do with it?" asked my friend in the next seat. "Let's give credit where credit is due. Thank God we're down safely."

Because so many people say, "Thank God" so casually, it sometimes feels like taking His name in vain, but my friend was right. As Schroeder says in a "Peanuts" cartoon, "Thanking goodness isn't theologically sound, Charlie Brown."

We can't earn God's grace. It's His loving gift to us. We have a steady income, thank God. Our children are healthy, thank God. We have a home, food to eat, people to love and work to do, thank God. Our goodness couldn't get these things for us. Let's acknowledge the Source.

As the psalmist wrote, "Let everything that hath breath praise the Lord. Praise *ye* the Lord."

I thank You, my Lord. —D.S.

31

REMEMBER the sabbath day, to keep it holy.

—EXODUS 20:8

If you've already decided against going to church today, please check the appropriate boxes on the following form:

I'LL NOT BE AT CHURCH TODAY BECAUSE:

- ☐ I'm too tired. I need my rest.
- ☐ Too much work to do at home.
- ☐ Visitors are coming.
- ☐ The sermons have been boring lately.
- ☐ It's the only time I have for______________ (golf, picnicking, reading the Sunday paper, etc.)
- ☐ I can pray just as easily at home.

Now sign your name,
tear the page from this book
and mail to God. —V.V.

S	M	T	W	T	F	S
	1	2	3	4	5	6
7	8	9	10	11	12	13
14	15	16	17	18	19	20
21	22	23	24	25	26	27
28						

The Second Commandment

Thou shalt not make unto thee any graven image... —EXODUS 20:4

LORD,
When I think of graven images
I think of golden calves
wooden statues
saints of stone.
And I know I'll never bow
To one of these.
So I find it easy
To follow Your commandment.

But wait...
What about those other things
That people seem to worship
Like money,
beauty,
the power of the mind —
Images not carved of stone or clay
But sculpted, insidiously,
Inside the heart.

O Father, keep my adoration image free.
There cannot be another God for me.

1 *...PRESENT your bodies a living sacrifice, holy, acceptable unto God...* —ROMANS 12:1

Parables are not just the stories that Jesus told His disciples. Indeed people today tell all kinds of useful parables. One of my favorites concerns a chicken and a pig that were walking down a country lane. They stopped outside a little white church to read a notice advertising a bazaar in support of the church's program. At the bottom of the sign they read: "Ham and Eggs Will Be Served."

The chicken said, "See! Even you and I can help the work of the church."

"Yes," said the pig, "but yours is only a contribution. Mine is a *sacrifice*."

When I first read that little parable, my conscience was pricked. For so often my contribution to God's work came as easily as a chicken laying an egg. Rarely did I find my efforts in God's behalf in the realm of genuine sacrifice.

Now as I do my small part for God in this world, I'm more inclined to pause and ask myself...is it ham or eggs?

I want to contribute to You, Lord, but don't let me shy away from sacrifice. —S.M.K.

2 *WHAT a Friend we have in Jesus...* —JOSEPH M. SCRIVEN, HYMN

I used to be hesitant about saying grace obviously in restaurants. Feeling that I might appear overpious, I tried to get away with a barely bowed head and a quick "Thanks for this meal. Amen." But a college freshman recently gave me a new perspective.

"I was really scared my first evening at the university," she told me. "I didn't know anybody there, and the thought of walking into a huge dining hall and sitting down with strangers was almost more than I could face. But while I stood in the food line, trying to spot an empty table, I saw a couple praying. Not making a big deal about it, but quietly offering thanks. Right away I felt it would be okay to sit with them. After all, we had a mutual friend — Jesus. So I went over and sat down, and we started talking. They really helped me get through those first days, and we became good friends."

These days in restaurants I bow in prayer just as I would at home. I truly want to give thanks to God, and, who knows, some lonely Christian out there might want to join me and become friends through our mutual friend, Jesus.

Thank You, Jesus, for making strangers I meet into friends.

—P. H. S.

---

3 *OLD age, the crown of life, our play's last act.* —CICERO

A friend of mine never throws anything away. No matter how old it is or what condition it's in, she finds a use for it. For instance, handles of worn-out brooms stake up tomatoes in her garden. "Everything has value," she says, "no matter how old it is."

I was reminded of her words in a recent conversation with a retired professor in my church. Since he stopped teaching, he has spent days cutting brush on the church lawn, painting the sanctuary, visiting men in prison. "I think you're busier now than when you taught school full time," I said to him.

"Why not?" he answered with a twinkle in his eye. "I'm not retired — I'm just recycled."

What a beautiful philosophy — and, come to think of it, a tried and true one. Moses was way past retirement age when he led his people to the Promised Land. Abraham and Solomon weren't exactly spring chickens at their peaks. And one of my favorite Scriptures goes: "They shall still bring forth fruit in old age..." (Psalm 92:14)

Lord, thank You for the opportunities You have in store for me all the rest of my life. —B.R.G.

---

4 *...I AM with thee, and will keep thee in all places...*

—GENESIS 28:15

Sometimes I find myself remembering night sounds of my boyhood. A freight train in the distance. Crickets in the garden. Frogs in the creek down the road. Laughter from a passing car. Church bells.

I live in a big city now and, these days, the night sounds are the low rumble of traffic, the sudden scream of an ambulance siren, a telephone nagging to be answered. But late last night I awakened for no reason, and, lying there awaiting the return of sleep, I heard the chimes of a steeple clock in a church a few blocks away. I couldn't remember ever hearing those bells before. The other night sounds muffled them, I suppose. There was a certain comfort in it. And I needed comfort, for I was feeling lonely.

As a boy when I heard steeple bells in the night, I was quite sure that nobody would be going to church at that hour, and I would say a prayer so that God wouldn't feel lonely. Last night, when I heard the steeple bells above the noises of a big city, I remembered my boyhood habit, a habit I had lost, and I said a prayer. The difference was that, this time, *I* did not feel lonely.

Oh, Lord, how You fill the emptiness of my darkest nights.

—G.K.

---

5 *...LO, I am with you alway, even unto the end of the world.*

—MATTHEW 28:20

I drove to the beauty shop in a very bad mood. "Oh, God," I despaired, "where are You? If You could just touch me for a brief moment and lift my spirits."

I turned on the radio, and, almost as if they were heaven-sent, familiar strains of "Sweet Hour of Prayer" filled the car. Then a gentle voice read Scripture. At a red light I began to cry. Not sad tears, but tears of gratitude. God had heard my prayer and touched me through this radio program.

I got to the beauty shop, but just sat in the car. As the hymns and the soothing voice of the man reading Scripture continued to minister to me, I said to the Lord: "I really don't want to leave this car. It's full of You. In the shop loud music will blare, and people will be caught up in things not of You. I am aware of Your glory inside this car. I may just sit here all day in this parking lot."

It was just at that moment that the announcer quoted Jesus saying, "Lo, I am with you alway." And right away I knew I had to get out of my car. "Now you go into that shop and take Me in there," Jesus was telling me. "Start with a smile and love in your heart for anyone you meet, for I will be with you."

Nothing should ever separate me from Your peace, Jesus.

—M.B.W.

6

...VERILY, I say unto you, I am the door... —JOHN 10:7

My friend Bob's father was a Scotsman, and he used to enchant us with Scottish tales. A favorite was about a poor man who found a beautifully carved door from a castle ruin. He carefully built it into the front wall of his modest dwelling. But the longer he lived with it the more dissatisfied he became.

The old Scot would always finish the story by saying: "The canny mon go' the bonny door for naught, but couldna bear how dreary it made his poor hoose look. So it cost him a muckle to build a hoose 'round it fine enough to go wi' his beautiful door. And, laddies, that's how it is when the Lord comes t' live wi' us."

Isn't that true when Christ becomes the beautiful door of my life? His perfection makes me want to build the finest house I can around Him.

Oh, Lord, I want to be better. I want to live up to You.—C.M.D.

7

...THAT Satan tempt you not... —I CORINTHIANS 7:5

Once upon a time the devil decided to add a new product to his line of wares and snares. It wasn't that business was bad. Ever since he'd introduced his Satan's Seven Sensations things had been going especially well for him. People gobbled up Greed and Lust and Gluttony. Pride and Envy were perennial favorites; not to mention Wrath; even Sloth was a fast mover. But the devil believed in growth. It was time, he decided, to grab off more of the market with an even bigger crowd-pleaser.

The devil went to work and came up with something that looked encouraging, and by the time the reports came in from marketing research and testing, he was convinced he had a sure-fire item. He called it "Discouragement."

Discouragement did fine for a while. The price was sinfully low, or so people thought, and for a while they bought it as though there were no tomorrow. But little by little, as the sales figures came in, the devil saw that he wasn't going to do as well as anticipated.

Why?

It seems that his old competitor, God, had brought out a product of His own, a far more effective one. God called it "Hope," and He packaged it in a great number of shapes and sizes. Perhaps you yourself have seen it in Psalm 43 or Matthew 19:26 or Lamentations 3:26. It has numerous listings in the Catalog.

Of course, Satan — who never gives up — is still selling Discouragement. But Hope is a better buy.

Dear God, everything You've done — The Book You've caused to be written, The Son You sent to us — gives us reason for hope.

—V.V.

8

THE Lord will perfect that which concerneth me . . .

—PSALM 138:8

As a mother I made more than a few mistakes. I sometimes robbed my children of the joy of being givers. At times, I was a pushover when I should have been tougher, or too firm when I should have been flexible. The list goes on, but I've learned that a mistake remains a mistake only if I allow it to smolder in my mind.

If you find yourself dwelling on past mistakes, this prayer pattern may help you. First, write down the error, including your feelings of regret and self-blame. This helps to get it out where you can see it objectively. Then, on another sheet of paper, write down the psalmist's words: "The Lord will perfect that which concerneth me." Tape, staple or glue this paper over the first one, so that it covers it completely and permanently.

Now open your Bible to Psalm 138:8, place the joined sheets of paper between the pages, and *leave them there*. If the memory of your mistake returns, just open your Bible to that symbolic reminder that your mistake is, even at that moment, being transformed by His perfecting grace.

Take my mistakes, Lord, and transform them. —M.M.H.

---

9 *ALL true work is sacred; in all true work, were it but true hand-labor, there is something of divineness.*

—THOMAS CARLYLE

My hands are often chapped and stained — even hand lotion can't seem to keep them presentable. I've learned to accept this. With a family to care for and a large yard and garden to keep, my hands get rough treatment.

I don't mind — usually. But not long ago I was invited to a benefit card party. How embarrassed I was! I wanted to sit on my hands — anything to keep them hidden.

Then as my table became acquainted, we started chatting. One woman, it seemed, visited a psychiatrist weekly. "He wants me to get involved in volunteer work," she said. "But I don't feel up to it." Later her partner confided, "Getting and keeping a housekeeper is a constant headache. Domestic workers are so hard to come by these days." The third smoked constantly. "I know I should quit," she said, "but I don't have a family so it really doesn't make much difference to anyone else. Besides, it gives me something to do."

On the way home I looked at my hands again. I no longer felt ashamed of them. And I thanked God that I had so much to do that I didn't have to visit a psychiatrist, worry about household help or chain smoke. I could hardly wait to get home and put my unattractive hands to work again.

Thank You, God, for good, honest work to do. —A.J.L.

10

...BE rich in good works... —I TIMOTHY 6:18

The bell rang. Children streamed from the school and out into the falling rain. I sat in my car out front waiting to pick up my son.

A little girl hurried by, with a large stack of books and a lunch box. Suddenly her books toppled to the ground. Then almost as quickly a boy stopped, bent down and picked them up.

I was surprised. Seldom had I seen such chivalry in my school days. The girl smiled at him and rushed on. Then something peculiar happened. The boy reached in his left pocket and pulled out something gold and shiny. Like a large coin. He held it up a second, then quickly dropped it into his right pocket.

A few weeks later on Christmas morning, my son opened a small gift from a friend. Inside was the same kind of shiny gold coin I'd seen in the boy's hand. On it were engraved these words: "Secretly transfer me to your right pocket each day after your good turn has been done." On the opposite side was the Boy Scout insignia. All at once I understood. It was a good-deed coin.

A few days later I went out and bought a Boy Scout coin for

myself. For surely the spirit of the good-deed coin should be in every pocket.

Oh, Lord, keep me busy with the currency of kindness.—S.M.K.

---

11 *AND if we know that He hear us, whatsoever we ask, we know that we have the petitions that we desired of Him.* —I JOHN 5:15

My husband Plaford and I sat down for supper.

"Your turn to say grace," I said to him.

"Thank You, God, for this food," he prayed. "Bless us. Bless those for whom we should pray. Amen." We were practically bringing food to our mouths before he'd finished saying the last words.

As we cleaned up the dishes afterward, I found myself thinking back to the way we'd been saying grace lately. "You know, Plaford," I said, "I don't think God enjoys hearing our prayers any more. We've really gotten into a rut. I'm not sure why, but I know I'm giving God less than I should."

"We're not giving God our *whole hearts* when we pray," said Plaford. "Nor our whole minds. We're not specific in what we ask for."

Plaford had put his finger on it. When we prayed, we were thoughtless, literally thoughtless. *What* blessings did we need? And why couldn't we say *who* those people were "for whom we should pray?"

We began shaping up our prayer habits. I'm so glad we did, because talking to God is an incredible privilege, and I never want to take it for granted again.

I never want to take any of Your blessings for granted, Lord.
—Z.B.D.

12 *IN the world ye shall have tribulation: but be of good cheer; I have overcome the world.* —JOHN 16:33

Here are a few facts about Abraham Lincoln.

He was born in poverty.

His mother died when he was nine.

His much-loved Ann Rutledge died when she was 19.

His marriage proposal to Mary Owens was turned down.

He was defeated in his first run for the Illinois State Assembly.

His venture into business failed; it took him 17 years to pay off the debts of his deficient partner.

He had one term in the U.S. House of Representatives, but was not reelected.

He lost his race for the U.S. Senate to Stephen Douglas.

He had four sons. One died at the age of four, another at the age of 12. Another was born with a cleft palate.

He was vilified as few U.S. Presidents have been, before or since.

— BUT —

He was not bitter.

He was even-tempered.

He was calm.

He believed firmly in what he called "the Saviour's condensed statement of law and gospel: 'Thou shalt love the Lord thy God with all thy heart, and with all thy soul, and with all thy mind... and love thy neighbor as thyself.'"

In You, Father, I too find the strength to endure. —V.V.

13

GRACE is written across all I have and all I am...

—E. STANLEY JONES

I had worked all week on a Sunday-school presentation. Then late Saturday night the head of the deacons called and said, "Nita, we're canceling your program tomorrow. We've decided to show a movie instead." I was devastated. "Lord," I exclaimed, "I really didn't deserve that!"

Perhaps. But what else didn't I deserve?

Life. Health. This day to enjoy. Love of family and friends. Freedom. Riches beyond imagination. The list is endless. None deserved!

Above all, the forgiving and saving grace of Jesus Christ, Son of God!

O Lord, give me yet one more gift: a grateful heart. —N.S.

14

SO God created man in His own image... —GENESIS 1:27

I thought it was awful when my friend Fay sent herself a valentine the year we were in seventh grade. Just awful. The verse was most complimentary. It spoke to "a special friend whose heart was gentle, kind and true."

"How could you do such a thing?" I asked, in the full outrage of a 12-year-old.

"I don't know exactly," Fay said quietly. "Maybe I sent the card because it describes the way I want to be."

And, don't you know, that's exactly what Fay turned out to be—one of the gentlest, kindest and truest friends I have!

Fay was onto a truth that I can profit from. God made us in His own image. Why can't I see myself that way?

Lord, let me be Your valentine. —J.M.B.

---

15 *...FOR I will turn their mourning into joy, and will comfort them, and make them rejoice from their sorrow.* —JEREMIAH 31:13

I am standing at the bedroom window. It's a bitterly cold winter morning and the window is completely covered with frost. I can't see out. I scratch at the frost, but can't scratch my way through. What I do remove comes right back, anyway. I go to the kitchen to eat breakfast. When I come back to the bedroom a half hour later, all of the frost is gone. The morning sun has risen and is casting its rays. My room is now full of light.

Whenever I go through a disappointing experience in my life — a disagreement with a neighbor, a friend letting me down — a bitter cold sets in then, too. A chilling frost becomes indelibly etched upon me. It's then that I must work hard to place myself in God's light. It's then that I must work hard to live the way God wants me to. And sure enough, when I do, God's warm love melts the bitter cold away, and I stand there full of His light.

In the cold and dark I reach out to You, Lord, and I know You will come. —P.B.H.

16

I LOVE to tell the story
Of unseen things above,
Of Jesus and His glory,
Of Jesus and His love. —KATHERINE HANKEY, HYMN

The story is told that when John Wesley, the founder of Methodism, was a child he was a very slow learner. Once, in exasperation, the young Wesley's father said to his wife, "How can you have the patience to tell that blockhead John the same thing twenty times?"

And Mrs. Wesley answered, "Well, if I had told him only nineteen times, I would've wasted my breath."

When I think of all of God's slow-learning children, I'm sure He has even more patience than Mrs. Wesley. Maybe that's why He repeats the word "love" hundreds of times in His Scripture. He knew that if He had told us only once, He'd be wasting His breath.

Forgive me my slowness, Lord; I do want to love. —I.C.

17 When the Bible Speaks to Me

JOHN 21:15

Dawn hovered on the horizon around Galilee. The sea sloshed against Peter's boat where the tiny band of six disciples stared through the misted silence. The fishing nets were empty. As empty as their lives without the Master. He had been crucified.

As they rowed toward shore, they saw a man standing in the half-light of the beach. Beside him a charcoal fire flickered red and orange. There was something familiar about his outline, something familiar about the voice that called out to them. The memory filtered back from another time when a man had stood on the beach and called them from their boats.

Now it was John's voice that burst through the shadows. "It is the Lord!"

And so it was. They gathered together around the fire and shared breakfast. The last breakfast. The sun spilled over the rim of the little Galilean world and fell like golden beads upon their small circle. And then suddenly...the question. "Do you love Me?" Jesus asked it of Peter. Not once, but three times.

I always thought it curious that Jesus should repeat himself. Then one day a connection leaped in my mind. Three denials — three questions. Peter had denied his Lord three times. And now, there by the sea, where remorse snared Peter like a tangled fishing net, Jesus came with three questions of devotion, one for each denial. He seemed to be offering Peter the chance to make it up. How lovely and complete was God's healing, as love replaced sin!

Yet the mystery and beauty is that the question which broke through the dawn that faraway morning, is still echoing in the world. Again and again my life has caught its quiet vibrations. Each time I fail my Lord...in those low, sad moments which follow, somehow the question always comes to me. "Do you love Me?" And then the rush of healing as I answer, "Yes, yes. Oh, yes."

— SUE MONK KIDD

18

. . . WOE to him that is alone when he falleth; for he hath not another to help him up. —ECCLESIASTES 4:10

The other day I sat on my front steps and watched a neighbor of mine teach her young son how to ride a bicycle. The training wheels had come off, and the boy was making his first solo flights. His mom stayed right with him, though, offering him a light steady hand whenever the boy was about to topple over.

It was a lovely sight. The boy grew more and more exuberant, more confident in his ability to master this wondrous machine. The union of mother, boy and bicycle seemed to be one of those joyous occasions when you're sure that growing up is truly a beautiful thing.

Last night I was at a gathering of our Christian fellowship society. We had a new member, a man who had very recently come to Christ. The man was thrilled with his new faith, but he was not yet free of certain lingering doubts and questions. We all drew around him and offered him what we could. His confidence that God truly did love him grew right before our eyes. And, to tell you the truth, my confidence that God loves *me* grew, too, because God was so clearly in the room with us.

Do you know people who are still trying to find their balance as Christians ? Offer them a light, steadying hand; and then you'll both believe that growing up as a Christian is truly a beautiful thing.

Actually, Lord, we all need steadying hands. Help me find strong Christian friends. —I.C.

19 *THE words of the Lord are pure words: as silver tried in a furnace of earth, purified seven times.*

—PSALM 12:6

Whenever I'd start my annual reading of the Gospels, beginning with St. Matthew, I'd grit my teeth. The formidable genealogy of Jesus Christ, "the Begats," were monumentally boring. What purpose did they serve for modern readers, anyway?

Then I read something in a magazine that helped change my attitude: A missionary in Africa was making no progress in getting primitive tribesmen to listen to the Good News of Jesus. Even translated into their dialect, the Bible seemed beyond their ken.

Then one day the missionary began reading his restless flock the Gospel of Matthew: "The book of the generation of Jesus Christ, the son of David, the son of Abraham. Abraham begat Isaac; and Isaac begat Jacob; and Jacob begat...." (Matthew 1:1, 2). As he reeled off the list his congregation stopped fidgeting. They were listening with rapt attention.

The missionary could hardly believe it; then it dawned on him: The tribes of Israel were patriarchal societies, just as African tribes still were. These tribesmen understood perfectly that they *had* to know who their forefathers were because they formed a chain that linked itself back to God. Of course the tribesmen listened with fascination.

The more I learn about the Bible, the more magnificent it is.

Lord, You gave Your book to all *of us, and all of us find richness there.*

—W.D.

20 *HE performeth the thing that is appointed for me . . .*

—JOB 23:14

Little did I guess, when I asked the Lord to use me, that He would put me to work leading *four* prayer retreats in three different cities — all in the short month of February! "I'm not complaining," I said to my friend Judy. "It's just that I'm not sure I'll have the energy to do justice to all this." Judy spends many hours each week praying with and counseling troubled Christians, so I asked her, "How in the world do you keep on top of it all? What's your secret?"

Judy told me her secret, and it's a powerhouse. She said: "I just keep reminding myself, several times a day that, since the Lord gave me this work, *He* will see it through for me. There's a passage in Job that really helps me with this. It's 'He performeth the thing that is appointed for me.' Each morning when I get up, I say it over and over in my mind — as I'm getting dressed, while I'm brushing my teeth, driving to work, and while I'm working. Before I meet with each person, I repeat those words, trusting Him, every minute, to do His work through me. And He does!"

My first February retreat was only a week away when I talked to Judy. I started right in using the affirmation from Job every day, and I felt confident that He would carry the work through for me successfully. And, you know, He did. If the Lord has given you a job to do (and He does give assignments to all who ask), Judy's plan can help you to *know*, deep inside, that He will help you to complete it.

I trust You to complete what You have appointed for me, Lord.

—M.M.H.

21 *IN the multitude of my thoughts within me Thy comforts delight my soul.* —PSALM 94:19

It was the middle of the night, and the world seemed dark and lonely. Would I ever get back to sleep again? What was that? It seemed as though delicate music were playing outside in the rain. But that was crazy! The sound came again, and I smiled. Of course. It was the wind chimes that hung in the cedar tree, a recent gift from our eldest son and his wife. I lay quiet, listening, and the thought came, *That is Ted and Sue-Ellen's love for us singing in the rain.*

I felt better and decided to read a little. Turning on the light, I saw the clock on the bureau. *That* had been a present from our second son Fred. It said 2:30 and seemed to be ticking away with *his* love.

I looked around. In its corner niche stood the small wooden statue of St. Francis, and I thought of how shy our youngest son Doug had looked when he handed it to me. "We happened to pick this up in Mexico — and, uh, thought you might like it, Mother." Now my glance went to the candleholder on the windowsill, painstakingly fashioned in stained glass by our daughter Barbara.

I didn't read. I just lay there, feeling the love of my children radiating out from their gifts, soothing and quieting, banishing my loneliness. Then, turning out the light, I drifted into sleep, saying, "Thank You, Lord, for teaching me a new way to pray."

You, too, must have objects in your home that seem to reach out with their love. Look about you now and give thanks to God — not for those objects, but for the loving people who gave them to you.

Your love comes to me in so many ways, Father. Let me not be blind to any of them. —G.N.

22

NOW hear me while I pray,
Take all my guilt away,
O let me from this day
Be wholly Thine! —RAY PALMER, HYMN

A long time ago a friend and I were in a museum when we came across a reproduction of a painting of George Washington praying in the snow at Valley Forge. "You know," Dennis said, "Washington really wasn't all that religious. At best he was a Deist, one of those who believe in some vague Supreme Being."

And the more I thought about it, that seemed to be true. Whenever Washington referred to God, he used phrases like "Divine Providence," nothing specific, like Jesus Christ. Recently, however, I read an article about a little-known manuscript that George Washington had written. The article included several lovely prayers that Washington had written in his own hand under the title *Daily Sacrifice*. Here are two:

"Direct my thoughts, words and work, wash away my sins in the immaculate Blood of the Lamb, and purge my heart by Thy Holy Spirit... Daily frame me more and more into the likeness of Thy Son Jesus Christ..."

And...

"Thou gavest Thy Son to die for me; and hast given me assurance of salvation, upon my repentance and sincerely endeavoring to conform my life to His holy precepts and example."

Suddenly it was easy for me to see the tall general kneeling in the wintry wastes of Valley Forge. The father of our country was calling on the Father of us all.

Father, thank You for the men of faith who founded our country.

—R.S.

23

HE that is greatest among you shall be your servant.

—MATTHEW 23:11

My friend Stan was only 16, the son of missionary parents serving in Gabon, Africa, when Nobel Prizewinner Dr. Schweitzer invited him to his compound at Lambaréné. Stan told me how he accompanied the great doctor as he made his rounds, treating the people he cared about so much.

"Do you think those people ever realized what a great man Schweitzer was?" I asked Stan.

"No," Stan replied thoughtfully, "they probably didn't. They knew a man, full of compassion, who simply loved them. That made him great in their eyes."

Ever since that casual conversation with Stan, I've had a new respect for myself and what I can achieve. By lending a hand to someone who needs it, even I can be as great as Albert Schweitzer, for I believe that a small act can be great — in the eyes of God.

Lord Jesus, You have shown me that there is no greater deed than the one done for others.

—T.C.

24

ASH WEDNESDAY

AND many that believed came, and confessed, and shewed their deeds.

—ACTS 19:18

Ash Wednesday. Everywhere this morning I see people with a smudge of ash on their foreheads. They've been to church, where they've acknowledged their shortcomings as Christians. And now they are not afraid to be humble in public.

What about me? I know I do not hesitate to flaunt my virtues and successes, but when it comes to my failures — that's a different story.

This is the first day of Lent. Those ashes tell me that it is time to start bringing my weaknesses into God's light.

On this cold winter day, Lord Christ, give me the courage to believe that rebirth is drawing near. Help me prepare for that glorious day of Your resurrection. —G.K.

25

JUST as I am; Thou wilt receive;
Wilt welcome, pardon, cleanse, relieve.

—CHARLOTTE ELLIOTT, HYMN

I go to the kitchen sink to put some paintbrushes to soak. Standing there in my spattered jeans, hair in an old red bandana, I gaze through a dingy window upon a drab brown world. On the rusty hills the snow lies like dirty scatter rugs tossed out to dry. The trees stand tall and bleak, bare as bones. It's hard to believe that soon, in a few weeks, they will begin to rain rosy buds, be draped in a haze of green. That this dull empty stage will become transformed into a brilliant extravaganza of grass and flowers.

Right now, patience; the earth is resting. It has to have these periods in which to replenish itself, store up its juices, get ready for spring. *It can't be beautiful all the time*, I think. We can't change it, so we love it anyway.

Oh, dear, nearly five o'clock — time to start dinner and I look a mess! Ought to do something about your hair, Marjorie, change, put on make-up — but I'm so tired I just want to flop... Then, as I hear a car in the driveway, footsteps, I smile. A sense of grateful tenderness fills me. Because my family will understand.

My family knows that no one, especially me, can go through life always dressed up. Like nature, we, too, have days, even weeks, when we are drab and colorless and plain. But those who truly care about us don't mind. Or they forgive us. Like God Himself, they see the beauty within us or the promise of beauty to come.

Thank You, Lord, for showing me that You and my family love me, no matter what.

—M.H.

26

...THE Lord will hear when I call unto Him. —PSALM 4:3

The local hospital recently initiated a telephone-tape library. Tapes on over 200 subjects are available, everything from first aid and nutrition, to advice on various family problems.

I had never called until the other evening when I was particularly upset about a friend in the hospital. I dialed the number and asked for a tape on "Worry — What To Do About It." A recording told me to call back at nine in the morning.

I didn't need advice in the morning — I needed it that night!

Then I remembered — God has a number I can call. I opened my Bible to Jeremiah 33:3.

"Call unto Me, and I will answer thee, and shew thee great and mighty things, which thou knowest not."

I placed my call. His line wasn't busy. And I got an answer. I didn't need to wait until the next morning! In fact, God is there, no matter the time of day or night.

Calling You, Lord, is like calling home. You are always there. You always listen with love.

—S.P.W.

27

. . .REJOICE with me; for I have found my sheep which was lost.
—LUKE 15:6

The stories in the Bible repeat themselves in our lives every day. The story of the Good Shepherd finding his lost sheep never meant so much to me until the night our eight-year-old didn't come home from soccer practice.

I had driven him down in the afternoon, but it was dinner time when practice was over. Because I was busy in the kitchen, my husband went to pick him up.

He returned without him. "The coach said he'd gone home in a car pool."

"We're not in a car pool!" I cried.

Frantically, I called every team member's house — no, our son was not with any of them.

It was dark now, and my heart was pounding. I grabbed the car keys and flew back to the deserted field. *Oh, please, God, let him be safe.*

Two blocks from the practice area I spotted a small, dejected figure in a soccer shirt sitting on the curb. In seconds he had flung himself into my arms, his small face wet and smudged.

"Oh, Mom, I thought I was losted!"

For a long time we just stood, locked tight together. In those moments, when the preciousness of this child and my love for him swept through every part of me, I knew how God felt when one of His children was "losted." And I also knew the triumphant, flooding joy He feels when one of them is found.

Oh, Jesus, thank You for loving and finding us — all Your lost sheep.
—D.A.P.

28 A GRACE FOR THE FIRST WEEK IN LENT

Let this food, Lord,
Remind us of the forty days You fasted.
Let these brimming glasses,
Remind us of the bitter cup You drank.
Let this bread we break together
Remind us of Your body broken
For us.
And let our grateful hearts be filled
With sorrow — and with love. AMEN.

S	M	T	W	T	F	S.
	1	2	3	4	5	6
7	8	9	10	11	12	13
14	15	16	17	18	19	20
21	22	23	24	25	26	27
28	29	30	31			

The Third Commandment

Thou shalt not take the name of the Lord thy God in vain... —EXODUS 20:7

LAST week
I answered the door
And there was another salesman.
"Oh, God," I said aloud,
"I don't need a brush!"
And firmly told him so.

I meant it about the brush, Lord,
But I never meant to use Your name
That way — as my outlet
    for exasperation.
Surely You know
How mindless it is,
How everybody does it...
    but...then...here I am
Making excuses when
All the while I know I'm wrong.
You've set it down
    so simply and so clearly,
Your name, Your precious name,
I should not take in vain.

The next time that I say
"Oh, God,"
I won't stop there.
I'll make it be a prayer
That starts
"Oh God...how great Thou art!"
For how really great
Thou art.

1 *...AM I my brother's keeper?* —GENESIS 4:9

George Lewis, a spry, 83-year-old Californian, was fishing an isolated mountain stream last year when he lost his balance on a ridge and tumbled into the icy water. He managed to drag himself to safety, but he had broken a hip. He propped himself up on some rocks and reconciled himself to dying.

But late that afternoon an electric company crew found him. George was incredulous. "Whatever prompted you to come looking for me?" he asked. The men told him that they remembered his friendly wave as he passed them on his way into the stream. Then, they explained, they worried when he never passed them on his way out.

Have you ever wondered what a friendly gesture is worth? To the construction crew it was worth quite a lot because they spent two hours looking for George Lewis before they found him. It was worth a lot to George Lewis, too. It saved his life.

Help me to remember, Lord, that I can enlarge my world every day with the simple gesture of a friendly wave or smile.—N.V.P.

2 *NEITHER give offence to others, nor take offence from them.* —ST. AMBROSE

When I was a little girl of nine or ten, one of my friends did not invite me to her slumber party.

I narrowed my eyes and poked out my lips. "I'll show her," I told my mother. "I won't invite her to *my* party."

"Maybe," Mother said, "there's a good reason why Alice didn't invite you."

Then she sat me down on her bed and told me this story. "Once there was a little girl who was walking along the sidewalk with her mother. After a while an old bulldog waddled toward them and stopped in front of the girl. The girl stared at the dog and, all of a sudden, stuck out her tongue, making a horrible face at him.

"'Don't make ugly faces at the dog,' scolded her mother.

"'But he started it!' cried the little girl."

I giggled and interrupted my mother's story. And she smiled, too. Then she said, "See how silly it is to take offense at every ugly thing that comes your way."

I never did find out why Alice didn't invite me to her slumber party. But, thanks to Mom, she came to my next one, and I always went to hers after that.

When I've received a slight, Lord, help me to give a kindness in return. —S.M.K.

---

3 *JESUS saith unto him, I am the way...* —JOHN 14:6

There's a college professor in our town who raises homing pigeons. I've always been fascinated by the ability of these birds to find their way home, traveling hundreds of miles over unknown terrain. My friend says that "there seems to be an invisible force in the universe that guides and directs living things homeward."

I'm part homing pigeon, too. I have a deep inner yearning to find my way home to my Heavenly Father. Yet how crooked my flight path! How many wrong turns I take! Why can't I be more like a pigeon that allows itself to flow with the invisible force of the universe? I could try because, as you and I know, that invisible force is the will of our Heavenly Father. My goal is to attune myself to Him. Just for today I'll stop whenever I face a decision, no matter how large or small, and offer it to the Lord! I'll ask Him to dissolve my shortsighted, stubborn will into the perfection of

His will. I'm hoping that by day's end I'll begin to sense that invisible force, nudging me, drawing me, guiding me Godward.

You are the way, Lord; I must follow. —M.M.H.

4

LORD, when saw we Thee an hungered, and fed Thee?... —MATTHEW 25:37

Charlie was the town drunk. A more unsightly drunk there never was. He used to sleep in an abandoned car near our church. Whenever there was a church supper, Charlie would be there, looking for a free meal or a handout. We'd reluctantly give him something to eat at our kitchen door, and occasionally I'd drop a coin into his grimy palm.

One night, an evangelical group visited our church. Our staid congregation was overwhelmed by their joyous singing of the old spirituals. The mighty sound rose up to heaven — and over to Charlie's ears. Pretty soon he came shuffling in, roused from his drunken slumber by the singing.

"Welcome, brother!" cried Aunt Ada, the leader of the visiting group, rushing up to Charlie and embracing him. Then, looking into his eyes she asked, "Do you know the Lord Jesus?" Charlie shook his head no. Embarrassed, I studied the tiled floor.

That night, Aunt Ada got Charlie to accept Jesus Christ as his Lord and Saviour. Neither I — nor anyone else — who had known Charlie for years had ever bothered ourselves about his soul.

But Charlie didn't hold it against us. Within a year he was an usher, greeting people at the church door. Sober and cleaned up, with a handsome head of silver-gray hair neatly combed, he looked for all the world like a banker.

It had taken a stranger to look beneath the drink and the dirt and see Charlie as he really was — a son of God, like the rest of us.

Lord, open my eyes to the needs of others, and let my heart respond to what I see. —W.D.

5 *. . .HE that is without sin among you, let him first cast a stone at her.* —JOHN 8:7

One day, while lunching in a restaurant with my friend Sue, I asked her how it could be that in the four years I had known her, I had never heard her speak an unkind word about anyone. She just smiled and, reaching into her purse, pulled out a small, flat, ordinary-looking stone with the word "First" written on it in fading blue ink.

"My mother gave this to me years ago," she explained. "Whenever I open my purse, there it is to remind me that I'm not yet qualified to throw it."

Later that afternoon, at home, I picked up a small stone from our backyard and with a felt tip pen I wrote "First" on it, then put it in my handbag. Now, when I see that stone, I remember that an unkind word or a gossipy remark can bruise, can hurt the same way a stone can — all the more reason for not throwing it.

You did not cast the stone, Lord; let me not lift my hand either. —B.H.

6 *. . .JESUS is tenderly calling thee home.*

—FANNY J. CROSBY, HYMN

One of my happiest memories of childhood is the one of my mother calling me home about dusk. Playing was fun and I loved being with my friends. But when the sun began to fade and the first hint of darkness appeared, I'd hear my mother calling, "Maaar-i-on, come on home now." What security I felt in her voice!

Even running toward home, I could see the lights on in my house and I'd run faster. My mother would stand with the door open, waiting for me.

Now, just about the time the street lights begin to flicker on, I stand on my front porch and call my children in from their play. Having children of my own makes me keenly aware of how fast time passes.

One day Jesus will call me, "Come on home now, child. It's time to come in." It should be a time of intense joy and anticipation. I'll know without a doubt Who is calling me and that I'll be warmly welcomed and loved in my Heavenly home.

I work and play so much more easily, Father, knowing that You are there. —M.B.W.

---

7 A GRACE FOR THE SECOND WEEK IN LENT

At this meal, Lord,
We're imagining ourselves
Guests at Your table.
May the warmth and humor,
Fellowship and love
That reigned at tables
Where You sat so long ago
Be present here today. AMEN.

8 *...LET God's sunshine into your heart.* —OLD HYMN

For me, one of the nicest moments in the day is simply going about the house in the morning drawing back the draperies, opening up the shades. It brings back the memory of my mother doing this same thing as she waked us. And how often she'd sing out that rousing song from Sunday school: "Let God's sunshine into your heart, let God's sunshine into your heart! It will cheer you all the day, drive the cares of life away if you let...God's sunshine...into your heart!"

I smile just to think of it, and that too helps bring a sense of love and joy and hope into my being. The knowledge that the Lord really wants me to be happy, to let the sunlight of His love flood every moment of my life, just as the sunny rays of a new day sweep the shadows from waking rooms. Yet how often I turn my back on its light and plunge off to my work, preoccupied, burdened, anxious.

Or I shut out that warm presence with worries and grudges. It's like pulling down the shades. In fact, that's what Mother used to call it whenever I'd be grousing and things got too glum. "Come on, Marjorie, let's change the subject — it's getting dark in here, let's open up the shades!" Sometimes she'd go to the window and stand, breathing deeply, as if to draw more of God's sunshine in.

Try it. It helped her — all of us. And it helps me even now.

Lord, help me to remember You want me to be happy. Keep my heart open to Your sunshine. —M.H.

9

LOOKING for that blessed hope, and the glorious appearing of the great God and our Saviour Jesus Christ. —TITUS 2:13

Something in the newspaper last month left me looking at my life in a new way. I read about a management professor at Purdue University who'd done a study of women workers in a dress factory. She found that half the workers appeared exhausted and strained at the end of the day, while the other half were bright-eyed and spirited. All the women had done the same work for the same length of time.

The professor's research showed that the alert ladies were the ones who'd made plans for the evening and were looking forward to a good time. The tired ones, on the other hand, tended to have nothing special in mind for the night ahead.

Over the next few days I charted my days and evenings to see if I followed this same pattern.

I did! No matter how trying my workday was, I always found myself less tired if I had an event to look forward to. So I began to see to it that my evenings were more interesting. It wasn't just a matter of scheduling "fun" things like movies or eating out, but creating special times to expand my mind and spirit — organizing a Bible study group or attending evening meetings of the town council, informed and ready to speak out. In a few months I found that by creating something worthwhile to look forward to most evenings, I'd created hope.

Having faith in You, Lord, is my surest way of having hope. And oh, how grateful I am for that! —I.C.

10 *BUT we speak the wisdom of God in a mystery...*

—I CORINTHIANS 2:7

The letter was addressed to the General Electric Company from a little girl in third grade who had chosen to investigate electricity for her class project. "I'm trying to get all the information I can," her letter ran, "so please send me any booklets and papers you have. Also, would it be asking too much for you to send me a little sample of electricity?"

When I heard about her innocent letter I laughed, as have three generations of executives at General Electric, where the letter is now legend.

Yet, maybe I was laughing at myself as well. For how many times have I wanted concrete examples of the great mysteries? How many times have I asked God to give me tangible proof that He is there?

I think that what that little girl and I need to learn is that there are some mysteries in this life that we must accept — it is the mystery that is their glory.

Lord, I am an innocent, but I accept the mystery that is You, and I believe. —J. McD.

11 *...YE are of more value than many sparrows.*

—LUKE 12:7

I once lived in a neighborhood where a woman took in any lost dog or cat. She would mend its hurts, feed it, and then either keep it or see that it found a welcoming home. Yet this kind woman never paid a call on a lonely, elderly couple who lived right next door to her.

One day recently I mentioned this woman to a friend. "It's odd," Don said, "that it's easier to be kind to stray animals than it is to stray people."

"Yes," I agreed. "I've seen a person pick up a wounded bird and nurse it back to health, even though that bird pecked its rescuer's hands until they bled." The more we talked about it, the more we saw the challenge. It *is* easier to be kind to animals. Sure, we're expected to show compassion to His lesser creatures, but Jesus has commanded us to love one another.

Even though people were spiteful to You, Jesus, You still died for us. Remind me of this when I encounter a spiteful person who needs my help. —B.R.G.

---

12 *...FOR ye are all one in Christ Jesus.* —GALATIANS 3:28

There is a sadness in me tonight, as I sit at the desk in my little basement office. That final glimpse of my friend waving as the airplane taxied out of sight is etched on my heart. So many miles. Such a short time together. We may never meet again.

And yet, in those last moments before my friend boarded the plane, we had joined our hands and prayed together, affirming that we were — and are — one in Jesus Christ. In that moment, another hand touched ours, binding us together, and that sustains me. It is the hand of the One Who said, "I will never leave thee, nor forsake thee." (Hebrews 13:5)

Parting is never easy when you care about someone, but all of us have to face good-byes. If you and the person you love will affirm your oneness in Jesus at the moment of farewell, *He* will be the link between you...a link that can span distances as great as infinity.

I praise God that my friend and I are joined forever in the love of Jesus! —M.M.H.

---

13 *HEAVEN and earth shall pass away, but My words shall not pass away.* —MATTHEW 24:35

As a lonely teenager I used to seek advice and help from a sprightly octogenarian named Mother Gibson. Barely five feet tall, with snow-white hair, she was always sparkling, full of sunshine.

One day I asked Mother Gibson how to handle a thorny problem of temptation I faced.

"Temptation!" she cried, "Why, honey girl, that's just another name for the devil. And when the devil comes around I just read the Bible to him."

I stared at her. "You what?"

Right then and there Mother Gibson picked up her Bible and held it high. "I tell him, 'Temptation, you old devil, all the promises in this Book are mine. See that? Read it.' Then I read it to him, and say, 'You just skedaddle on out of here.' Try this. It works!"

I have teenagers of my own now, and through the years, when temptations come, I remember Mother Gibson holding her Bible high, pointing to God's promises, and reading the Bible out loud to the enemy.

Father, thank You for all those promises. I claim them today. —A.C.

14 A GRACE FOR THE THIRD WEEK IN LENT

Father:
Someone put the seed into the ground,
Someone watched it grow,
Someone harvested the grain
That eventually became
The flour, the dough, the bread
We eat today.
We thank You now for all the someones
Who give, that we may live.
And for the gift of life itself
We thank You,
Father.

AMEN.

15

BEHOLD, I stand at the door, and knock: if any man hear My voice, and open the door, I will come in to him, and will sup with him, and he with Me.

—REVELATION 3:20

When I worked as a nurse on the pediatric ward, before I listened to the little ones' chests, I would plug the stethoscope into their ears and let them listen to their own hearts. Their eyes would always light up with awe.

But I never got a response to equal four-year-old David's. I gently tucked the stethoscope in his ears and placed the disk over his heart. "Listen," I said. "What do you suppose that is?"

He drew his eyebrows together in a puzzled line and looked up as if lost in the mystery of the strange tap-tap-tapping deep in his chest. Then his face broke out in a wondrous grin. "Is that Jesus knocking?" he said.

I smiled. Somewhere, maybe in Sunday school, David had obviously been told that lovely old illustration about Jesus standing at the door of our hearts, knocking.

Dear little David. You were exactly right. Inside your heart, and every heart, there is the faint persistent sound of Jesus knocking. For Jesus comes to each of us every new day, wanting to share its moments with us. And maybe it is only those with the faith and wonder of a David who hear it beneath the clamor of a busy world, and open the door.

I'm listening, Lord. —S.M.K.

16 *When the Bible Speaks to Me*

II SAMUEL 12

It is one of the most dramatic passages in the entire Bible, a moment of such high drama that the account of it in Second Samuel still has an eyewitness ring after almost 3000 years.

The great and gifted King of Israel, David the psalmist, David the Goliath-slayer, David the hero of his people, has taken another man's woman — Bathsheba, wife of Uriah the Hittite — to be his concubine. Worse, he has arranged for Uriah, a brave and loyal soldier, to be killed in battle so that he can bring Bathsheba openly to his palace.

These are barbaric times. Who dares question the actions of the king? Nothing can be done — unless the king can be persuaded to judge himself.

Now comes Nathan the prophet with a story of injustice to lay before the monarch. A certain poor man, says Nathan, had one little lamb, more a pet than common livestock, the only animal he had. A certain rich man had many sheep and lambs. But when he needed meat to entertain a guest, he took the poor man's lamb from him and killed it, rather than use one of his own.

David is enraged. His eyes flash and his voice rings out like thunder. Who has done this unpardonable thing? He deserves to be punished. He deserves to die! Who is he?

And Nathan, standing there gaunt and grim among the courtiers and the soldiers of the guard, raises his arm and points one long accusing finger straight at the king. "Thou art the man!"

And everyone standing there knows that the conscience of the nation has spoken.

A lesser ruler would have had Nathan killed on the spot. David is man enough to accept the rebuke, admit his fault and resign himself to the punishment that Nathan foretells: that the child Bathsheba is carrying — David's child — will die.

And what does the story say to us? Not merely that sins committed in darkness have a way of coming to light, but also that before we condemn the actions of others we had better ask ourselves if we are flawless. Because we seldom are. — ARTHUR GORDON

17 *NOW the serpent was more subtle than any beast of the field...* —GENESIS 3:1

One of the things I have always enjoyed about St. Patrick's Day in New York is that, for one day at least, everybody is Irish. Everybody wears something green. Bosses give secretaries green carnations. Everybody eats corned beef and cabbage and a boiled potato, with hot mustard. There is a parade of thousands up Fifth Avenue, the traffic divider painted green for the day. Nobody notices that half the marchers are blacks and Hispanics. This day, they are all blue-eyed Irishers.

So I was surprised to find out that St. Patrick himself was not Irish at all. He was an Englishman, of all things, who was educated in France and sent to Ireland in the Fifth Century as a missionary to evangelize the country. He is credited with driving the snakes out of Ireland, but this is a symbolism for the paganism he drove out as he won converts. One thing he did has a special meaning for me. In trying to explain the Holy Trinity to the people, he plucked a three-leaf clover and held it up, saying that the Trinity — the Father, the Son, the Holy Spirit — was like the clover — three Divine Personages in one Entity — God.

What I like most about March 17 is that all New Yorkers are Irish. They're like St. Patrick's three-leaf clover: a variety of people finding unity in the Brotherhood of Man.

Heavenly Father, Creator of the world and everything in it, help us always to remember that despite our differences we are all Your children and must love each other as You love us.—G.K.

18 *O WORD of God Incarnate,*
O Wisdom from on high . . . —WILLIAM W. HOW, HYMN

No one likes to visit the dentist and I'm certainly no exception, yet when I'm summoned for one of my semiannual checkups, I go with some anticipation, all because of a little calendar that stands on a counter top in my dentist's examining room.

This daily calendar, in addition to giving the day and the date, notes one new but uncommon word, along with the pronunciation and meaning. Committing the "word of the day" to memory has become an excellent way for my dentist, his assistant and his patients to increase their word power.

I liked the idea so much I decided to copy it. Each morning I searched the dictionary for one unfamiliar word, jotted it (and its meaning) down on paper, and kept the note in front of me on my desk all day. It has worked wonders. Yesterday I memorized the meaning of "intransigent." (Look it up!)

The nice thing about my little dictionary exercise was that it started me doing something similar with my Bible. I began placing a Bible passage on my desk each day. Yesterday's message was: "Fret not thyself because of evildoers..." (Psalm 37:1) Today's passage reads: "What doth it profit...though a man say he hath faith, and have not works? Can faith save him?" (James 2:14)

So now I not only increase my word power each day, but my spiritual awareness too!

Lord, thank You for Your holy Word. It never fails to bring me strength and joy. —E.V.S.

19 *BUT when ye pray, use not vain repetitions...*

—MATTHEW 6:7

It was not my favorite kind of day, with errands to be done all over town. The bank, the library, the supermarket, the dry cleaner's. Everywhere I went I was told, "Have a nice day," when my transactions were completed. Each time I heard the phrase I felt more annoyed; it seemed such a mindless kind of remark, with no real meaning.

At my last stop, the dry cleaner's, the bored clerk said it without even looking up as she thrust my dresses at me: "Have a nice day."

Again the mechanical remark irritated me. She said it without even thinking, much less feeling.

On the way home, passing our parish church, I began to say the prayer I always say when going by. And then I caught myself. It was just as automatic, just as mechanical, as the clerk's "Have a nice day." Did I really feel it? And I wondered how God felt when He heard it.

Lord, let me mean, truly mean, everything I pray to You.—A.F.

20 *NOW when they saw the boldness of Peter and John, and perceived that they were unlearned and ignorant men, they marvelled; and they took knowledge of them, that they had been with Jesus.* —ACTS 4:13

"O.K. It's your turn! Jump in!"

The Outward Bound instructor stood on a rock beside a deep creek, beckoning me toward the icy water. It was March and it was cold. Maybe 35 degrees. I was already shivering in my bathing suit. This was madness!

But I had agreed beforehand to at least *try* all the different exercises on this Christian version of Outward Bound, a week spent braving outdoor challenges.

Not giving myself time to think, I plunged in. I felt numb. I'd forgotten how to breathe. I let out a shriek before thrashing my way to shore.

Then I felt a rush of warmth. It was my own blood, there all the time, but working overtime to reheat my body, surging to the surface of my skin. I stood there in the crisp air, encouraging my bundled-up companions who had not yet taken the plunge.

So the reason for this particular exercise became clear to me. Christians must take risks that seem unpleasant, even impossible, risks that dare us to step out of our comfortable, everyday behavior into unknown waters. And, when we do, there is a rush of His spirit to warm and sustain us.

Today, Lord, let me risk something for You. —C.C.

---

21 A GRACE FOR THE FOURTH WEEK IN LENT

Father in Heaven:
The true bounty of this table is more than the food that strengthens our bodies; it is the love, Your limitless love, that nourishes our souls. For that, and all the abundance in our lives, thank You, Father, thank You.

AMEN.

22 *LET your light so shine before men, that they may see your good works, and glorify your Father which is in heaven.* —MATTHEW 5:16

Ben Franklin felt that the streets of Philadelphia needed to be lighted, but he knew the city officials would never go the expense of the project. Not willing to give up on his good idea, he said nothing, but hung an attractive lantern on a long bracket outside his front door.

People carefully picking their way down the street at night would come upon the bright area in front of the Franklin home and think — that's a good idea. Soon his neighbors had lanterns hanging in front of their homes and it wasn't long before the whole city had caught on to the idea of street lighting.

As I look around me I see the need for the light of the Gospel, but I feel so inadequate for the task. The job of bringing God's light to this dark world is staggering in its magnitude. Of course I could say to myself that there's nothing I can do about it, but I know that isn't so. I can be a light to my family, to my fellow workers and to my neighbors. I can be a Ben Franklin for God.

Dear Lord, may the light that shines from me be the light that helps others find their way to You. —B.M.

23 *...IN whatsoever state I am, therewith to be content.* —PHILIPPIANS 4:11

When I was quite young a carload of us traveled one night to hear a colorful preacher, Gypsy Smith, who was holding evangelistic meetings in a nearby town. That night he told of a woman who came up to him after one of his services and said, "Gypsy, I feel the Lord is calling me to preach — if only I didn't have these ten children!"

"Why, that's wonderful, sister," Gypsy replied, "the Lord *is* calling you to preach, and He's given you your own congregation. Now go home and preach to them!"

For years that story has served as a little warning signal for me. Whenever I get an attack of the "if onlies" — if only I weren't tied down to the house; if only I had more talent — then I'm reminded to get on with the business of the Lord. He's given me my own "congregation" that nobody else could serve as well. And if I fail, then who will do it?

With Your help, Lord, I can make the best of all situations.

—T. B.

24

AND forgive us our debts, as we forgive our debtors.

—MATTHEW 6:12

My 13-year-old son came in from school with his first almost-black eye. I noticed it because he kept turning his face away from me. "What happened, Jon?"

"Aw, I got in a fight."

"Jon! Fighting at school. You've never done that before."

"Am I going to have a black eye, Mama?"

"Probably not, if you take care of it," I answered, handing him an ice pack. "Really, I'm more concerned about the condition of your heart."

"Huh?"

"Tonight and tomorrow will be very difficult if you don't make it right today. I want you to call the boy you fought with and apologize."

"Aw, Mama. It was his fault. He hit me first."

"It doesn't really matter whose fault it was. You will feel better on the inside and I'll bet your eye will heal quicker if you call."

"I'll tell him tomorrow at school."

"Jon, it will be one of the hardest things you've ever done, but I want you to call now and say that you are sorry about the fight."

He started up the steps so he could talk in private. His head was down as he held the ice pack to his eye. His shoulders slumped. In just a few moments I heard a loud, enthusiastic, "Hi, Bill. It's Jon. I'm sorry about the fight. Can we still be friends? Great. See ya tomorrow. Bye."

I walked upstairs. Jon was sitting by the phone staring straight ahead. Quickly he pretended to rub at his face. I knew he was wiping tears away, so I looked in another direction. "By the way, if you cry a little, that's normal," I told him. Then I remembered a time after I apologized to a neighbor that I cried all the way home — out loud.

After one long, loud sniff Jon bounded down the steps three at a time, opened the refrigerator. Smiling, almost glowing, it seemed, he asked, "What's to eat, Mama?"

Ah, forgiveness, that's the greatest Christian virtue!

Father, surely the two most difficult words in the world are, "I'm sorry." Give me the strength to say them. —M.B.W.

25 *AND His face did shine as the sun . . .* —MATTHEW 17:2

Early in the spring, when the sun first begins to spread its gentle warmth over the sleeping earth, my daughter Karen starts sunbathing, just a few minutes every day. She fits sun time into her schedule and never misses a day. Slowly, almost imperceptibly, she develops that lovely golden glow that whispers to the world that she has spent time soaking up the transforming rays of the sun. Karen says that regularity is the secret, and that you can get just as much tan on a cloudy day, even when it seems that the sun isn't there.

I know some Christians who have a lovely golden glow about them, don't you? If we asked them, they'd probably tell us they developed it a little bit at a time, sitting quietly in the presence of the Son, bathing in His radiance. I'm sure they'd also tell us that there are cloudy days in their prayer lives, when nothing seems to be happening and the face of the Son seems to have disappeared. Yet gradually, quietly, their lives have been transformed, and they radiate a kind of inner beauty that reflects the light of Jesus on all whose lives they touch. The secret is regularity.

Is letting the Son shine in a part of your daily schedule?

Keep me faithful, Jesus, to my daily time in Your light. —M.M.H.

26 *. . . WHAT house will ye build Me? saith the Lord.* —ACTS 7:49

My grandmother often told the story of a very rich, but stingy man who appeared at the Pearly Gates. He was greeted courteously. An angel was summoned to escort him to his eternal residence. They passed stately marble mansions with sweeping green lawns. As they walked, the houses gradually became smaller. Finally they came to a small, unfinished tar-paper shack.

"This, sir," said the angel, "is your heavenly home."

"What!" snorted the man. "There must be some horrible mistake. I'm a wealthy man. This will never do."

"We're sorry, sir," the angel said, "we did the best we could, but these are the materials you sent us."

And whenever my grandmother told me this story, she would end it by saying, "You don't have to be rich, child, to build a stately mansion — either here or there."

Lord, let me always try to give You my best. —C.M.D.

27

O JESUS, I have promised
To serve Thee to the end... —JOHN E. BODE, HYMN

We can all use some help in developing more effective ways to pray. Quite by accident I learned a little technique from my young son. Bryce had a bulletin board in his room on which he tacked up class assignments and all kinds of personal projects. He used to ask us to look at his bulletin board from time to time.

"Did you check out my board today?" he'd ask us often.

Finally one day I asked him, "Why is this so important to you?"

"Because when I let you and Daddy know about my assignments, I know there's no backing out. I feel that I'm letting you down if I don't do the work."

Our son, the psychologist! But there was a lot of wisdom in his theory. For after all, when you make a commitment to someone, even as simple a one as, "I'll put a patch on your pants this afternoon," or, "I promise to get that recipe in the mail to you," you feel obligated to do it.

I've found that this works for me in my prayers, too. When I tell God what I'm going to do, there's no backing out. If I don't follow through, I feel that I'm letting God down.

What power there is in commitment, Lord; it's the power I gain from being true to You. —J.M.B.

---

28 A GRACE FOR THE FIFTH WEEK IN LENT

At the last supper, Lord,
You said, "One of you will betray
Me, one who is eating with Me."
We are about to eat with You now,
Lord Jesus,
About to ask for Your trust.
We pray that we may be worthy of it
Always. AMEN.

29 *THROW out the Lifeline across the dark wave,*
There is a brother whom someone should save.

—EDWARD SMITH UFFORD, HYMN

When men decided to build a bridge across the river at Niagara Falls, they had a problem. They needed one rope across the river to start the suspension bridge. But the river was too deep to wade, too wide to throw the rope across, and too swift and turbulent to take it across by boat. Finally they came up with an ingenious idea.

They flew a kite across the river. Once it had been caught on the other side, a cord was tied to its string. Eventually the cord was used to pull the rope across the river. That was the beginning of the suspension bridge that now spans Niagara Falls.

There are times when I have had a falling-out with someone and a gulf has widened so that I felt it couldn't be bridged. But I've found that if I pray about it and truly accept Christ's admonition to forgive, there is always a way to make amends. A telephone wire can be the string of my kite, for instance. Or, any number of tiny gestures can be the start of my bridge of reconciliation.

Lord, give me the courage to take that first small step.—L.E.W.

30 *BE not overcome of evil, but overcome evil with good.*

—ROMANS 12:21

I stopped at a traffic light on my way to buy a birthday present for a friend. The very instant the light turned green, a loud honk came from the car behind me.

"Well, give me a chance, buddy," I muttered angrily, looking in my rearview mirror at a scowling man.

I was determined to get even with him. Sneaking my car up behind his at the next light, I waited with a delicious feeling of anticipation.

Blink went the light! Honk went my horn! Jump went the man!

Soon after I pulled into the parking lot of the store, but I didn't get out of the car. I just sat there. My conscience was troubling me.

For the rest of the day I felt uneasy and disheartened. It's amazing, if you've known even a little of God's grace, how instantly you dislike yourself when you do something mean-spirited.

Don't honk, I tell myself now. Pray, instead, for those who wrong me.

Oh, Lord, give me control over my temper. Let me use its wasteful energy for positive things. —S.M.S.

31

AND now abideth faith, hope, charity, these three . . .

—I CORINTHIANS 13:13

Hope! What a wonderful and mysterious power it is. And how handicapped we are if we ever lose it.

Some time ago I read a report by Dr. Harold G. Wolff in which he reported as a medical fact that when a man has hope he is "capable of enduring incredible burdens and cruel punishment."

One of Dr. Wolff's studies involved the 25,000 American soldiers imprisoned by the Japanese during World War II. These men were subjected to long months of harsh treatment, poor food, forced labor. Many died, and almost all were sick. But there were a very few who, with identical treatment, showed but slight damage from these nightmare months in prison.

Now here is the important thing. Interviews with these men revealed no physical superiority, but simply a far-above-average ability to hope! In prison they drew word pictures of the girls they would marry; they designed their future homes; in the middle of the jungle they organized seminars in business management.

Dr. Wolff believes it was hope that kept these boys well — indeed, in some cases, kept them alive at all.

What do we learn from this? We learn that hope, as the Bible says, is the twin sister of faith. Hope is *wishing* for a thing to come true; faith is *believing* that it will come true.

And when you wish strongly enough, and believe firmly enough — why then, the impossible happens.

Dear Jesus, You are our hope of salvation — we thank You.

—N.V.P.

S	M	T	W	T	F	S
				1	2	3
4	5	6	7	8	9	10
11	12	13	14	15	16	17
18	19	20	21	22	23	24
25	26	27	28	29	30	

The Fourth Commandment

Remember the sabbath day, to keep it holy.
—EXODUS 20:8

WHAT once was called the sabbath
is now a long weekend.
What once was called a holy day
is thought of as a holiday.
Strange, isn't it, how we alter things,
forgetting — or ignoring —
the reason for their being?

O Lord, You said
The sabbath was made for man,
And so it is;
But now I work so hard at play
I tire myself for labor days.

Remind me, Lord,
Tell me again,
That even You required a time
to rest and be renewed.
Now when I hurry through the sabbath day,
Stop me!
Stop me and let me know
That You, the mighty God,
expect a great deal more from me
than just a fleeting nod.

1

WILL all your worries add a single moment to your life?

—MATTHEW 6:27(LB)

One year not so long ago when I was in college, our dormitory council decided to sponsor an April Fool's Day contest. Each of our floors was to submit a prank that, if selected, would be played on one other floor. Each student was to submit an idea for a prank. The winner — whose identity was kept secret — got to choose the floor that would become the butt of the joke. My floor was it.

For seven long days my floormates and I kept a wary eye out for preparations or secret meetings. We sent spies to other floors looking for anything that might betray the perpetrator of the forthcoming dastardly deed. Then on April Fool's Day, our every step was taken with extreme caution, looking out for short-sheeted beds, sewn-up pants legs, or buckets of water cascading from booby-trapped doors. But nothing happened. The whole day passed with no atrocity. Finally, at the 11 p.m. dorm meeting, the winner was announced. His gag? — not playing a gag at all. He simply wanted to make us sweat and worry for nothing. His joke had worked to perfection!

My worry has not been limited to that one April Fool's week. Often I seem to fret about problems, like the April Fool's gag, that never materialize. It is only when I concentrate on the blessings I receive each day, rather than the problems I may never experience, that I know the comfort of my God.

On this April Fool's Day, Lord, help me to admire beauty, cherish friendships, count blessings and laugh! —J.J.

2

'TWAS I that shed the sacred blood
I nailed Him to the tree
I crucified the Christ of God
I joined the mockery!

—ANONYMOUS

I recently read about a great painting of the Crucifixion by the Dutch master, Rembrandt. If you were to look at it the first thing you would see would be the figure of Christ hanging upon the cross. Next your eyes would probably move down to the mob gathered beneath, to the people who had helped to crucify our Lord. But if you were very keen and let your eyes drift to the edge of the painting, you would notice a man standing in the shadows. And you might even recognize this man as Rembrandt himself. For Rembrandt painted himself into the mob as if saying to all the world, "I, too, helped crucify Jesus. He is hanging on a cross for *my* sins."

We are often called to remember that dark and holy scene on a skull-shaped hill called Golgotha. Usually we recall it as a sad day in history when a mob crucified our Lord. Perhaps today we should look a bit closer, over in the shadows, beside Rembrandt. Aren't you and I there, too?

Lord, remind me that Your death was a sacrifice for my sins. Thank You.

—S.M.K.

3

CHRIST has turned all our sunsets into dawns.

—CLEMENT OF ALEXANDRIA

My family's Easter message that year came unexpectedly. Tindy, our gray-and-white Persian cat, leaped nimbly to the kitchen stool and from there to the refrigerator top. She sniffed at the hard-boiled colored eggs which had been left in a rack to dry. *Crash!* The eggs, intended for the children's Easter baskets, rolled on the floor. I gathered them up, but cracks and lines now spoiled the colorful surfaces.

"They're ruined!" cried Jenny.

Granny thoughtfully studied the situation. Then she sat down, picked up an egg and a wax crayon and began following the crack with a line of green. Soon a vine circled the egg. Then she added tiny green leaves and red and yellow flowers. Like magic, the cracks were transformed. She then went to work on the others and soon all were bright with colorful designs.

"Why, they're prettier than before," Jenny cried.

And they were.

The Easter message? Broken eggs, like broken people, can become more beautiful than ever. The eggs needed Granny. Broken people need Jesus Christ.

Because I love You, Jesus, and because You have died for me, I am made whole and beautiful once again. —D.H.

---

4 A Note from the Editors

Matthew, Mark, Luke and John give detailed accounts of the last week of Jesus' life on earth, from his triumphal entry into Jerusalem to His resurrection. Through all the pages of the Gospel, there is one disciple who seems more vivid than the rest: Peter, that always impulsive, quick to speak, quick to act, quick to repent Simon Peter.

This year, as we worked on *Daily Guideposts, 1982,* we began to wonder how Peter would have reported the historic events of that life-shaking week. What, say, if Peter had kept a diary? What happenings would he have recorded? What incidents would have been most significant to him?

It seemed an intriguing idea, and so we asked one of our favorite writers, Marilyn Morgan Helleberg, to put herself in the shoes of the Big Fisherman for those eight days that changed the world.

Here are the results.

Palm Sunday

So many voices echo in the silence of my heart tonight. I can't seem to get Jesus' words out of my mind — the ones He spoke on our way to Jerusalem: "The Son of Man will be betrayed... crucified..." *O God, no! He's changed my life. I need Him so! Don't let it happen!* But then I hear those other voices — great multitudes of people, gathering on the outskirts of town at the Mount of Olives, shouting, "Blessed is He who comes in the name of the Lord. Hosanna in the highest!" A shout of praise — not condemnation! *Thank You, God!*

Pictures of the day flash through my mind: Jesus riding into the city on a donkey, people waving palms, running ahead and laying down their cloaks, cutting branches, making a carpet of greenery for Him to pass over. Oh, how proud I am to be numbered among His disciples! It's been three years now since I left my fishing boat to join Jesus. Finally, it seems, the people are coming to realize that He is not an ordinary man. Many say He's a prophet. A few are whispering that He might even be the Messiah.

Now a voice from the past interrupts my thoughts. It's *His* voice. "But you, who do *you* say I am?" It seems uncanny how clearly the answer came to me that day in Philippi: "You are the Christ, the Son of the living God." There was such a certainty in me, such an absolute *knowing*. Jesus said it was because His Father in heaven revealed it to me, and I know that's true. Yet I can't rest on that one-time profession of my faith. Every day I must ask myself, anew: "And you, who do *you* say I am?"

Jesus my Lord, as I raise my palms of praise to You in the streets of my life, speak Your word of certainty in my heart so that I may affirm again this day — and every day — "You are the Christ, the Son of the living God."

5 The Second Day

For as long as I can remember, merchants have sold sacrificial animals at the temple during Passover time. That's why I was so stunned, today, when Jesus went striding into the temple, His jaw set and His dark eyes flashing. With an air of absolute authority, He overthrew the tables of the money changers and upset the chairs of those who were selling pigeons. Coins clattered to the floor. Birds' wings flapped madly. Merchants shouted in indignation. Then there was a shocked silence, and many stood with gaping mouths as Jesus said, "It is written, My house shall be called the house of prayer; but you have made it a den of thieves." Oh, what power! What mastery! What courage!

What is it about today's event that grips me, thrills me, makes me want to stand up and cheer? I know! It's that my Jesus, so gentle, so kind, is also a mighty and vigorous...*fighter*! As long as I stay close to Him, He will defend me, fight for me, purge my inner temple. If material things begin to clutter up my life, He will come striding in and overthrow the tables. If others try to rob or cheat me, He will be there to knock them out of their chairs. If my carnal nature leads me into temptation, I can call His name and He will drive the animals out. Oh what blessed security it is to have a gentle Friend Who is also a fearless warrior in the battle against evil!

I call on You now, Lord, to cleanse the temple of my soul, so that it may truly be a house of prayer.

6 *The Third Day*

There's something ominous, foreboding, in the air tonight. I feel a chill stab at the center of my chest. After yesterday's episode at the temple, I saw scribes and priests whispering, plotting against my beloved Jesus. Today in the temple, the Sadducees and Pharisees fired cunning questions at Him. Each challenge shot fear through me. Would they be able to trap Him into saying something that contradicted Jewish law, something that could be considered blasphemy? Yet, through it all, my Master's face remained calm, His body relaxed, His voice sure and steady. He spoke in parables, answered questions with deeper questions, always expressing a higher truth — one that was beyond the mere letter of the law. Squinting smugly, a lawyer in the crowd asked, "Master, which is the greatest commandment of the Law?" I gasped. How could Jesus possibly choose one law out of 3600? I was afraid they had Him for sure.

But then, without a moment's hesitation, this God-made-man reduced all those laws to two simple statements: "First, love the Lord your God with all your heart, soul and mind. Second, love your neighbor as yourself."

That sense of foreboding is still with me, and some kind of deep inner sorrow I can't explain has begun to stir within me. But I know that, if I can just remember those words of His, using Love as my guide and my measure, I'll be able to face whatever comes.

Help me to open myself, Lord, to Your infilling Love. Then let it overflow the bounds of myself, returning to You and spilling itself on others.

7 The Fourth Day

My Master said it again tonight: "It will be Passover in two days' time, and the Son of Man will be handed over to be crucified." His words pained me like a fishhook in my flesh as we sat for dinner at the home of Simon the leper, in Bethany. The mood at the table was one of quiet solemnity, when suddenly, into the room swept a woman, carrying an alabaster jar filled with costly ointment. We all watched, startled, as she walked straight over to Jesus, broke the expensive jar, and poured the ointment on His head! My mouth fell open. Other disciples jumped up angrily. Someone — I think it was Judas — shouted indignantly, "Why wasn't this ointment sold and the money given to the poor?"

My Lord's reply nudged that ache in me: "You have the poor with you always, but you will not always have Me. She did this to prepare Me for burial."

Through all this, the woman seemed oblivious to the stir she had caused. Lovingly, caressingly, she continued to anoint the body of her Lord. And Jesus? He accepted her act with love, and gratitude, and a promise that wherever the Good News is proclaimed, this woman's act will be told.

Oh, to be as honest and as generous as that woman was! To give the best without worrying about the cost, without caring what other people might think! To be willing to appear foolish in the eyes of men, for the sake of Christ!

Lord, give me a heart like that woman of Bethany, and the courage to obey its loving impulses.

8 Maundy Thursday

What a wretched man I am! How miserably I have failed my Lord! I am so sick at heart, I can hardly breathe. As we walked toward the Mount of Olives tonight, my Jesus told me that I would deny Him three times before the cock crew. I couldn't believe such a thing! So I answered, "Even if I have to die with You, I will never disown You." I was so sure that I meant it!

Now I am so ashamed. I fell asleep when He asked me to watch while He prayed, slashed off a man's ear in a moment of terror, and fled when they arrested my Master. *O my Lord, why do I always do the wrong thing?* Then, while Caiaphas questioned Jesus on the balcony of the palace, I warmed my hands by a fire in the courtyard below. Suddenly someone tossed some dried thorns on the fire. As they flared up, I noticed a servant girl staring at me. With terror I heard her say, "Aren't you another of that man's disciples?"

"No, I am not!" I exploded, and I went out into the forecourt to avoid further questions. I sat, stood, crouched low, paced. My nerves were raw. Then another accusation came, "This fellow is one of them!" Again I denied it. The third time it happened, I began to swear and call down curses upon myself, as I spat out the words, "I know not the man." That was when I heard, from somewhere in the distance, the sound of a cock crowing, and the terrible realization slammed on my heart like an anchor falling into the sea. I felt the eyes of Jesus upon me, and I knew that He had heard it all. Turning toward the balcony, I saw Him standing there, His hands bound, His face swollen and blotched with bruises, in His eyes an infinite sadness. *Lord God, if only I could die instead of You!* Hot, bitter tears filled my eyes and I ran out into the night, sobbing.

Now as I think back on it, an amazing thing occurs to me. As my Master's gaze held mine, there was not a trace of anger in those soft eyes — only sadness, forgiveness... love!

As I write this, I know there will be other times when I will fail Him. But I know, also, that He understands my humanness and that He stands waiting, with unutterable compassion, to welcome me back.

For Your faithfulness, Lord, in the face of my unfaithfulness, I am amazed — and so very grateful.

9 Good Friday

My hands tremble as I write these words. The horrors of this day will torture me forever. The monstrous cries of the crowds shouting, "Crucify Him!" The mocking of the soldiers, striking my Lord, spitting on Him, jabbing a crown of thorns onto His head. The jerk of His body as the spikes were driven through His hands and feet, the sudden eerie darkness, the blood, the agony etched on His face. And then that shattering cry from the depths of His soul, "My God, my God, why have You forsaken Me?" *O my precious Lord, I, too, have felt that kind of desolation.* How human is my God!

Yet, through all the trials of this week, He has continued to move *out of Himself.* He truly is the Man for others. "If I am the one you are looking for, let these others go."... "Daughters of Jerusalem, do not weep for Me."... "Father, forgive them."... "Today you will be with Me in paradise."... "Woman, behold your son."... and that final giving of Himself, "Father, into Your hands I commit My spirit."

Last night I wanted to die with Him. Now I know that part of me has. Yet there is still too much of *self* in me. I want to die with Him every day, by making a total offering of myself to His Father, and through Him, to other people.

Lord God, as I carry my own little crosses of rejection, hardship and pain, let me be as self-giving as Jesus was upon His cross. I ask for the grace to move out of myself — toward You — toward others.

10 *The Seventh Day*

Two nights ago, I wept. Tonight I am numb. My world has turned as gray as a rain squall in Galilee. All meaning has drained out of my life. My Jesus is dead.

I had been so sure that He truly was the Son of the living God. From the time He cured my mother-in-law with a touch of His hand, I knew He was more than a simple carpenter. He filled my nets with fish, walked on the water and saved me from drowning. There are blind who now see, deaf who now hear, lame who now walk, because He lived. And yet, this Man who raised Lazarus from death is Himself unbelievably...and yet undeniably ...DEAD. How can this be?

I think, now, of that day we stood on Mount Tabor and I saw Him transfigured, His face shining like the sun and His clothing made of light. A voice from the clouds said, "This is My Son, the Chosen One." That body on the cross yesterday was twisted, disfigured, inhumanly marred. How could this Man — now dead — be the Son of God, the Chosen One?

And yet...yet, He did say that on the third day He would rise again. Oh, I desperately *want* to believe that, but my faith wavers. The only prayer I can voice tonight is the one I heard the father of an epileptic child pray:

Lord, I believe. Help my unbelief.

11 Easter

It was not yet dawn when I heard the frantic pounding at the door. I stiffened, cast an anxious look at John. Soldiers? I stood frozen as John cracked the door open just wide enough to see...Mary Magdalene!

"Come quickly," she panted. "The body of Jesus is not in the tomb! A young man in shining robes told me He is risen!"

John hesitated, glanced at me, then dashed out the door. As fast as I could, I ran after him to the tomb. Only the intact linen cloths remained. Incredible! We tried to recall His exact words. "On the third day..." We counted. Could it be? Could it possibly be? Afraid to risk believing, yet churning with suppressed hope, we ran to tell the others.

As we all waited behind closed doors for fear of the high priest's men, Mary came again. Her face was luminous. Her eyes glistened with tears of joy. "I have seen Him! He is risen!" Still we held back, afraid to chance another crushing grief.

But as we stood talking, suddenly there He was, among us — or was it a ghost? No. He asked us to touch Him, showed us His hands and feet, even ate a piece of grilled fish. *Oh my Lord, my precious Lord Jesus! You ARE alive!* The realization burst upon me, splitting open the darkness that surrounded me, radiating outward, beyond time, beyond space. Never again will I fear to risk believing. The shining truth of this day must surely span the centuries.

He lives!
He has won the victory!
He is truly risen!
Hallelujah!

---

12 *...HE is risen...* —MARK 16:6

Was yesterday, Easter Sunday, a day of absolute hope and joy for you? It was for me. It is the day on which Jesus rose from the dead, the day that Jesus proved His spirit can never be destroyed.

My faith tells me that the story of His resurrection is undeniably true. But if I ever needed additional proof, I'd recall something I once heard a minister tell his congregation. "Some people," he said, "aren't quite convinced by the disciples' reports about their having seen Jesus after He emerged from the tomb. They want more proof. But the thing these people fail to grasp is that the disciples verified their claims, not by what they *said*, but by what they *became*. From a poor, bedraggled band of friends in complete shock and despair, they soon became bold men, confident and strong. And they changed the world."

What a powerful thought!

Easter day was the day of Your glory, Lord. I bask in its glow every day of my life. —C.H.

---

13 *IF we confess our sins, He is faithful and just to forgive us our sins, and to cleanse us from all unrighteousness.* —I JOHN 1:9

When I recall the events of Christ's last days on earth, I think of two of His disciples. Both of these men failed Him during that crucial time, but we remember one with affection... and the other with loathing. Why? What was the difference?

Peter denied Christ, denied he ever knew Him three times. When the rooster crowed, Jesus turned and looked at Peter. And Peter remembered Christ's prediction of these denials. Peter went out and wept bitterly.

Peter became the Rock on which Christ's church was built.

Judas betrayed Christ. When he saw Jesus had been condemned and would be crucified, he tried to repent by giving back the 30 pieces of silver he'd been paid to betray Jesus. And when rebuffed by the chief priests and elders, he went out and hanged himself.

What was the difference between these two men? One stayed on to work for the Kingdom of God on earth. The other gave up.

Lord, when I fail, let me work all the harder to succeed for You.
—L. E.W.

14 When the Bible Speaks to Me

GENESIS 6:14-16

I'm a weekend sailor, and I've always loved all manner of boats — everything from a dinghy to an ocean liner. So a part of the Bible that has always held a fascination for me has been the section of Genesis where God describes to Noah how he should build his ark. In the sixth chapter of Genesis the Creator of the Universe becomes a Naval Architect, specifying the details of a magnificent three-deck vessel, 450 feet long, made of resinous woods and composed of rooms designed to accommodate all the living things on earth.

In the time of Noah, a three-deck, 450-foot ship was an awe-inspiring creation. But we have our own awe-inspiring creations today. Last April, as I watched the space shuttle Columbia make its majestic, flawless descent from outer space, my mind harked back to Noah piloting his fabulous craft through uncharted waters.

What comfort and hope it gives me to know that life is an endless chain of miracles. I'm thrilled by the continuity of man's achievements, by the thought that what started in Genesis will continue, and continue and continue. — JAMES McDERMOTT

15

JOYFUL, joyful, we adore Thee,
God of glory, Lord of love. —HENRY VAN DYKE, HYMN

On my way to church on Easter morning, I made two new friends at a bus stop — Shelley and her Seeing Eye dog, Princess. As we waited we chatted, mostly about Princess, a large, reddish-brown Chesapeake retriever. "She just loves to go out," Shelley told me. "It's really *her* bus, *her* church, *her* job, *her* friends at the office. I'm only tagging along."

And then she told me how the night before she and Princess had been at an Easter Vigil in her church. Princess had slept quietly at Shelley's feet until the close of the service at midnight. "Then the bells rang," Shelley said, "and the choir burst into song, and all over the congregation people called, 'Happy Easter! Christ is risen indeed!' Princess woke up, and she caught the joy and excitement in the air. She began barking, and tugging at the leash, trying to bounce and frolic. It was her way of saying that she was glad, too."

I loved that conversation with my bus-stop friend. It got me excited about Easter — for after all, isn't that the way it should be? Bells ringing, people joyful, dogs barking — hallelujah! Christ has risen!

Yes, Lord, You are risen, hallelujah! —J.E.

16

...SPEAK, Lord; for Thy servant heareth. —I SAMUEL 3:9

Lying in bed, halfway between being awake and asleep, I knew that one of those marvelous early spring days had dawned. The day before I'd heard a sermon about asking the Lord, first thing in the morning, what He'd have you do with your day and then rejoicing over whatever He told you. I tried it.

Out of the blue, He seemed to say to me: "Get up and take your boys fishing." It sounded peculiar. Nevertheless, I got out of bed and called out to my 13-year-old twin sons, who were home on spring vacation: "Boys, what do you say we pack a lunch, and I'll take you to the river fishing. We can take the dog." Immediate shouts of joy pierced my ears.

What have You got me into, Lord? I said to myself. I'm not a fishing-type mother. I don't like mud, worms, fish, dirty hands or waiting for the fish to bite. My husband usually takes the twins fishing. I tend to stay closer to our girls and their cleaner activities! My sons were amazed at my offer, but no more so than I was.

We found a pleasant stretch of river. The tall trees seemed to be holding hands high over our heads protecting us from the morning sun. We waded in the creek and walked through the woods. The boys caught some fish, but they were small and much to my relief they threw them back. I was able to overlook their muddy hands while we ate lunch.

The trip was a delight. The boys were open with me and we talked a lot, which I loved. When we got home, they said, "Thanks, Mama. That was fun. We didn't know you could be such a good sport." The rest of their Easter vacation went unbelievably smoothly. We enjoyed one another. That experience made me think that there are probably many unique experiences the Lord would give me if I'd check with Him early each day.

Your ideas are always better than mine, Father. Keep me open to them. —M.B.W.

---

17 *...A DOER of the work, this man shall be blessed in his deed.* —JAMES 1:25

I owed a friend an apology, but knuckling under is hard for me. I was embarrassed by the situation, but worse, I wasn't able to find the words.

I described my problem to my elderly neighbor Mrs. Rigsby, as we sat in her spice-scented kitchen and shared her fresh gingerbread. "Well, does your friend like gingerbread?" she asked.

"Why...I suppose. I mean, anybody would. But what does that have to do with the problem?"

Mrs. Rigsby smoothed her apron. "Ben Franklin once said, 'Better well done than well said.' Don't worry about finding the right words for your friend. Just take her some gingerbread and she'll understand what you're trying to say."

The next day I used Mrs. Rigsby's apology recipe. When I handed the gingerbread to my friend, no word was needed.

I guess St. Paul had the same idea in mind when he told the Corinthians that though we speak with the tongues of angels, it means nothing unless we show love. And that's why when our Master reckons with me maybe He'll say, "Well done (not well said), thou good and faithful servant."

So make me a doer, Lord. A sayer won't get Your work done.

—J.M.B.

18

...And give them compassion... —I KINGS 8:50

Beside the elevator in the surgical wing of the Regional Hospital in Longview, Texas, there is one object that seems out of place. Waiting amidst all the cold steel apparatus — IV stands, cardiograph machines, oxygen tanks, and flashing lights — there is a little red wagon.

The wagon is there for children. Young patients are wheeled into surgery in the little red wagon.

Whenever I see that little red wagon, I know that the world is never so cold, efficient and bureaucratic that there is not room for a quiet touch of compassion.

Show me, Lord, how to bring gentleness to the hard places.

—F.F.

19

RUN the straight race thro' God's good grace
Lift up thine eyes, and seek His face.

—JOHN S.B. MONSELL, HYMN

"What's wrong?" I asked my doctor, as he prodded my knee. "I've been running three years; how come my knee's acting up now?"

"I think you're pushing yourself," he said. "Ever hear of the old running cliché, 'train but don't strain'? Running should be easy, fun — joyful."

"Joyful?"

"Right. Like when you were a kid and ran just for the fun of it. If your running becomes a chore, it means you're trying too hard. So take it easy!"

Out for my morning run the next day, I looked at the faces of my fellow joggers. Many showed strain and fatigue. No wonder running looks like self-inflicted torture to nonrunners!

Same way with Christians, I thought. Some of us just try too hard, and are so stern and grim-lipped in our efforts to follow Christ that we exhaust ourselves and become useless for doing God's will. And think of the people we must turn off!

Let me run the course for You, Jesus, joyfully. —C.C.

20 *HE must increase, but I must decrease.* —JOHN 3:30

All through my youth, I suffered from shyness. One evening, at a church fellowship I belonged to, I was asked to stand up and introduce some newcomers to the rest of the group.

"Oh, no!" I said. "I can't. I'm too shy."

They let me beg off. A little while later, though, I happened to overhear my friend Sally telling another girl: "I don't think people are shy. I think it's just another name for ego."

This bewildered me. As soon as she was alone I approached her and asked her what she meant.

"Well," Sally said, embarrassed, "I really think that some people are so self-centered, so worried about what other people think of them, that their fear makes them say that they are shy. To tell the truth, if you'd been thinking more about making these newcomers feel at home here, and less about the impression you were making, you wouldn't have had time to be shy. You'd just get up and welcome them."

Ever since then I've been trying to get out of myself by reaching out to others, sincerely. And, you know, I'm not really afraid to show myself as I am. After all, God made me in *His* image. Why should I be ashamed of that?

The more I fill myself with You, Lord, the more confident I become. —E.V.S.

21

TAKE time to be holy,
Speak oft with Thy Lord. —W.D. LONGSTAFF, HYMN

I watched him from the window... my five-year-old son galloping across the grass on an imaginary horse. His head bobbed under a heap of Indian feathers, looking as if a giant peacock had landed in his hair. He was Chief Big Eagle, or so he said. And in his hand he clutched his brand-new bow and arrow, the harmless, rubber-tipped kind.

He reined his invisible horse to a stop under the maple, placed the arrow into his bow and took aim at the sky. But the arrow took a limp little nose dive to the ground a few inches in front of him. He tried again and again. But the arrow refused to take off. It just fizzled to the ground like a deflated tire.

"My arrow won't shoot," he whined, as he dragged his bow behind him into the house.

I smiled at him under all those drooping feathers and shook my head. "I know," I said. "You didn't draw back."

His eyes lighted up. Then he went back out and sent an arrow onto the neighbor's roof. But at least he'd discovered the secret of flying arrows.

It's a secret I need to remember, too. For life is the same way. Only as I draw back to God, to the Source of my strength and power, does my life soar to full potential. For like the arrow I must withdraw in order to go forward, or else I usually fall on my face. My flying power comes from retreating into His presence.

Lord, pull me back on Your gentle string. —S.M.K.

22 *...YEA, I have loved thee with an everlasting love: therefore with lovingkindness have I drawn thee.*

—JEREMIAH 31:3

It was a beautiful spring day. As I headed home at the end of a day of teaching, I heard two young girls giggling. They were sprawled on the lawn, pulling petals out of a daisy and chanting: He loves me...he loves me not...he loves me...he loves me not....

Silly game, I said to myself. Someday they'll know that true love isn't ruled by chance.

But a little farther on a stab of guilt shot through me. You know, old as I am, I'm often just as foolish when it comes to God's love for me. I get a raise at work; God loves me. My hours get cut back; He loves me not. I get a good grade on my test; God loves me. I can't get into a class I want; He loves me not.

How silly of me! Why don't I remember that God loves me *all* the time, that even my disappointments are part of the love. I don't need a daisy to tell me that!

Lord, I know *You love me all the time. Just help me to remember, especially when things seem dark.* —J.L.H.

23 *...DAILY shall He be praised.* —PSALM 72:15

My desk calendar lay open to April 23. Not a single appointment dotted the white expanse. I took a handful of pages and flipped back through March and February. I couldn't believe how many blank pages there were. "All these days gone by and so little to show for them," I said to myself.

But then I flipped to April 22. There was my notation of a lunch date with friends. What a pleasure that lunch had been!

Quickly now I scribbled down these words: "Lord, I give thanks that You brought these wonderful friends into my life."

And on April 24, when my office was alive with sunlight, I leaned over and wrote on the calendar, "Thank You, God, for this bright shiny day."

It's autumn now, and as the days have gone by, I've come to know that what I have to show for them isn't the important thing. What's important is what God has shown me. Not a day passes that my calendar doesn't reveal my praise for one of His gifts to me.

Why not try making your desk or wall calendar into a day-by-day record of God's abundance in your life? You'll be amazed how blessed you are.

And daily shall I praise You, Father. —L. V.

---

24 *WHATSOEVER thy hand findeth to do, do it with thy might...* —ECCLESIASTES 9:10

Recently I read a study conducted by a large university that mentioned four characteristics common to highly successful business leaders. According to the study, decisiveness, persistence, self-assurance and discipline were all-important executive traits.

I've often thought that these good business qualities are not out of place when applied to our spiritual lives. For instance, have you made your decision (1) for Christ? That's the biggest decision of all. Do you persist (2) in your prayers when you think God isn't listening? Do you have the self-assurance (3) to remain unswayed when others scorn or deny your belief? And, finally, do you have the discipline (4) to live your life as your Savior would have you live it, as well as expecting those close to you to pursue this ideal?

If you don't measure up, perhaps you might think about applying some sound business principles to your spiritual life.

The most important "business" of my life is You, Lord.

—C.M.D.

25

AND whatsoever ye do in word or deed, do all in the name of the Lord Jesus, giving thanks to God and the Father by Him. —COLOSSIANS 3:17

One Sunday my friend, Si Anthony, drove by our house, his old, green pickup truck loaded down with furniture. An hour later he passed by again with a different load. The third time he passed, I hailed him down.

"Hey, Si," I said, "I thought Sunday was a day of rest!"

"Yes," he said, "it is. But it's also a day of worship, and I've divided worship into two categories. This morning I worshiped in church. This afternoon I'm putting into practice what I learned there. I call this 'workship.'" He tooted his truck's ahh-ooga horn and was off.

Later Si told me that furniture belonged to a widow who was moving to a smaller house. Some of his other Sunday "workship" projects included planting a flower garden for his daughter and straightening out his elderly neighbor's garage. "I love to be outdoors," Si told me, "and anything that gets me there, I enjoy. So, in a way, 'workship' is rest, too."

I think Si has chosen a creative way of "resting," and I'm going to try to find a few "workship" projects of my own. Perhaps you'd like to, too.

I'm learning, Lord, that resting doesn't exclude helping others.

—J.McD.

26

...HOLY, holy, holy, is the Lord of hosts: the whole earth is full of His glory. —ISAIAH 6:3

One day everything seemed to be going wrong in Edna Albrecht's life: Her husband was laid up with a broken hip; two sons were squabbling; and a broken water pipe had just flooded her kitchen. Just when Edna was about to take out her frustration by yelling at her boys, she stopped. A childhood memory of something an old nurse used to say to her came to mind. The old nurse was crippled and was often in pain, but was never known to complain. "I don't talk about my troubles to people," she'd tell Edna, "I save my complaints for God."

That gloomy day Edna went upstairs and bowed her head in prayer. But just as she began to tell God about her sorry state, something strange happened. She found herself listening to the rhythmic sound of the rain outside. *Well, complain. Go on, complain!* she said to herself. But she couldn't. The rain, how beautiful it was...she found herself thanking God for the rain.

Then, on the floor she saw some crumpled sheets of paper that her boys had left — another example of their untidiness! But kneeling to pick them up, she read the composition that one of them had written. In it she saw a miracle of maturing, thoughts and feelings coming of age. It made her proud just to be a part of her son's life.

And that's the way it went, until it came to her what her old nurse had meant. Who can linger in our mighty God's presence and still dwell on the small, the unimportant? Who can pray without cherishing the gift of life that He has given us? Yes, saving complaints for God meant forgetting all about them.

Oh, Lord, we can never stand in Your presence without feeling a deep sense of gratitude. —N.V.P.

27

AND I was afraid, and went and hid thy talent in the earth . . . —MATTHEW 25:25

Last week somebody sent me a pencil with erasers on both ends.

Of course there was a joke attached: "Two heads are better than one, when it comes to erasing mistakes."

With this kind of pencil you cannot make any mistakes. But neither can you write. I'm afraid my playful correspondent was poking fun at a failing of mine. Fearing mistakes, I'm a little too careful. A little bit like that fellow in the Bible who buried the talent his master had given him instead of putting it to work.

I keep my nonwriting pencil handy now to remind me to trust God more and myself less. God, I'm certain, doesn't approve of lives with erasers at both ends. He wants me to take a few chances. He wants me to try.

He wants you to try, too.

Father God, I trust You to approve of my honest efforts, even if they fail. —M.A.

28

NEITHER do men light a candle, and put it under a bushel, but on a candlestick; and it giveth light unto all that are in the house. —MATTHEW 5:15

It was a typical spring thunderstorm with spurts of lightning, thunder rumbling and rain swirling against the windows. And, as so often happens, the electricity went off, plunging the house into darkness.

"Stay where you are until I get a candle," I instructed my daughter and her little playmate.

I fumbled in the cupboard drawer and came up with a stubby white candle that I lit. Standing in the small circle of its light, I asked, "Now, isn't that better?"

"It's too small," my child whimpered. "Most of the room is still dark."

"Don't you have a candlestick?" her friend asked. "Mama always puts our candle in a candlestick and sets it in the middle of the table. That makes the light go all over the room."

What she said was true. As soon as I placed the candle in a tall candlestick, the light shone into the dark corners.

Many people spend their lives stumbling about in darkness, a spiritual darkness, because the Light of the world has not reached them. Truly, Jesus is the Light, but we can be His candlesticks. Unless we stand erect to hold the Light high, some corners of the universe will always be dark.

How high do you hold His light?

Use me, Lord. Let me help You bring light to the darkness.

—D. D.

29

ALL Scripture is inspired by God and is profitable for teaching . . .

—II TIMOTHY 3:16 (ML)

I was stuck in a hospital bed, recuperating from surgery. The previous patient, a little girl, had left her coloring book and crayons. When I couldn't take any more television, I picked up the coloring book.

This might sound strange, but I loved coloring the drawings of cats, and, when I'd finished the book, I wished there were more.

Back to the television, I thought, but then one of my daughters dropped in. I showed her the book, said how much fun I'd had with it, and told her I was sorry to be finished with it.

"Well, Mom, maybe you're not quite finished with it." She pulled a pocket Bible from her purse. "Let's find an appropriate Scripture for each picture, a verse that expresses its feeling."

We started with a picture of two kittens lapping up milk and wrote, "God shall supply all your need..." (Philippians 4:19).

Every picture called forth a verse. We had a wonderful time, and afterward I wished I'd played this game with my children long before.

So, I'll have to play it with my grandchildren when they get a little older. Then they'll soon learn how to use the Bible, and they'll also learn how to look for the true feelings in life's little moments. And — so will I.

Father, please show me new ways to bring Your word to light.

—M.B.W.

30

...BE sure your sin will find you out. —NUMBERS 32:23

Once upon a time a little girl named Mary had a rag doll which was stuffed with wheat straw. One day early in the spring — just about this time of year — Mary and her brother Billy had a fuss. Mary ran crying to Mother. When Billy saw that Mary had dropped her doll, he ran off and buried it.

The next day Mother asked Billy, "Have you seen Mary's doll?"

"No, Mom," Billy said fearfully. He was ashamed; he'd told a lie. But no one found the doll, so he thought, *Nobody will ever know*.

Several weeks went by. One day Mother was surveying the garden for spring planting. Suddenly she said, "Look at this bunch of wheat coming up right in our garden plot!"

"And it's just the shape of my old doll," Mary exclaimed.

That's an old tale I tell to my little grandchildren, but there's a big truth inside it: A lie or cruel act that you try to hide has a way of coming to light.

Whenever I'm tempted to say, "No one will ever know," I try to remind myself that *Someone* always knows.

Let me always find my way by Your light, Lord. —I.C.

S	M	T	W	T	F	S
						1
2	3	4	5	6	7	8
9	10	11	12	13	14	15
16	17	18	19	20	21	22
23	24	25	26	27	28	29
30	31					

The Fifth Commandment

Honour thy father and thy mother...

—EXODUS 20:12

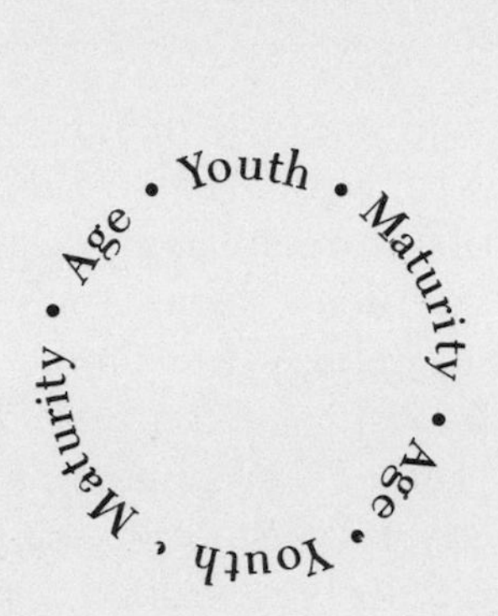

THIS is the way the world goes round:
In tender continuity,
Generation after generation
Caring for the other,
Age for youth, maturity for age,
Each in its time.

Youth. Maturity. Age.
This is the way the world goes round:
We, God's grateful children
Held together by an endless chain,
Linked with love,
Honor bound.

1 *...LET every man be swift to hear, slow to speak, slow to wrath: For the wrath of man worketh not the righteousness of God.* —JAMES 1:19, 20

I had repeatedly explained to the neighborhood children that I didn't want them ringing the doorbell during the baby's nap time. One May afternoon, therefore, I was especially irritated when the bell rang. I dashed to the door, threw it open and was ready to let the kids have it — but nobody was there.

As I stood there, something fell off the door handle. It was a lovely straw basket. Then I saw some lilac blossoms and tulips scattered on the porch, and out of the corner of my eye, I could see six-year-old Nancy peeking around a tree. She was frightened. And I was embarrassed. So embarrassed that I picked up the flowers, and made a quick retreat into the house.

There, I'd let my temper flare again, I thought. *And without just cause.* I knew I'd have to make it up to Nancy later. But I wondered how many blessings I had missed because I had acted or spoken in haste.

Once a friend had told me how she dealt with her temper. "Instead of counting to ten, I just repeat slowly, 'In the name of the Father...and of the Son...and of the Holy Spirit.' It takes the same amount of time, and gets better results. That was the second gift I brought into the house that May Day afternoon.

In the name of the Father... —S.P.W.

2 *DAVID said to Saul, "Let no one lose courage..."*

—I SAMUEL 17:32 (MLV)

In May, 1940, the first spring of World War II, Adolf Hitler suddenly unleashed his *blitzkrieg* against the Allies. In a short and stunning campaign, the panzer divisions swept through Holland, Belgium and past the Maginot Line; France was overrun; British soldiers were pushed into the sea at Dunkirk.

On the day that France surrendered, the darkest day of the entire war, Winston Churchill called his cabinet together in emergency session. This bulldog of a British prime minister looked down the conference table at the somber faces of his ministers.

"Gentlemen," Churchill said, "we now stand alone. And let me say that I find it inspiring."

Some people might call that statement an example of foolish optimism. I wonder, however, if it isn't really a wonderful example of courage and faith. I wonder if it isn't what young David was feeling when he went out to meet his giant adversary. I wonder if it isn't what *I* should be feeling when I face troubles that seem overwhelming.

O, Lord, the more faith I have, the more strength I have. Thank You.

—V.V.

3 *...I WILL teach you the good and the right way.*

—I SAMUEL 12:23

That afternoon we were planning a party for some visiting relatives, but first my father and I had to pick rocks out of the newly plowed field. We wanted to plant corn in this field the next day, so we didn't have much time.

"We'd better hustle," I said to my dad, heaving rocks into the truck. They bonged off the steel like bombs exploding.

My dad winced at the horrible racket I was making, and said, "Come on, Edward, not so fast. Let's move with Godspeed."

"What's that mean?" I asked.

"It means, let's not get all out of breath and worried that we won't get this job done. Let's take our time, do the job right, and keep our presence of mind. Don't think, 'Gotta hustle, gotta hurry.' Think, 'It sure feels good working out in the air and sun. Thanks, God, for a strong back and this rich field to work in.' Then the morning will move with Godspeed."

Godspeed. It means "successful journeying, going with God's blessing."

Godspeed to you. Godspeed to your day.

Don't let me get lost in a frantic pace, Lord. It's not how fast I go, it's how in tune I am with You that's important. —E.B.P.

4 *THEREFORE they shall come and sing in the height of Zion, and shall flow together to the goodness of the Lord...*

—JEREMIAH 31:12

I watched a television show the other night about gorillas. One segment showed a zoo keeper teaching a mother gorilla how to take care of her baby. I'd always assumed that breeding, giving birth and caring for young was instinctive in animals. But this isn't quite so. These abilities are inborn, an expert explained, but a gorilla must be in its natural habitat if the abilities are to develop naturally.

In the African forest, each gorilla can learn its instinctive behavior from its elders and peers. In a zoo, though, a gorilla often has no elders to learn from. Fortunately, there are caring zoo keepers to help them.

We human beings are smarter than gorillas, but later I thought about how we often unnecessarily cut ourselves off from our healthiest, most natural habitats.

When I'm tired on a Sunday morning I sometimes say, "I can be a Christian without going to church." This might be partly true, but why should I make life harder? Why deny myself the chance to learn from other Christians about the wonders of God?

I like to think my Christianity is instinctive in me. And most likely it is. But I can't forget that I'll be a stronger Christian by living in a Christian habitat.

Thank You, Lord, for the rewards of Christian fellowship.

—D.D.

5 *TO every thing there is a season, and a time to every purpose...* —ECCLESIASTES 3:1

The other day my friend Martha was telling why her six-year-old son wanted to give up piano lessons so soon after he'd started. "He said he just doesn't have time to practice every day."

"How long did his teacher ask him to practice?" I asked.

"Fifteen minutes!"

We laughed at the idea of a little boy too busy to practice the piano a mere 15 minutes a day. What on earth could he have to do that was so important?

But later I began to wonder. Does God also laugh — but sadly — at me when I think I don't have 15 minutes to give to Him every day? What else do I have to do that is so important?

Let me always find time for You, Lord. —P.H.S.

6 *LET the beauty of Jesus be seen in me.* —OLD HYMN

When Mother Teresa of India won her Nobel Prize, she exhorted us to "recognize Jesus in the disturbing disguise of the poor" in her acceptance speech. This is good advice, but I learned a while back that it can apply to more than the poor.

There's a man in my office who does his job well, but he's unbearably rude to his co-workers. For a long time I thought there was no way to reach him. But then I wondered if it was possible to "recognize Jesus in the disturbing disguise of the *selfish*."

Of course it's possible. Just as faith dwells deep inside those who are starved for food, faith also dwells deep within those who are starved for love and warmth.

I'm learning that if I make myself see through his disturbing disguise of selfishness, I'll see Jesus deep within that man in my office. He's been impoverished, but, as with Mother Teresa's poor, I'm finding he can be made rich with love if I help nurture God's seed within him.

Dear Lord, let me always see Jesus in those who don't even know He is in them. —M.A.

---

7 *...LET thine heart keep My commandments: for length of days, and long life, and peace, shall they add to thee.* —PROVERBS 3:1,2

The other night a television program taught me how to compute my "body age." Body age, I learned, may be more or less than my age in years.

The program pulled no punches. My life span, it said, could be diminished five years or more by obesity, tobacco, lack of exercise, or too much stress. My blood pressure and cholesterol count would tell me if I was a lot older than I thought I was.

But the program did give me hope: Good habits *do* lengthen life span.

As I analyzed my health habits, something else occurred to me. What's my "spiritual age"?

Just as bad health habits age the body, bad spiritual habits age and wither the soul, making it lifeless. To check on my body age I can go to my doctor, my bathroom scale, or do a few exercises and see how out of breath I get. But how to check my spiritual age?

I can go to my minister and join the Bible study group he's conducting. I can check myself with the Commandments, and then the Beatitudes. And the "Love chapter" in I Corinthians (Chapter 13) is a good measuring stick, too!

Oh, Lord, when I'm in harmony with You, I'm forever young.

—J.M.B.

8 *HAVING eyes, see ye not? . . .* —MARK 8:18

While Mother and my aunts prepared the 50th anniversary dinner for my grandparents, I took my six-year-old self to the vacant lot and picked a bouquet of lavender blooming thistles. After climbing on a chair to get Mother's cut-glass vase, I put my "flowers" on the table, next to the centerpiece from the florist.

Just as Granddaddy opened his mouth to say grace, Aunt Alta looked up and said, "Well, for heaven's sake, who put those weeds on the table?" I was too embarrassed to confess, but as Aunt Alta started to carry away my bouquet, Granddaddy said, "No! Leave them there. It's been a long time since I've really *looked* at a thistle in bloom. They're quite pretty, aren't they? Let's thank the Lord for the gift of seeing with fresh new eyes!"

I don't remember anything else about that day, but the cut-glass vase now sits on my kitchen window sill, reminding me of a very old man with fresh new eyes. It even prods me, now and then, to look for something I usually take for granted and try out "Granddaddy's eyes" on it — the painting on the living-room wall that I walk blindly by each day, the dance of the willow in the March wind, the crinkles around my husband's eyes when he laughs. What taken-for-granted, God-given things can you find, today, to see with fresh eyes?

Not all the wonders of Your world are grand and dramatic, Lord. Let me see and feel and delight in the little ones, too.

—M.M.H.

9

A MERRY heart doeth good like a medicine...

—PROVERBS 17:22

God didn't put us on this earth to be bored. He wants us to have fun — to be stimulated and excited by life. My mother knew this better than anyone. She was a real companion to her three girls. I can't remember her ever being too busy to get the car out of the garage and run us around — to a music lesson, the public library, a friend's house. Or maybe just to the drugstore for ice cream.

One day we were cruising along Washington Avenue in that old car, heading for the Pig 'N' Whistle. Leila was about 12 years old then, I about 10 and Bette 4. We older girls were in the back seat and Bette was up front with Mother. Leila had been very quiet for a time, just staring at the back of Mother's head. Suddenly she blurted out, "Mother, I wish you'd get rid of that hat."

Mother's hand touched the flower-bedecked brim on her head. "You don't like my hat?" she asked.

"I hate it!" Leila said. "It makes you look tacky!"

Mother's eyes darted to the rearview mirror. No cars were coming behind her. Without a word, she snatched the hat off and pitched it out the open window.

Leila and I gasped in amazement and whirled to look out the back window at the hat dancing merrily down the middle of the street. Then we all burst into laughter.

"No more being tacky," Mother said.

Silly? Of course it was silly. And, strictly speaking, her impulsive act may have violated some very valid ordinance against littering. But it was fun. Mother confided much later, the hat was old, its flowers faded, and she was going to discard it anyway.

What a beautiful childhood Mother gave us, built of love — and laughter.

Father God, so many of Your gifts have come to me through my mother. Thank You both. —D.D.

10

...FOR every one that asketh receiveth...

—MATTHEW 7:8

My nine-year-old daughter and I were jumping waves in the Gulf of Mexico, when Kate said, "Mother, I can't touch!" I grabbed her hand to pull her toward me and realized suddenly that I couldn't touch bottom either.

I'm a competent swimmer, so I was not overly worried. "Hang onto my shoulders," I said to Kate, "and I'll tow you in."

But there was a bad undertow. No matter how hard I swam, we remained in the same spot. All around us others were romping in the water. I didn't want them to see my helplessness. I knew that if I could manage to move only a few feet closer to shore I would be able to touch bottom.

A few minutes later and no farther in, I had to face the truth. The current was too strong for me. Incredible as it might seem, right there, a couple of yards off a public beach, Kate and I could very well drown.

"Help!" I cried. "Help!" People turned to stare, apparently thinking I was playing some sort of game. Then Kate, catching my panic, began to scream also. A lifeguard strode out from shore and easily drew us to safety.

Why is it so difficult for me to ask for help when I obviously need it? Maybe it's because I haven't learned the difference between honesty and pride. Pride is so often blind, but honesty can mean admitting when I'm powerless. I won't be a sensible swimmer until I learn this. And I won't be a sensible Christian, either.

Lord, give me the sense to know when it is time to ask for help from others ... and from You. —L. D.

11

AND these words ... shall be in thine heart ... when thou liest down, and when thou risest up.

—DEUTERONOMY 6:6,7

Years ago my son, then four, and his four-year-old playmate Margie were playing a lively game of "slam the door" when his finger got caught. "Bad old Margie," John, Jr. wailed, holding his throbbing, badly cut finger.

The "bad old Margie" litany continued at top volume all the way to the hospital emergency room until the anesthesia wore it down like an old windup Victrola running out of steam.

The surgeon was skillful, and soon the anesthetist was bringing John, Jr. around. "Bad old Margie," he murmured. Then, when he found his voice, he was off again, loudly berating his playmate.

That was over 20 years ago. The hapless Margie has been long forgiven, and the incident probably forgotten by John, Jr. But I haven't forgotten its message: What was on my child's mind when he went to sleep was on his mind when he woke up.

I've found that this is often true in my own life. If I carry my concerns with me to sleep at night, they're likely to be there in the morning. But there's no need for this. If I surrender my burdens to God before I go to bed, I awake refreshed, surrounded by His love.

Lord, when I lay me down to sleep, I'm always Yours to hold and keep. —I.C.

12 When the Bible Speaks to Me

PSALM 119:105

The late President Chiang Kai-shek was my personal friend. This great Chinese statesman literally lived the Bible. He would walk a long terrace every morning at five o'clock for an hour or more, repeating Bible verses as he walked. He told me that he wanted to be sure the Bible was "inside of him." By memorizing verses and saying them over and over, he believed they would "soak" deeply into his consciousness.

I myself make a practice of walking two or three miles every day and I repeat aloud as many Bible verses as I can think of at the time. Not all are letter perfect, word for word, but the essence and the message come through.

"If you will fill your mind with God's words," my grandmother used to say to me, "they will come back to bless, guide and help you in every time of need."

It's true. As I take my many walks, the old words seem to reveal new meaning and fresh insights. They minister to my personal needs. And, even more significantly, they move me into action.

Indeed the Bible speaks to me — and I am convinced that it will to anybody who learns to speak the great words.

— NORMAN VINCENT PEALE

13

LOVE divine, all loves excelling,
Joy of heaven, to earth come down...

—CHARLES WESLEY, HYMN

Toward the end of World War II, as a young bride, I was on a train, enroute across the country to meet my soldier husband in El Paso, Texas. We were in a Pullman car for three days and nights, so most of the passengers got to know one another very well. Soon everybody knew about my husband and how excited I was to be joining him. I couldn't stop talking about how wonderful he was.

When the train wheezed to a stop in El Paso for a brief layover, all of my train mates, the entire group, left with me and pushed through the crowd to meet this one who was so greatly loved.

Suppose all Christians were as enthusiastic in expressing their love for Jesus? What a different world this would be! Soon everyone would want to meet this One so greatly loved. Suppose we start it, you and I? Suppose this very day we begin to tell the world about this greatest love of all!

To love You, Lord, is not enough. Such love must be shared.

—D. D.

14

SEE, the streams of living waters,
Springing from eternal Love,
Well supply thy sons and daughters,
And all fear of want remove. —JOHN NEWTON, HYMN

Not long ago Guideposts sent me to interview marathon runner Bill Rodgers. At the end of the interview, I mentioned that I would be handing out water to runners in the next New York City Marathon.

"Great!" he said. "You have no idea how important water is to us runners."

Then he told me how, early in his racing career, he ran the first ten miles of a marathon without stopping for water. He was running well and he thought he didn't need it. At 17 miles, however, his muscles cramped and he "hit the wall"; he had to stop.

"I now know," he explained, "that you have to keep replacing the water that you lose in sweat. And if you don't take any water early in the race, you'll dehydrate later on. The point is," Rodgers summed up, "you have to take water even when you think you don't need it."

What an obvious parallel between running a marathon and living the Christian life! How often I've felt so strong and confident that I didn't seem to need Jesus, yet Jesus said, "If any man thirst, let him come unto Me and drink." (John 7:37)

And Jesus might have added: "Even when you think you don't need it."

Lord, You are the source of all my strength. If I am to run a good Christian race, I must come to You often. —C.C.

15 *...BECAUSE thou hast seen Me, thou hast believed: blessed are they that have not seen, and yet have believed.* —JOHN 20:29

Last spring Amy, my three-year-old niece, rode in my truck as I hauled wheat from the field to the elevator.

"Where does it all go?" she asked, as she watched grain pouring from the truck.

I pointed to the towering elevators. "Way up there."

"No it can't!" she said. "I see the wheat going down into the ground!"

Patiently I explained that the grain went first into an underground pit, then was carried by a huge auger up into the elevators. Amy still didn't believe me.

"I see it going down," she insisted.

My, this little girl is being silly, I thought. But as we rode for another load I remembered all the times *I* had refused to believe in what I couldn't see.

The next day I arranged to have Amy tour through the grain elevator. As soon as she saw the auger, she understood. I put my arm around her and said, "Someday soon you'll begin to trust in things you can't see." And that's how we began Amy's first lessons in believing — lessons we're never too old to learn anew.

Someday, Lord, I'll see it all. But for now — I believe, I believe. —P.V.S.

16 *I NEED Thee, O I need Thee,*
Every hour I need Thee. —ANNIE S. HAWKS, HYMN

Puffing my way up the stairs of a new watchtower overlooking New Hampshire's Lake Winnipesaukee, I saw the fresh boards were already acquiring the graffiti that had scarred the old ones. These scrawlings seemed especially vulgar in the serene lakeside setting. Yet, on one railing, I noticed these poignant words, "I'm lonely, Chris. I need you."

At first I thought it odd that someone would write such a heartfelt appeal way out in the middle of nowhere. Then it occurred to me that there was one letter left out of the message, a letter shaped like a cross, that could make all the difference for the writer. By including that letter, the call for help would reach the only One Who could be counted on to hear the needs of the writer.

"I'm lonely, Christ." This would find a response in the tender, caring love of the One Who died on that cross so that we would not feel estranged and lonely because of our sins.

Wherever we are, whatever circumstances we face, Christ is as close as the wood on which some people scribble messages...as close as our whisper, "Christ, I need You."

You are always there, Jesus. The next time I feel lonely, help me to remember that. —P.B.H.

17 *Jesus calls us from the worship*
Of the vain world's golden store,
From each idol that would keep us,
Saying, "Christian, love Me more!"

—CECIL F. ALEXANDER, HYMN

When I read a report that the average American gives 15 percent of his time to watching television and less than 1 percent to the church, I mentally dismissed it as applying to "the other guy." Then I began figuring my own time. One, sometimes two hours in church each week? And then, how many hours did I give to television? I *was* the other guy!

Then I began comparing what I received from each. Too often TV wore me down with violence and foolishness, while time spent with God always calmed and comforted me.

And now do you know where I keep my Bible? Answer: On top of my TV.

Lord, You've given me all kinds of choices of what to do with my life. Help me to choose wisely. —R.S.

18 *OPEN my eyes, that I may see*
The gifts of love Thou hast for me.

—CLARA H. SCOTT, HYMN

My husband and I had moved to California. I was miserable about leaving green Oregon for this dry, brown place. "One year and we're leaving," I told myself.

After a few months, still feeling bad, I met a woman who lived in the desert near Barstow. She told me she'd lived there ten years. I asked, how had she done it?

"I was bitter when we had to move here," she said, "but when I saw that my children were sad, too, I realized I couldn't just mope and forget about them. So I decided to act as if Barstow were the peachiest place on earth. I tried to make my kids see the beautiful things: the magnificent sunsets, the desert plants and animals, the brilliant stars in the black-velvet sky. Well, the kids started getting excited, and before I knew it I was getting excited, too. Barstow really *did* have its own special beauty. I guess I got to love my new home when I started making it seem lovely to others."

That attitude has kept me in California for 20 years. Once I really looked, I saw so much!

Lord, remind me always that showing Your goodness to others is the best way of showing it to myself. —J.M.B.

19

CHARITY [*love*] *suffereth long, and is kind...*

—I CORINTHIANS 13:4

The most important Bible lesson of my childhood came about because of a holy terror named Wilfred. Our whole block was filled with little girls, and little girl activities. There was just one flaw, Wilfred, the lone boy on our street. He teased us constantly. Whenever we played house or had tea parties, Wilfred was a menace. He stood on his side of the fence and bombarded the playhouse with heavy clods of dirt. We were always complaining bitterly to my father about awful Wilfred.

"Sounds to me like Wilfred just wants to be where the action is," said Father. "Why don't you ask him to join you?"

"To play house, or have a tea party?" we asked scornfully.

"Why don't you invite him to your pet show?" suggested Mother. "This is a good chance to put 'love thy neighbor' to work."

We didn't think much of the idea, but we agreed, reluctantly, to invite Wilfred. And he came! He brought his pet hamster, and politely admired our kittens and Meg's parakeet. His mother sent some pink lemonade and we had our own circus.

That's the day I found that even holy terrors respond to love.

We all need love, Father — especially the unlovely. —D.E.

---

20 *FOR I am persuaded, that neither death, nor life, nor angels, nor principalities, nor powers, nor things present nor things to come; Nor height, nor depth, nor any other creature, shall be able to separate us from the love of God, which is in Christ Jesus our Lord.*

—ROMANS 8:38, 39

He came clutching a handful of daisies. He came just as he did every day, passed the nurse's desk, where I was working, down the hospital corridor to his daughter's room. She was nearly six now, shut away in a world of unconsciousness and coma. Yet sometimes I heard him, as he sat by her bedside, talking to her about her dog or her brother or even the weather.

I came into the room that day as he was stroking her hair with his hand and telling her a story. The daisies drooped over the sides of a little plastic cup, positioned where she would see them if she opened her eyes. He paused at my entry and patted his daughter's hand. She was still, so still that for an instant I looked with relief at the rise and fall of the sheet over her chest.

I wondered how he sat here day after day, without ever getting a thank-you for the flowers, without her eager eyes to follow his stories, without a smile to meet his, or a hug or even the flutter of her eyelash. He gave his love and all he ever got in return was her slow, comatose breathing and the awful stillness.

"It must be hard to keep giving so much love when she's... like this," I said, gently.

"I suppose," he answered. "But I'll keep coming and bringing the flowers and telling these stories even if she's oblivious to it because, you see, I love her whether or not she loves me back."

And suddenly there was a whisper tugging in my heart. When I am oblivious to God, when I ignore His gifts and fail to return His smile, when my response to His love is not so much as the blink of an eye, still He keeps coming back, loving me anyway. For His love does not depend on my return. It is unconditional and eternal, yet as tender as a father's, who strokes my hair, and waits.

As I slipped away, the tears swimming in my eyes were for the little girl who was loved so sublimely. But they were also for myself.

Don't let me keep You waiting, Lord. Wake me up to Your glorious love. —S.M.K.

21

WHEN I consider Thy heavens, the work of Thy fingers, the moon and the stars, which Thou hast ordained; What is man, that Thou art mindful of him? and the son of man, that Thou visitest him?

—PSALM 8:3, 4

Almost anything can be rendered as a scale model, except the universe. If the earth were represented by a ball only an inch in diameter, the nearest star (Alpha Centauri) outside of our solar system would have to be placed nearly 50,000 miles away!

It's hard for my mind to consider such boundless distance. Fifty thousand miles is more than twice around our equator.

The universe — what an awesome thing to comprehend. Even more awesome is the thought that out of the four-and-a-half billion people on the earth, God cares about me. And yet He does.

Oh, Lord, how great Thou art. —I.C.

---

22 *UNTO Thee lift I up mine eyes...* —PSALM 123:1

I first came to love ballet when I was taken to a performance of "Swan Lake" at the age of five. I was thrilled by the beauty and grace of the dancers as they swirled and leaped and pirouetted about the stage, and yet, I was bewildered, too. *How do they keep from spinning right off the stage and onto the floor in a dizzy heap?* I wondered. And I kept right on wondering until one day I asked a ballet teacher how the dancers kept their balance in pirouette after pirouette.

"Easy," he replied. "They just fix their eyes on one spot and return to it with each whirl. So long as they have that, they can keep going on and on."

I had reason to remember those words — and to put them to use — not long ago. On a balmy Saturday afternoon in New York City I was trying to make my way down Fifth Avenue, but it was so crowded with shoppers that the going was difficult. I was buffeted and shoved, and as I crossed 53rd Street I was almost pushed into an oncoming car. Angrily I whirled around, ready to hurl harsh words. But just then my eyes were caught by the spires of St. Thomas' Church with its cross silhouetted against the sky. *Jesus*... I thought,... *fix my eyes on Jesus, that's the way to keep my balance in this dizzying world.*

The harsh words never came.

Help me not to lose sight of You, Lord, especially when I'm running around in circles. —E.V.S.

23

...HE gave to the sea His decree, that the waters should not pass His commandment... —PROVERBS 8:29

Walking the beach at sunset, I watched a sandpiper gathering his supper from the sand — small sea creatures which had been carried in, sand creatures uncovered by the sweeping water. The sandpiper scarcely moved as the fringes of tide touched his feet — it was as if he knew that even the thundering waves could come only so far, could not really harm him. I admired this small bird's trust and tranquility: frail and alone in an enormous world, he stood his ground.

Sometimes the waves of trouble threaten to swamp me. Yet I know the same Hand that controls the ocean's flow controls my life as well. I believe that both the little sandpiper and I are precious to God. He stands his ground by instinct; I stand my ground by faith.

Trouble is always near, Lord, but You are nearer still. —J.E.

24

"HE who believes in Me, as the scripture has said, 'Out of his heart shall flow rivers of living water.'"

—JOHN 7: 38 (RSV)

The Sea of Galilee teems with plant and animal life. Today, just as in Jesus' time, many an able fisherman earns a living from its bountiful waters. In startling contrast the Dead Sea, to the south, is incapable of supporting life of any kind at all. In fact, so deadly are its waters, it's reported that birds won't even fly over them. The Sea of Galilee thrives because it not only receives water from the River Jordan, but passes it on as well. The Dead Sea receives water from the River Jordan, too, but since there are no significant outlets for it, the water merely stays and stagnates.

People are like those two seas. Those who receive and give in return are healthy, but those who receive and never give are doomed to stagnation.

Make me a giver, Lord. —K.B.S.

25

DRAW nigh to God, and He will draw nigh to you.

—JAMES 4:8

I used to feel cheated when I heard friends say that God talks to them, giving guidance and direction. What's wrong with me, I wondered, that I could not also hear His voice?

Then at a retreat which I attended last year, one of the speakers told us quite seriously that God writes him a letter each morning. He explained that after his prayers and Bible reading, he takes pen in hand and jots down the first words that come to his mind. "It's as if God were speaking to me personally," he said.

Now, morning after morning, I invite Jesus to write me a letter in my notebook. "Visit Jean," He said recently. And, sure enough, Jean was ill that day. "You've been a little cranky lately," I wrote about myself another morning. "Tell your husband you love him." How exciting to think about what He might be writing me next.

Write to me and through me in Your heavenly language, Jesus, drawing me closer into the circle of Your love. —J.S.

---

26 *FEAR ye not, neither be afraid...* —ISAIAH 44:8

On our flight to Lake Tahoe, the stewardesses were nervously pacing the plane's aisle.

"What's wrong?" I asked.

"We seem to be missing a passenger," one of them said. Then she stared at the tiny, blanketed mound beside me.

"Oh, I'm sorry. You're missing my son," I said, lifting the blanket to reveal a scared three-year-old. "He's afraid of flying."

In a minute the stewardess, having run off for something, returned and drew the blanket back. She said to Gary, "Hey, you almost missed the gift I have for you!" Gary reluctantly sat up, but the stewardess soon had him laughing and wide-eyed as they browsed through a comic book together.

It was a simple incident, but it got me thinking of how often I try to hide from my fears. But then God comes along. He pulls off the blanket of fear for a moment and says, "Stop dwelling on all the bad things and think about the good." He shows me a moment of warmth and kindness from a friend, blooming dogwoods tossing on a breeze. And all my fears begin to melt away.

I reached over and smoothed my son's tousled hair. *How lucky we are, Gary,* I thought, *to be safe...and found!*

Thank You for seeking me, Lord. Thank You for finding me!

—D.H.

---

27 *SEND the light!...the blessed gospel light.*

—CHARLES H. GABRIEL, HYMN

As we were finishing lunch and I was putting the tip for the waiter under my plate, my elderly luncheon guest reached into her purse and placed something under her plate. It was a little card with a Bible verse penciled on it: "Giving thanks always for all things unto God and the Father in the name of our Lord Jesus Christ." (Ephesians 5:20)

"When my husband and I moved into town from the farm," my friend explained, "I was very lonely all winter long. Our house just seemed so drab. Then, in the spring, green shoots started coming up everywhere — crocuses, tulips, irises, daffodils — all planted by the previous owners. What a blessing those people left us! I don't expect to ever move again, so I can't pass on the *same* favor, but I *can* leave a blessing for the next person by doing this. I always carry several Bible verses in my purse, leaving them in doctors' waiting rooms, taxis, restaurants...wherever I go."

It was such a blessed idea that I went home and typed some of my favorite Bible verses and put them in an envelope in my purse. I hope to plant these little blessings wherever I go. You never know who might pick them up and have a better day — or a better life — because of it!

Bring special blessings, Lord, to those who find these verses.

—M.M.H.

28 *HE that hath ears to hear, let him hear.* —MATTHEW 11:15

What a wasted day this has been! Here I am exhausted, and I haven't accomplished one single item on my long list of "To Dos."

First thing, an old man called and rattled on about his ailing dog. And a friend came by full of worries about her runaway daughter. And my husband showed up for lunch filled with enthusiasm about a new business venture. And my four-year-old came home from preschool determined to tell me about everything that had happened in class that day. And even the baby kept calling to me with peremptory "Uh-uh-uhs" that mean "Come play with me."

Now, in less than an hour our prayer group is going to meet at our house. Automatically I start to straighten the coffee table; I pick up the Bible; it falls open to the Book of Job. I see this verse; it's Job crying out, "Hear diligently my speech, and let this be your consolations." (Job 21:2)

A wasted day? Well, maybe I haven't accomplished one of the things I wanted to. But all day I have listened. If just one person has been consoled, and loved, by my listening, then this has been one of my better days.

Lord, some people think that when you're listening, you're not doing anything. But You've shown me that listening can be a labor of love. —P.H.S.

29 *...ON Thee do I wait all the day.* —PSALM 25:5

As a baby, Jon, one of our twin sons, had a mysterious illness that caused him to become dehydrated. One day my husband and I labored to follow our doctor's instructions at home so Jon wouldn't have to go to the hospital. "Feed him one-fourth teaspoon of crushed ice every twenty minutes, slowly," the doctor had said. "You must wait the entire twenty minutes each time."

I myself couldn't follow the instructions. Inevitably, I'd give Jon the ice too quickly and he would get sick to his stomach. Then, despite my protests, my husband took the baby from me and held him. Jerry glanced at his watch and held Jon quietly. Time passed. I worried. I crushed ice. Finally, Jerry studied the second hand on his watch and then, very slowly, placed a few slivers of ice between our baby's dry lips. This time Jon didn't get sick to his stomach. All afternoon and into the night, Jerry repeated the process of waiting exactly 20 minutes. By morning the crisis had passed.

Jon is now 13 and weighs 100 pounds. When I watch him gulp down an entire glassful of milk without pausing, I often remember the time his daddy held and painstakingly fed him a few pieces of ice every 20 minutes. My husband has always known how to wait. I am still learning. It is an important lesson, and I want to master it. For God seems to keep presenting me with situations that demand: "Wait on Me. Do nothing but wait. Cease all your anxious efforts."

Father: I *will* wait. —M.B.W.

---

30 *O SPEAK to reassure me,*
To hasten or control,
O speak, and make me listen,
Thou Guardian of my soul. —JOHN E. BODE, HYMN

Do you believe that God has His own way of giving little messages? I do.

For instance, the car won't start. At one time I would have

cursed it. But now I say to myself that maybe God is trying to slow me down.

Company's coming. And the kids have spilled hot chocolate on my brand-new carpet. Once I would have got into a yelling match, but now I check my priorities. What matters most? Company or my children?

I'm going to a new restaurant. But from habit I take the wrong freeway exit. As I fight traffic to get back onto the freeway, I stop and think. How often do I drift along, doing things by habit? Should I be more aware of the direction my life is taking?

What kind of messages does God have for you?

Hearing is a matter of listening, isn't it, Lord? —L.E.W.

31

...FOR it is in giving that we receive...

—ST. FRANCIS OF ASSISI

When we moved to the farm, I discovered several columbines blooming in a weed-filled flower border. I was delighted. They were the same as the ones my mother had lovingly nurtured in the garden I knew as a child.

I weeded, fertilized and gave them loving care. One day an elderly neighbor told me that she, too, recalled this hard-to-find columbine hybrid in her *own* mother's garden.

I longed to give her some, but I had so few. I didn't want to risk losing them. Then, on impulse, I grabbed a spade and dug up the largest plant. After wrapping it carefully in damp newspapers, I handed it to her. "Here," I said, "I want you to enjoy them, too."

Several years later, during an especially bitter winter, my columbines died. When the snow melted, I watched in vain for the first green leaves and searched the border for seedlings. Nothing remained.

One May morning the telephone rang. It was my elderly friend. "I understand your columbines winter-killed," she said. "I planted mine by a south wall, and they're coming up beautifully. In fact I just discovered several dozen seedlings. I'll bring some over this afternoon."

So again I have my beloved columbines — because I shared.

Give and it shall be given you, the Bible says.

Yes, of course.

Grant me the wisdom to know that sharing doesn't mean losing.

—A.J.L.

S	M	T	W	T	F	S
		1	2	3	4	5
6	7	8	9	10	11	12
13	14	15	16	17	18	19
20	21	22	23	24	25	26
27	28	29	30			

The Sixth Commandment

Thou shalt not kill. —EXODUS 20:13

WHEN I was young I fashioned
A slingshot from a maple fork
And a slice of inner tube.
My first shot
Was an idle one
Aimed at a catbird.
Astonishingly, the bird toppled from its perch
Dead.
Stunned, I tiptoed to it.
Caught in the unseeing glare of its
Yellow-black eye, I wept.
And, oh, Lord,
A dark corner of my heart has mourned
Ever since.
More lately I've been wondering
What other things I've killed,
Not meaning to, along the way.
By withholding an encouraging word,
How much enthusiasm
Have I killed, Lord?
By being a spoilsport,
How much joy?
By condemning
How many reputations?
Yes, Lord, I am grown now,
And I've learned to love life more.
And loving life
Means helping all living things
And all things living
In hearts and minds
To flourish and grow.

1 *GIVE unto the Lord the glory due unto His name...*

—I CHRONICLES 16:29

I know that I should never say "Oh, God!" unless I really mean to be talking to Him, but nonetheless, I sometimes catch myself saying "Oh, God," when I really should be saying simply "Oh, no," or "Oh, my," or "That can't be!"

It's a very bad habit. I try never to do it, but for those times when the sauce pan boils all over the stove, and I realize I've said "Oh, God!" in horror, I've discovered a new way of making amends. My exclamation, "Oh, God," becomes the beginning of a spontaneous prayer. After "Oh, God," I'll say, "please help me not to lose my head before this dinner party even starts."

What surprises me about this new technique of mine, is that when I let an "Oh, God" slip, either because of fright, worry or wonder, it really is a time to call on the Lord. What was once a bad habit has become a reminder of Whom it is I really need to turn to.

Oh, God, I want to honor Your name, always. —P.B.H.

2 *THE happiness of your life depends upon the quality of your thoughts.*

—MARCUS AURELIUS

I was invited to a local recording studio one afternoon recently to meet country singer, Tom T. Hall. He entertained us with several of his songs and explained how he came to write the one entitled, "I Love."

He told us that he heard a psychiatrist say that the way to have a good day is to sit down first thing every morning and make a list of everything you dislike, everything that bothers you and everyone who bugs you. Then, by tearing up the list and throwing it away, you can help rid yourself of all your grievances.

"But that," Mr. Hall said, "seemed too negative. I couldn't see starting my day off by thinking of all those ugly things. It seemed that I should try to think of happy things, things I love. So I made a list, and part of that list became a song."

We all listened while he sang, enumerating things he loves — little yellow ducks, old pickup trucks, slow-moving trains and summer rains, country streams, sleep without dreams, coffee in cups, little fuzzy pups. And every now and then he added, "And I love you!"

A happy, loving list can easily grow longer than a mean, hateful list. And everyone's loving list is unique. Why not make out your own? You might find, as Tom T. Hall did, that it's a great way to start off every day.

Father, help me to center on the happy things of life, not just early in the morning, but all day through. —D.D.

---

3 *FOR God hath not given us the spirit of fear; but of power, and of love, and of a sound mind.*

—II TIMOTHY 1:7

One time, when I was younger, I had to go door-to-door in our neighborhood selling magazine subscriptions for a church charity fund. When I got back to our house, my mother asked me how I'd done. I told her that hardly anyone had been home. I'd only sold two.

"Then you'll have to go again tomorrow," my mother said.

"No way," I exclaimed. "Once is enough. It makes me nervous."

"You need to be braver about facing people," Mother advised.

"But, Mom, in church last Sunday, the priest said, 'Blessed are the meek, for they shall inherit the earth.' I'm meek. That means I'm okay, doesn't it?" I pleaded.

"Wait a minute now, Edward. You're not understanding that verse quite right. In the Beatitudes, meek does *not* mean timid or cowardly. In fact it means that you have strength because you have submitted yourself to God's will and are living under His rules. So if you want to be meek, I suggest you ask God for the courage to do well during tomorrow's rounds."

Well, I did go out again the next day. I didn't get over my timidity right then and there, but over the years I've learned that God doesn't want us to be timid. As it says in the Bible, God hath not given us the spirit of fear. He wants us to be courageous. He wants us to be meek.

When I'm fearful, Lord, it means I've wandered from You. Please help me to stay near. —E.B.P.

---

4 *FOR the beauty of the earth,*
For the glory of the skies, ...

—FOLLIOTT S. PIERPOINT, HYMN

Last June our community hosted the fifth World Hot-Air Balloon Championship. One Tuesday we were wakened at dawn by the roar and hiss of the balloons' burners. My family rushed outside and what a sight greeted us! Over one hundred balloons filled the blue sky. They floated low over our farm, countless colors shimmering in the June sun. We watched, entranced, until they drifted far to the south.

Then we went in for breakfast. Over the radio an excited announcer said, "They are so beautiful! A once-in-a-lifetime spectacle. Probably few of us will ever see such a sight again!"

My thoughts still on the balloons, I sat at the kitchen table, sipping coffee. Outside the window, a stalk of sky-blue delphinium reached high above the garden fence, its lovely petals translucent in the early morning light. *How lovely,* I thought. *Not as spectacular as the balloons, but truly more beautiful, more miraculous.* And God's beauty is not once in a lifetime. He gives it to us to enjoy every day.

God, please open my eyes to all the undiscovered beauty around me. —A.J.L.

---

5 *REMEMBER now thy Creator in the days of thy youth...* —ECCLESIASTES 12:1

When I lived in the suburbs of Chicago I helped start a youth group at our church. It was one of the most satisfying things that I ever did. Sometime later, after I'd moved to the Northwest, I received a letter. "We're disbanding the kids' club at church," my friend wrote. "We don't need the group anymore anyway, because Scouts have started now."

I was thinking about that letter one day as I walked along the edge of the ocean. I watched the surf erase my footprints, and I felt sad. The youth group seemed so pointless now — a waste of time and effort.

And suddenly I realized I was missing the point. Had I given the young people in that group a glimpse of the joy of Christian life and the pleasure of the company of fellow Christians? That was the real point.

I've heard that every footprint in the sand, or any seashell picked up, forever changes the contour of the beach, however slightly. If I had, even once, brought those children into the presence of a loving Heavenly Father, God's footprints would be forever imprinted in their lives.

We can all make enduring contributions, Lord, because You endure.

—D.S.

6

I LOVE to tell the story;
For those who know it best
Seem hungering and thirsting
To hear it, like the rest.

—KATHERINE HANKEY, HYMN

For over a year the husband of a close friend of mine waged a battle with cancer which, in time, he lost. But for all the months of his illness, my friend went out every Wednesday evening as part of a door-to-door evangelistic team for her congregation.

"How can you do it?" I asked her one day. "Here you are in more distress than anyone I know, yet you keep going out week after week to talk about the love of God. Why don't you give that up for a while, until all this gets settled and you can be calm again?"

"Because," she replied simply, "I desperately need to hear the Good News myself. And *telling* it, is the best way to *hear* it."

Father, in one of the most beautiful of all prayers, St. Francis said, "For in consoling we are consoled." How grateful I am that that is so.

—P.H.S.

7

THROUGH Thy precepts I get understanding: therefore I hate every false way. —PSALM 119:104

Several years ago when I was introduced to John Philip Sousa, I thought someone was pulling my leg. Hadn't the great bandmaster died 50 years before? John Sousa laughed good-naturedly and said, "I'm the composer's grandson."

Then we got talking and he told me how as a young man he used to get big-money offers from impresarios to lead bands. "I couldn't read a note of music, but the Sousa name would pack houses. At first I thought it a lark, and had a good laugh that people couldn't tell that the band was leading me instead of me leading the band."

But, after a few engagements, Sousa stopped the charade and started in at the bottom of the heap in publishing. He didn't want to go through life pretending to be something he wasn't.

The truth that he learned is one that Jesus preached when He emphasized the commandment: "Thou shalt not bear false witness." Now John Sousa is a respected publishing executive. By being straight with himself and others, he's made a little history of his own — instead of just remaining a footnote to another man's.

When I fool another, Lord, I fool myself — and betray You.

—J. McD.

8 *I WILL sing unto the Lord, because He hath dealt bountifully with me.* —PSALM 13:6

When my four-year-old son Adam and I came out of the grocery store we were caught in a sun shower. It was raining where we were, but the sun was shining a short distance away. We dashed into the car and, as we dried ourselves off, I said to Adam, "Now is the time for a rainbow. Let's find one." I craned my neck out the side window and searched the sky. Then I looked straight ahead, muttering to myself, "If I can just find the right spot..."

"But, Mommy," Adam said, "our rainbow is right here."

I looked where he was pointing, and there on the dashboard of our car was a lovely patch of shimmering colors. The sun was shining through the rain on the window and indeed we did have our own rainbow. Adam was right; I was looking too far afield for our rainbow. As the colors danced in Adam's eyes I thanked God for the little lessons He so often gives me.

"Yes, Adam, our rainbow is right here," I said.

Help me to see all the rainbows You send, Lord, especially those close by. —L.A.L.

9 *DON'T let anyone think little of you because you are young. Be their ideal....* —I TIMOTHY 4:12 (LB)

We found the bleachers packed with relatives and friends. The faculty was seated on a center island. And the honor students occupied chairs at either end of the South Rich High gym — among them our two grandchildren, Marinell and Paul Mark.

As their names were called, the students walked to the center to receive their awards. Proud eyes followed them. The young men, forsaking their wordy T-shirts and canvas shoes for white shirts, ties and "hard" shoes tried to seem casual, ho hum, but there was a pride in their stride. And the young ladies: no tight blue jeans — sheath dresses, ruffles, pearls, perfume, their shoulder-length hair fanned back by the haste of their step. Some, in their first five-inch heels, walked like baby deer on ice. But every parent knew how hard earned this had been. Politely and with thanks the students received awards for sports, music, poetry, research, business, math, science, shop, homemaking.

Do you despair for the youth of America? I don't. I thank God for them.

Let me see, Lord, the strength and beauty — and future — that all our children have.

—Z.B.D.

10

I, PAUL, write this greeting with my own hand.

—I CORINTHIANS 16:21 (RSV)

"I wish you'd write to me sometimes," said my mother, as we lingered over coffee in the restaurant near her retirement home.

"Hey, Mom," I protested, "I phone you every week!"

"Yes," she replied, "but I can't share your calls with anyone. I only remember bits and pieces..."she smiled apologetically.

I felt resentful. Hadn't I just flown halfway across the country to see her? Wasn't I spending far more than I could afford on air fare, lunches and dinners just so that I could be with her? And my weekly calls to her were convenient. Why write? Weren't my actions enough?

We didn't discuss it again. But on my flight back to New York I took out my Bible and started to read. When I got to the fourth chapter of Colossians I read, "And when this letter has been read among you, have it read also in the church of the Laodiceans..." *Funny*, I mused, *I'd never thought of Paul's thoughts as letters.*

But I can't share your calls with anyone, Mother had said. Only then did I understand her request. I took a piece of airline stationery and began. "Dear Mom..."

Father, help me to remember that telephone calls are just words, but that letters are deeds. —M.C.J.

11

I EXPECT to pass through this world but once;
any good things therefore that I can do, or any
kindness that I can show to any fellow creature,
let me do it now; let me not defer or neglect it,
for I shall not pass this way again.

—Attributed to ÉTIENNE DE GRELLET

One day, arranging flowers from the garden, it suddenly occurred to me, "Why, I learned how to do this from Bett!" And I began to comprehend how much I'd learned from her — this dear friend now so far away. How my life had changed because of her... The old pine table on which I set the jug of daisies — she'd helped me find it, refinish it. Had taught me, in fact, to appreciate antiques.

As I dusted books on the shelves — here and there I spotted authors I'd have missed except for her enthusiasm — I remembered the fun of hunting down favorites together in secondhand bookstores. Her taste, her attitudes, her philosophy had helped shape mine. And through her I'd made other wonderful friends.

I began counting them up as I ran the sweeper, thinking, as I did so, of what they had contributed to me or my family. From shortcuts in cooking to help in getting a child into college. I thought particularly of Hope, who'd brought me a book that deepened my faith. Then became a spiritual mother to our daughter in a way that profoundly changed her life.

Suddenly, half-amused yet challenged, I wondered what effects my friendship had had on them? How much help had I provided? How many of my impassioned opinions possibly colored their views? What friends had they made because of me? How far had these circles widened? Were any of them healthier, happier, better people because of me?

I have found that pausing to take such an inventory now and then is a very good thing. It has given me a new appreciation of my friends. It has made me more aware of how inescapably we influence each other. And what a responsibility I have to them.

Friendship is an incredible gift, Lord. Let me treasure it.

—M.H.

---

12 *...ALL things are possible to him that believeth.*

—MARK 9:23

Not long ago at a backyard picnic, a friend played a little trick on me. When I picked up a new pickle jar and tried to open it, the lid wouldn't budge. So I tried harder, straining at it without luck.

"I can't open this pickle jar. Would you mind loosening it?" I said to Tom.

He took the jar, grunted and groaned as he struggled with the lid, finally handing it back to me. "There you go," he said.

Then with hardly any effort at all I twisted off the lid as if it were greased. Whereupon Tom began to laugh.

"Sue," he said, "I really didn't do anything to the jar. I only pretended to loosen it."

So there it was again, another example of the tried and true adage: "You can if you think you can."

Keep me aware, Lord, that the first step to believing in myself is believing in You. —S.M.K.

13

THY body, broken for my sake,
My bread from heaven shall be,
Thy testamental cup I take,
And thus remember Thee. —JAMES MONTGOMERY, HYMN

When I was about ten, I spent a week with a friend and her family at a lakeside cabin deep in the woods. We had a great time, but when Sunday came I suddenly realized I'd forgotten all about church, and for the first time, I felt a little homesick. Then my friend's mother put a basket of homemade bread on the table in front of her husband and sat down. He closed his eyes for a moment, then took a slice from the basket, broke off a small piece and passed the remainder of the slice to his wife. She did the same thing and then passed the piece of bread to my friend's little brother, who pinched off a tiny portion and handed the rest to me.

I wasn't sure what was going on, but I followed suit, passing the bread to my friend, who broke off her piece and returned the remainder to her father, all in silence. Then my friend's father said, "This we do in remembrance of Him." There was a shared "Amen," and then all ate the now-blessed bread. Somehow, I sensed that Jesus Christ was fully present at that meal in the out-of-the-way cabin, and my homesickness melted.

That experience taught me that, though I'm far away from church, I can always draw close to Him.

There are so many things that I can do in remembrance of You, Lord. —M.M.H.

14

WE who together held sweet fellowship...

—PSALM 55:14(ML)

After our first child married, I adjusted well. I got used to setting only five plates at the table. Julie's sister moved into her room. After a while I learned not to expect her to come home at the end of the day. She lived nearby, so I saw her several times a week and we talked on the phone. But one day for some reason I missed her so terribly that I ached to see her. The "attack" was sudden and unexpected. She was just up the street, less than five minutes away at the veterinary clinic where she worked. Neither our dog nor cat needed to go to the vet. I couldn't think of any reason to go see her. Finally I drove to the clinic and asked to see Julie. She appeared from the back room like a burst of sunlight. She had on her lab jacket and held a kitten. Quite professional.

"Yes, Mother. Did you want to see me?"

I nodded.

"What is it? I'm pretty busy."

"I just wanted to see you."

"About what? Here I am." There was just a slight hint of impatience in her voice.

"I don't have a reason. There's no need pretending I do. I just had to be with you for a few minutes."

"Mother!" she exclaimed, glancing around to see if anyone had heard. But then she smiled a warm smile and added softly, "See, I'm okay. I don't understand why you came by, but thanks."

Completely satisfied, I drove home happily.

Sometimes I think God's Holy Spirit comes to us, His beloved children, because He longs for fellowship for just a moment or so. These moments are unexpected and often I believe I miss many of the times that He comes just to gaze on me. I'm not accustomed to such intense love and can't imagine that God would want to visit with me. But I'm trying to be more watchful for His Spirit and to respond immediately with love and joy.

It's incredible that You desire my fellowship, Father. But I thank You.

—M.B.W.

15 ...*RESIST not evil*... —MATTHEW 5:39

With my family away on a canoeing trip, I was feeling a little nervous about being home all alone. That night about midnight I woke to the sound of my bedroom door slipping open. "Who's there?" my voice trembled. Silence. *Yet I felt a presence in the room.* THUD! A body landed beside me on the bed. I screamed and jumped up. Then I saw two glowing, green eyes in the dark — my daughter's cat!

Ordinarily I would have been amused, but now I was only angry. "Oh, you cat," I said as I grabbed him and shook him. Rather, I tried to shake him.

Have you ever tried to shake a cat? It's impossible! A cat's pliable body simply refuses to resist. And this big cat began to purr and purr and snuggle in my lap. How could I be angry at it?

A few days later I started to get angry at a comment my neighbor made, but I had learned something from that big black cat: anger needs resistance. Now I tried the cat's response. I refused to get angry, and soon our near argument turned into a productive conversation.

Lord, fill me with Your love, enough to smother my moments of anger. —J.H.

16 *When the Bible Speaks to Me*

JOHN 5:39

Among the many ways the Bible speaks to me is the guidance it gives about personal problems. I have found it truly the Book of the solved problem.

It is my habit to "search the Scriptures," for answers and insights when I need to solve a problem. If I come to a passage that seems to be germane, I write my problem on a piece of paper and put it at that particular place in the Bible. Sometimes I have had as many as a half-dozen problems in my Bible at the same time.

Then every day I hold the Bible in hand and ask the Lord to guide me. And the Heavenly Father always answers that prayer — not necessarily quickly, nor for all the problems at the same time, but always ultimately and surely. As I gradually remove each slip from the Bible, how amazing, how wonderful it is to find the number of problems that have been solved. Today I have a large file marked "Answered Prayers." That file is proof that the Bible has really spoken to me! — RUTH STAFFORD PEALE

---

17 *FOR in that He Himself hath suffered...He is able to succour them...* —HEBREWS 2:18

When my son announced that he was going overseas as an aerial photographer for the U.S. Air Force during a time of international crisis, I was sick with worry about his safety. It was the kind of worry that I felt I had to endure alone because I thought no one else would understand.

Then came the day I was talking to my husband about my feelings of loneliness. "You just don't understand," I blurted out.

"You know better than that," he said gently as he took me in his arms. "Have you forgotten that I, too, served overseas during the war? Or that Bryce is *my* son, too?"

Yes, I had forgotten — momentarily. I guess we all forget in our own suffering that others do understand. And those who understand most of all are those who have experienced sorrow, frustration, despair. Isn't that one reason why I feel so at ease with Jesus? He knows about suffering.

Jesus, I feel Your understanding — and Your compassion.

—J.M.B.

18

. . .THOU shalt shine forth, thou shalt be as the morning. —JOB 11:17

Many disgruntled souls waited for the tardy Third Avenue bus to take them to work. I was one of them.

Many sour faces reflected dark thoughts about the rundown Manhattan transit system. I was one of them.

Many bodies pushed aggressively through the doors of the already bulging bus when it finally arrived. I was one of them.

Many groaners turned to grinners when the hearty voice of a woman passenger trying to get *off* the crowded bus rang over the surly scene: "Make way, please, I'm not Twiggy."

I was one of them.

Thank You, Lord, for the people who brighten gloomy moments with a ray of humor. Help me be one of them. —N.S.S.

19

. . .I BID every one among you not to think of himself more highly than he ought to think, but to think with sober judgment . . . —ROMANS 12:3 (RSV)

I heard that a parishioner at my former church was seriously ill and in the hospital. I wanted to visit her, but I had a problem: The hospital was in another part of the state and I don't drive. I did pray for Lilla, but my conscience began to nag me; I told myself, *You can get to see Lilla, if you really try.* I felt I was letting Lilla — and the Lord — down.

Then, a few months ago, a mutual friend from my old church mentioned her again.

"Uh... how is Lilla doing?" I asked, not sure I wanted to know.

"Didn't you hear?" my friend said, "She's completely recovered. She just never gave in; simply told the doctors that the Lord was going to heal her. By golly, she was right! What a wonderful faith Lilla has!"

I was overjoyed to learn that Lilla was well, but I had made the mistake of thinking that if I didn't personally hold Lilla's hand at her bedside, my prayers wouldn't be enough. I know I should still try to do everything I can for those in need, but I also know that God hears our sincere prayers whenever — and wherever — we pray them.

Lord, keep me from falling into the trap of thinking the whole show depends on me. —W.D.

---

20 *FOR God so loved the world, that He gave His only begotten Son...* —JOHN 3:16

One Father's Day morning we four kids proceeded into the kitchen in a group, my brother carrying the fishing rod we'd bought for Dad. To our surprise, we each found on our plates a colorfully wrapped package. As we opened the gifts eagerly, my brother said, "Dad, this is *your* day. You're not supposed to give gifts on Father's Day!"

"Are you sure of that?" my dad asked.

We didn't know what he meant with his odd answer. We just knew that the gifts were our dad's way of letting us know that he loved us.

But, later, at church, it came to me — that God, the Father, gave all of us the gift of His Son. It was His way of letting us know that He loved us.

We're honoring fathers everywhere today, Lord, and especially we honor You, the Father of us all. —G.K.

21

TO him that overcometh,
A crown of life shall be. —GEORGE DUFFIELD, JR., HYMN

Going over my midyear budget, I was depressed to see how far I'd overshot my projected expenditures. How would I get through the rest of the year with what I expected to earn? There just didn't seem to be enough money to go around. Dismayed, I shut my expense book. I just couldn't balance it.

That afternoon I went to lunch with a friend who is a professional cellist. In the course of our conversation she remarked that a friend, a very successful piano accompanist, had lost the use of one of his fingers.

"How terrible!" I said. "What will he do now? Teach?"

"Oh, no! He's still playing," she said. "It happened years ago. Last night I was at his concert, sitting very near the stage. As I watched his hands, I noticed that one finger never moved. Afterwards, I asked him about it. He said he'd had arthritis and that the finger had become completely stiff. Undismayed, he just transposed all his music for the right hand so he could play it with four fingers. He did such a good job that almost no one ever noticed, and so he never bothered to tell anyone!"

I couldn't help but think of the words of St. Paul: "For I have learned, in whatsoever state I am, *therewith* to be content." (Philippians 4:11)

That evening I went home and did a little "transposing" of my own. That pianist had taught me that I did have the wherewithal to balance my budget, if I would only adapt a little.

How about you? Strapped for money or time? Why not try a "four finger exercise"?

Remind me, dear Lord, that I'm bigger than all the lacks that stand in my path.

—C.C.

22 *...LET us draw near hither unto God.* —I SAMUEL 14:36

There's a magical bridge available to all of us that can span time or distance. Its name? Association.

For instance, my father died many years ago, but whenever I turn on the television and stumble on a baseball game I sit and watch it, even though I don't like baseball all that much. It makes me feel close to my father again. How he loved baseball!

When my friend Marian and I were in boarding school together we were inseparable. Today Marian lives in California and I live in New York. We don't write very often, but whenever I want to feel close to her I take down a Gilbert & Sullivan album and let the music bring her back to me. How Marian loved *The Pirates of Penzance!*

I have a Father — a Friend — in Heaven Who sometimes seems far away. But whenever I take down my Bible and read it I feel close to Him again. And, oh, how He loves — me!

Oh, Lord, thank You for Your nearness — and Your love.

—E.V.S.

23 *SIMPLY trusting every day,*
Trusting through a stormy way;
Even when my faith is small,
Trusting Jesus, that is all. —IRA D. SANKEY, HYMN

We'd prayed for direction before deciding to move, and everything had seemed so right. But now when it was time to pack and say good-bye to the known, the loved and the familiar for a strange, friendless place, it all seemed wrong.

As I stood at the kitchen window scanning the backyard, Obie, our flop-eared dog, saw me and came running toward the house carrying in his mouth a well-worried bone bleached white from the sun.

That awful bone, I thought as I stepped to the refrigerator to get the meaty ham bone I'd kept for him from last night's scraps. *Wait till he sees this!*

I called him to me and held out my succulent treat. But instead of eagerly running up to take it, he drew back, loyally guarding his old white bone. He didn't even look to see what I had. He didn't trust me enough to trade the familiar for the unknown.

"But I'm not trusting God enough either," I mused out loud. "By resisting our move, I'm really rejecting all the good things He has in store for us in our new home."

I left the bone on the grass for Obie to accept when he was ready. I went inside to decide where to start packing.

Lord, I trust You today — and tomorrow. —P.R.P.

24 *BEHOLD, how great a matter a little fire kindleth!*

—JAMES 3:5

Before we went backpacking on the Appalachian Trail, I envisioned all the things that could go wrong out there. I could die from exposure, be eaten by a bear, get lost, fall off a cliff... Needless to say I was overly cautious. I looked for a snake under every rock. I boiled my drinking water in case of contamination. And once I took a half-mile detour to skirt a rocky ledge.

But despite all the precautions, my trip on the outdoor trail was a disaster. I was finally done in by a wee little half-centimeter blister. I limped along, miserable.

Often I travel the spiritual trail the same way. I stay cautious not to let the big, obvious sins befall me, but overlook the tiny dangers along the way...a small resentment, a tiny lie, a little thread of gossip. And like the blister, it's these lightweight sins that ruin the trip.

Let me be cautious of the small sins, Lord, as well as the big ones. For they are all sins. —S.M.K.

25 *AND He said unto them, Where is your faith?*

—LUKE 8:25

Today, when I went to get our five-month-old son Michael up from his nap, he was sobbing loudly. Somehow he'd become caught between the bars of his crib, and the blankets had inched up over his head. He was terribly frightened and even though I held him close and spoke lovingly to him, he continued to sob with his eyes tightly closed. It was several minutes before the crying stopped and he realized everything was all right.

It made me wonder: Isn't that what I do during troubled times? All the while God is there, holding me and speaking lovingly, but my eyes are closed and all I hear is my own wailing.

Lord, let me stop complaining long enough for me to hear Your reassurances. —R.R.S.

26

LIKE a mighty army
Moves the Church of God.—SABINE BARING-GOULD, HYMN

The other morning I heard a clamor of birdcalls in our backyard. When I looked out I saw that our kitten had climbed our large oak tree and was making his way toward a bird's nest. The parent birds stood screeching in front of their nest, but what impressed me was an assortment of nearly 30 other birds of various kinds that had rallied to the cause. Some chirped, some cawed, some screeched, but they all had one fierce, common intent: Turn back the enemy.

And they did. They backed him down the branch until, with great relief, he scrambled into my outstretched hands.

The birds had won! As I brought my frightened kitten into the house, I thought: *How wonderful it is when Christians band together like that, determined to defeat the enemy, Satan.* This is what churches are all about — a fellowship, standing together, doing the job, succeeding where a single individual would fail.

Father, keep reminding me that when I join others in a common cause I'm not losing my identity, but rather gaining stature in Your sight. —M.B.W.

27 *GIVE to every man that asketh of thee . . .* —LUKE 6:30

"Of course I'll pray with you. Come on over. No, you're not imposing."

I'd said the words, but as I hung up the phone, a twinge of annoyance flashed through me. I'd set aside this time to be alone with God. The rest of my day was scheduled full. I tried to remind myself of the desperation in Carol's voice, of her deep need to know that someone cared; yet some voice in me said, "Well, what about *me*? I *need* my private prayer time!"

By the time Carol arrived, I'm afraid my annoyance was bordering on resentment. She poured out the pain of her family problems and then we joined hands, closed our eyes, and began praying. Up to this point my heart had not really been present, but when we started calling on God I could feel my heart both fill with God and go out to Carol. As we prayed together, our petitions for Carol and her family gave way to praise and thanksgiving. I meant every word.

As I said good-bye to Carol, I knew that my own prayer time had been used up, but it had been used properly. It's true, isn't it, that you can't pray for someone else without being blessed yourself?

When I visit with You, Lord, help me to remember that my friends are always welcome, too. —M.M.H.

28 *HE loves each of us as if there were only one of us.* —ST. AUGUSTINE

Setting the table for dinner, I was lamenting a string of minor misfortunes that had seemed to zero in on my little corner of the world. Our family's medical bills were so large that we had to make an installment payment arrangement. Our lawn was dying from some rare infestation, and our neighbors on both sides were unaffected. My list went on and on. I silently asked the Lord why I was being singled out.

One of my sons interrupted my thoughts. He looked at his place setting and said, "You don't love me as much as you love Billy, do you? You gave me the chipped plate again."

"I love you both the same," I assured him and started to exchange his chipped plate for mine.

"No, don't change it," he said, "as long as I *know* you love me as much as Billy, it's okay."

Strangely, his words repeated themselves in my mind... *as long as I know you love me, it's okay.* Suddenly it dawned on me. Didn't God love me? Of course! Then all the bills and the lawn and the petty annoyances — the "chipped plates" — were okay. I wasn't being singled out by the Lord or by anyone or anything else. "Chipped plates" just *happen* to be set at my place, and I must use my confidence in my Father's love to help overcome them. Impulsively, I gave my son a hug.

Father, I know you love me. So everything's okay. —D.C.C.

29

SEE what love the Father has given us, that we should be called children of God; and so we are. —I JOHN 3:1 (RSV)

"Say, aren't you Bunko's son?"

Bunko's son! I loved my father very much, and he did have that unique nickname, but I was annoyed. One day I boiled over to a classmate. "Why do I always have to remind people of my father? Just once I'd like to be Jeff, not 'Son of Bunko'!"

My friend picked up a Bible. "Here," he said, "read this."

"'...Truly, this was the Son of God,'" I read. And I said, "So?"

"So, did you know that at least three hundred times in the New Testament, Jesus is identified as the Son of God, Son of Man or, simply, Son."

Son of God, I thought. The greatest Man ever to walk the earth was known as "Son of..." I had never seen it that way before.

On my way home that night I met an old neighbor of ours. "Do you remember me?" I asked. "I'm Jeff Japinga...ah, Bunko's son."

He smiled and began shaking my hand vigorously. And secretly I smiled. Of course I needed to develop my own identity. But meanwhile I was proud to be Bunko's son, just as Jesus gloried in being the Son of God.

Father, I glory in being Your son. —J.J.

30

NOW there are diversities of gifts, but the same Spirit. And there are differences of administrations, but the same Lord. —I CORINTHIANS 12:4, 5

My wife and I are both voracious readers, and like us, our first two sons also loved to read. But as our third son Doug was going through grade school and then junior high school, we couldn't get him interested in reading.

Then one day I was out on the patio trying to put together the pieces of an unassembled wheelbarrow. I had just started to read the instructions and was searching for each described item when Doug came out to join me.

"Hey, Dad, how about letting me put it together?" he urged.

"Do you think you can?" I said.

"Sure, it's easy," Doug answered, and immediately started in.

Alarmed, I interrupted, "Don't you think you ought to read the instructions first?"

"Naw, that'll just slow me up," he replied. And, to my amazement, he soon had the whole thing assembled perfectly.

In the parable of the talents Jesus spoke about the gifts of heaven given us, urging us to use them wisely. Maybe Doug didn't need to read as much as I thought he did. So I decided to stop fretting about what I thought was Doug's lack and start appreciating him for the abilities he had. And that, as it turned out, was exactly what I should have done.

Lord, all talents come from You. Help me to recognize them in others, as well as in myself. —H.J.H.

July

S	M	T	W	T	F	S
				1	2	3
4	5	6	7	8	9	10
11	12	13	14	15	16	17
18	19	20	21	22	23	24
25	26	27	28	29	30	31

The Seventh Commandment

Thou shalt not commit adultery.

—EXODUS 20:14

YOU meet quite by accident,
Two warm-hearted Christians
Who know each other pleasantly.
It happens that your marriage partners are away.
You've always liked each other,
So why not plan to meet for dinner?
A quiet restaurant, the food's not bad...

But wait.

On second thought, better not.

Why not?

Because you risk too much.

Because emotions are too...well...
    Too unpredictable.
    Too easily ignited.
And if a spark should blaze up,
Who gets burned?

    Everyone.

O God, help me to remember
The commitment I have made
To forsake all others
As long as I shall live.

And thank You for the peace
That Your commandent brings
    To all who stop and heed it.

1

THIS is my Father's world:
I rest me in the thought
Of rocks and trees, of skies and seas;
His hand the wonders wrought.

—MALTBIE D. BABCOCK, HYMN

During my first years in New York, I lived on a street that had no trees. Not even a blade of grass. I lived on a high floor, and when I looked out my windows all I saw were the backs of other buildings. I got used to this after a while, but now and then I would get the feeling that I was missing something.

Then a friend of mine invited me to spend a weekend at his home in the suburbs. Walking along, old delights struck me. The smell of freshly cut grass. The surprise of a rosebush in bloom. The coolness in the shadows of trees in full leaf. At dinner, the centerpiece on the table was a burst of violets moments out of the garden.

As soon as I could, I moved. I now live across the street from a park. I am on a low floor and, despite the sometimes roar of city traffic, I see trees and grass, spring bushes in flower, and, beyond, the Hudson River. It comforts me to know that, whatever man's efforts to foul the world with the mechanics of modern life, God is there. We can see Him, if we try.

Yes, Lord, I need only look out my window to see the wonder of Your gifts. Thank You. —G.K.

2

ARE we weak and heavy-laden,
Cumbered with a load of care?
Precious Saviour, still our Refuge —
Take it to the Lord in prayer! —JOSEPH SCRIVEN, HYMN

It had been an hour since my husband had gone into surgery. I sat in the waiting room, suspended in that unbearable time when life dangles in uncertainty.

What if there's been a complication, I thought, twisting a button on my sweater. What if they found something awful?

Suddenly I could sit no longer. I paced across the room to the window. Next to it sat a woman, waiting as I was. Yet she sat there placidly reading. I glanced idly at the book she held in her hands, then glimpsed a bookmark lying across an open page. On it, printed in a child's hand with red crayon, were the words — LIFE IS FRAGILE. HANDLE WITH PRAYER.

Why, of course, I thought. Life *is* fragile. And there *is* a way to approach its most anxious moments.

I returned to the chair. "Dear Lord..." I began.

Into Your gentle hands, dear Lord, I give my worries — and myself. —S.M.K.

3

...IN quietness and in confidence
shall be your strength... —ISAIAH 30:15

One balmy evening last summer my husband and I attended a performance of *The Unsinkable Molly Brown* at the San Diego

Starlight Theatre. The first act had barely begun when a jetliner roared over on an approach to nearby Lindbergh Field.

The noise of the low-flying jet was deafening — and maddening! I covered both ears, squeezed my eyes shut and silently deplored commercial air travel. Then I heard the audience applauding.

Onstage, the performers had stopped statue still, looking like an old tintype photo. Then as soon as the noise of the plane died away they resumed their act.

During the performance the actors repeated this pause whenever a plane approached. Instead of complaining, as I had, or trying to outshout the planes, they had merely paused.

I loved the show, but it was the pauses that made the biggest impression — and taught me something. Whenever I feel overwhelmed, instead of complaining or thrashing wildly against forces I can't control, I pause and bring them to the Lord. So often, in this interim, they seem to melt down to size.

Still me, Lord, when I am troubled. —J.M.B.

---

4 INDEPENDENCE DAY

LONG may our land be bright
With freedom's holy light;
Protect us by Thy might,
Great God, our King. —SAMUEL F. SMITH, HYMN

Virgil Mullinax, a dealer in rare coins, asked me one day, "Did you ever realize how much of the Almighty is in the 'almighty' dollar?" Then he took out a dollar bill for me to look at.

He first pointed out the two circles representing both sides of the Great Seal of the United States. "Thomas Jefferson, Benjamin

Franklin and John Adams spent six years designing the seal," he said. "Congress approved it June 20th, 1782. The pyramid in the left circle represents material strength and endurance. Its unfinished top signifies that there's more work to be done. The all-seeing 'Eye of God' on top of the pyramid emphasizes the importance of putting spiritual welfare above material things. The Founding Fathers believed that our strength was rooted in God, and our progress must be under His watchful eye.

"The words '*Annuit Coeptis*' circling the top of the seal mean, 'He (God) has favored our undertakings,'" Virgil continued. "Three Latin words under the pyramid, '*Novus Ordo Seclorum*,' meaning 'a new order of things,' signify the freedom of the people to exercise self-government. The Roman numerals at the base of the pyramid are a reminder of our nation's birth date: 1776.

"Now look at the right-hand circle," Virgil said. "The eagle became our national emblem in 1782, chosen as a symbol of strength and victory. The shield on its breast signifies self-reliance; it contains thirteen stripes for the thirteen states. In one talon is an olive branch with thirteen leaves, meaning peace; in the other talon is a bundle of thirteen arrows, symbolic of power and protection. Above the eagle's head is a ring of light surrounding thirteen stars, denoting a new state taking its place among sovereign powers.

"It is up to us who believe in God and country to keep reminding the world of these things," Virgil told me. "Especially the words, 'In God We Trust.'"

Not just this great holiday, Lord, but every day, let us put our trust in You. —Z.B.D.

5 *And ye shall seek Me, and find Me, when ye shall search for Me with all your heart.* —JEREMIAH 29:13

When I discovered that I had lost my beautiful Pi Kappa Delta key, my heart almost broke. I knew that I was wearing it that evening when I got out of the car in my mother's driveway. Shortly after I entered the living room, I missed the key. I must have lost it as I crossed the front yard.

My mother, my sister, and I traced and retraced my steps from the car to the porch. We kicked at the grass, bent low to examine the ground where bits of sticks lay from the limbs above; but to no avail. That bright, shiny, jeweled key seemed lost forever.

Then my brother-in-law stopped by. He took a flashlight, then on his hands and knees retraced the distance we had covered. His painstaking efforts soon paid off. He turned up the key hidden under a clump of leaves.

I felt ashamed of myself. Why hadn't I made the kind of effort my brother-in-law had? After all, it was *my* key that was missing. Could it be that I am sometimes as careless about finding Jesus, Whom I hold most dear? Am I willing to get down on my knees and find my way to Him when He becomes hidden in the midst of a hectic day?

Dear Jesus, when the jumbled circumstances of my life separate me from Your light, that's when I need most earnestly to seek You. —F.F.

6

GIVE us help from trouble: for vain is the help of man.

—PSALM 108:12

When my children were small, my younger son Brian was afraid to go into a swimming pool unless I went with him. I couldn't understand why he was so timid.

"Why do I have to be with you?" I said to him one day. "The lifeguard is right there. Don't you know that if you get into trouble, he'll save you much quicker than I?"

"But I don't *know* him, Mommy," Brian answered, clinging to my hand.

And so I took Brian and introduced him to the lifeguard. The two of them talked, and somehow that gave Brian the security he needed to swim without me.

A feeling of security — how we all yearn for it, yet how often we reach out to friends and loved ones, neglecting the One most qualified to provide it. People hesitate to turn to Jesus because they don't know Him. If they did, they'd trust Him with their lives.

Father, I know You are there, my Life-guard. —B.R.G.

7

I AM the light of the world. —JOHN 8:12

The seven of us had come to La Parguera, a fishing village on Puerto Rico's south shore, to witness a local wonder, but after a long, hot car ride our moods were very far from wonderful. We'd come to see a nighttime phenomenon known as *bioluminescence* — the luminous glow given off by tiny marine organisms in the waters of La Parguera.

When night began to fall, we boarded a charter boat, and as we chugged through the sea we were still tired and a bit irritable. Then the captain cut the motor and told us all to look astern. Our wake was brilliantly aglow.

"That radiance," our captain explained, "comes from thousands of little protozoa. When one tiny protozoan comes in contact with another, the nerves of one trigger the light of the other. They can't light up on their own. They have to touch one another to do it."

The captain bent over the gunwale, swept his hand through the water, and ignited a trail of fire. "There," he laughed, "I have just introduced thousands of tiny creatures to each other."

"They are getting along brilliantly," one of my friends joked.

We all began creating constellations in the water. We were now wonder struck. Later, as the boat headed in, we seven friends sat tightly together on a bench, laughing about how grumpy we'd been before.

And a thought came to me: We are so much like those tiny creatures. God has planted a light within each of us, but it's only when we touch each other in a loving way that this light shines.

In the darkness I sensed the light of seven smiles. I vowed to keep this secret of radiance always close to my heart.

What's the use of the light You've given me, Lord, if I don't shine it?

—N.S.S.

---

8 *SUFFICIENT unto the day is the evil thereof.*

—MATTHEW 6:34

A friend of mine has a peck of trouble with his garden. He'll read about mealybugs, then worry about them, and, next thing you know, his poor garden's infested with them.

Last year he bought a small tractor after a painstaking examination of over 40 models. He had heard that garden tractors were prone to transmission trouble, and he fretted that the model he chose would break down.

Even after he selected one with a guarantee against faulty transmissions, he still worried. "It'll probably break down the day after the guarantee expires," he told me gloomily.

It didn't. It wasn't until two weeks after the guarantee's expiration that his tractor's transmission failed.

I believe that when you worry excessively about something, you are really praying for it to come about. Excessive worry denies God's loving desire to give us what we want, and in so doing, actually "prays" for the opposite to happen!

Jesus reminded us of this in the sixth chapter of St. Matthew: "Take therefore no thought for the morrow: for the morrow shall take thought for the things of itself."

I say: Relax, God loves you.

Lord God, I believe that You want the best for me, and from now on I'm going to live as if I believed it. —M.A.

9

AND He said unto them, Why are ye so fearful? how is it that ye have no faith? —MARK 4:40

The second night of camp a thunderstorm came rolling and crashing across the lake, headed straight for our cabins. We counselors decided to make rounds of the cabins to make sure the youngsters were all right.

In one cabin I found three little girls huddled together on the same bunk, shivering in fright. "We're scared," Judy whimpered.

"What if lightning strikes us?" Roxy said.

"Don't worry," I said, "that won't happen."

"How do you know?" Cathy asked as a bolt cracked above.

"Do you remember," I asked, "our lesson this morning about the storm at sea? Jesus calmed the sea and He calmed the disciples. Because Jesus was with the men, they were safe, and because Jesus is with us, we'll be safe, too."

After a little more coaxing on my part, the girls went off to their own bunks and drifted off to sleep as the storm drifted away.

The next day was beautiful. I sunbathed on the pier as the girls dove and swam under the watchful eyes of the lifeguard. Cathy, Judy and Roxy kept asking me to jump in with them, but ever since a near-drowning incident in childhood, I had stayed away from water over my head. No thanks, I kept saying to the girls, I'll just stay here.

At last Cathy came over and, looking into my eyes, said, in the bravest voice a seven-year-old can manage, "You're scared, aren't you? Why don't you have faith like you told us to last night?"

I had no answer, and so before I really knew what I was doing, I took Cathy's hand and we jumped into eight feet of water.

That leap was a leap of faith, and it taught me that the power of Jesus to calm fears is a *challenge*, as well as a comfort. It's a leap we can all be ready to make, knowing He is there watching over us.

I'm not afraid, Lord. I have faith. —D.S.

10

THY word is a lamp unto my feet, and a light unto my path. —PSALM 119:105

While we were on a vacation in Central America, a friend of ours who lived in the area took us into a rain forest. We drove for several hours, and finally stopped on a narrow, dirt road. Our friend explained that from there on, we had to walk every step. Soon we could not see the sky, as the trees grew so thick and tall. We struggled uphill over rocky paths. Just when I felt that I could not take another step, we entered a huge clearing in the forest.

In front of us was a beautiful waterfall, cascading into a pool. Tropical flowers and shrubs grew all around, and gave off a sweet scent. Brightly colored birds flew through the mist from the waterfall. It was so lovely; never had I been so aware of the way God lavishes His beauty on the world.

But soon it was time to leave, and our friend led us away. You can imagine how surprised we were, when after just a few minutes of walking we reached our car just a short distance away.

"That beautiful waterfall was so close to the road. Why did you take us the long way around?"

Our friend answered with a grin and a wink, "Old Spanish proverb says that nothing in life is appreciated so much as the thing you must struggle for."

Lord, to reach Your beauty, I am ready to take the long, hard way.

—P.S.

---

11 *CAST out our sin, and enter in,*
Be born in us today. —PHILLIPS BROOKS, CAROL

A few years ago, I was a guest at a Mennonite farm in Mt. Joy, Pennsylvania. The days were long and lively, full of devoted prayer and hard, hard work.

After dinner one night, there was still some daylight and still some work to do, so we went out into the freshly plowed field to pick out stones. What surprised me was that this field was surrounded by a stone wall, decades old, that had been made of stones from this very same soil. Wasn't this field free of stones by now?

No. "Why are there still so many rocks in this field?" I asked farmer Nolt.

"The rocks are just part of the ground, ma'am," he replied.

That answer didn't really solve the rock mystery in my mind, but it did get me thinking about how little sins keep cropping up in my life, just like those stones, long after I thought I'd cleared my life of them.

But, of course, my life will never be free of those small, constant sins — they're just a part of me — and so I must be like that Mennonite farmer and from time to time pick them out, cast them away. Only then will my life become a good, fertile place, a place for God's love to grow.

Lord, give me the insight to remove those things that prevent me being what You mean me to be. —P.B.H.

---

12 *HE maketh the storm a calm, so that the waves thereof are still.* —PSALM 107:29

Our two cats, the Orange Brothers, rode in the car with us on the two-day trip to our new home. During stops, we put them in their cat carrier, but other times, we let them lounge around the car.

Sweet Face, completely relaxed and worry free in the strange surroundings, accepted the offer and napped on the seat or looked out the window.

But Wheezer, the kind of kitty who inspired the expression "nervous as a cat," refused to leave the box. During the entire trip he cringed in the back of the carrier with eyes wild and muscles tense, a nervous wreck.

Poor Wheezer! He's a dumb animal, yet how easy it is for me to identify with him, for I am the fretful type myself. The difference between this poor, dumb animal and me is that unlike Wheezer, I know I have God.

Thank You for Your promise of being with me always.—P.R.P.

13

ALL the way my Saviour leads me.

—FANNY J. CROSBY, HYMN

When I was growing up in an East Texas farming community, we had an old-fashioned custom of "walking a piece of the way home" with our visitors.

Guests were accompanied halfway home after visits.

As a little girl, I welcomed this extra time I could spend with a cherished friend. Often these were the most delightful moments of all.

I am a good deal older now, and life's day is growing shorter. I am nevertheless comforted that I have walked at least a part of the way home with a Friend — One who walks with me — always, everywhere.

Heavenly Father, thank You for the blessed assurance of walking me all the way home. —N.S.

14 When the Bible Speaks to Me
THE BOOK OF PSALMS

Picture this: a prison cell in the Greek city of Philippi, its cold stone walls wet to the touch. In the cell are two men, their feet locked in shackles, the flesh on their backs stinging with whip wounds. It is the middle of the night and in the blackness the two men are singing, joyously.

One man is named Paul; the other, Silas. Both are Roman citizens, both Jews, both Christians. They are the first men to spread the word of the Risen Christ on the European continent. The Greeks have looked upon them with suspicion, called them troublemakers, and jailed them on a spurious charge. Paul and Silas have no idea what will happen to them, whether they will be tortured again, or killed, but they are unafraid. It is midnight, and they are singing praises to God.

Now picture this: a room in a building in New York City. It is today, and the room is here in the apartment where I live. Sometimes, when I am discouraged, its walls seem to close in around me and I feel spiritually bound. I am no Paul or Silas, but for me it can seem like midnight.

Yet always at such times, I can find release — if I choose — for if I listen closely, I can hear singing.

The Lord is my Shepherd; I shall not want.

I can hear the songs that David sang 3000 years ago.

O give thanks unto the Lord, for He is good...
I love the Lord, because He hath heard my voice
and my supplications.

I can hear the same hymns of praise — Psalms — that Paul and Silas sang, and their words — powerful words of total faith — come surging across the centuries.

For Paul and Silas, an earthquake loosened their shackles and threw open their prison door. I need no such tumultuous happening to feel free and hopeful again. I need to sing. I need to sing out praises to the Almighty God, the same praises that two triumphant prisoners at Philippi sang.

When midnight comes, it is time for the Psalms again.

— VAN VARNER

---

15 *I CAN do all things through Christ which strengthteneth me.* —PHILIPPIANS 4:13

Our son Ron spent much of his spare time during high school fixing up a car. He tuned the engine until it nearly sang, and he finished the body as if it were a sculpture.

Less than a month after his graduation the car was sideswiped. Luckily Ron wasn't in it, but the car was judged a total wreck by the insurance company.

But Ron didn't think it was a total wreck. It was only half wrecked. So, instead of letting the car rust away in a junkyard, he decided to cut away the wrecked half, find a good half in a junkyard and weld the halves together.

I confess I had my doubts. "Why spend all that time and money?" I asked him. "Why not just take the insurance money and buy another car?"

But Ron said, "When I finish welding those fenders and panels together my car will be stronger than one right out of the factory. A good weld is stronger than the metal it joins, Mom. You'll see."

Well, I did see. Ron's car has held up perfectly and what he said about a good weld being stronger than the materials it joins has become a motto for me.

Whenever I have a falling-out with a friend or someone I love, I know it's welding time, time to forgive, because forgiveness creates a deep strong love that nothing can ever wear away.

Thank You, Lord, for making us stronger in the broken places.

—L. E. W.

---

16 *AND they brought yet unto him free offerings...*

—EXODUS 36:3

I'd mowed the lawn, then collapsed on the porch with a glass of iced tea in one hand and a fan in the other, when along came our young neighbor Bobby towing an adult-sized rake. To my surprise — and relief — he started to collect the grass I'd cut. In a little while he'd finished.

"Bobby," I called. "Come up here out of the sun and I'll fix you something to drink."

I gave him a glass of iced tea. We sat side by side on the steps and I said, "You did a good job. How much do I owe you for all your hard work?"

Bobby looked at me with big, brown eyes and said proudly, "Nothing, Mrs. Champ. This is one of my good-for-nothing days."

After he left, I stayed sitting on the porch with my empty iced-tea glass in one hand and the fan in the other. And I was wondering. *When was the last time I'd had a "good-for-nothing" day?*

When I'm good for nothing, Lord, I'm good for You. —I.C.

17

GIVE every flying minute,
Something to keep in store;
Work for the night is coming,
When man works no more. —ANNIE L. COGHILL, HYMN

I used to visit a tiny general store in the country. The proprietor had a clerk named Jake who I always thought was the laziest man ever created. Then one day I noticed that Jake was nowhere around.

"Where's Jake?" I asked.

"Oh," answered the proprietor, "he retired."

"Retired?" I said. "Then what are you doing to fill the vacancy?"

"He didn't leave no vacancy," the owner said without rancor.

Those words have stayed with me a long time. I think often of how sad it might be if Heaven's final judgment of my efforts here was: "He didn't leave no vacancy." Would I deserve it? I hope not.

Lord, I want to make You glad that You put me here on Your earth. —C.M.D.

18

...PAINT my picture truly like me, and not flatter me at all; but remark all these roughnesses, pimples, warts, and everything as you see me...

—OLIVER CROMWELL

It embarrasses me to tell you this, but I have some unsightly warts on one finger. I'm embarrassed about this because I'm afraid that if I let you know about my warts, you'll begin to think of me as a warty person instead of treating me as a nice person who, incidentally, has a few warts.

The only good thing about these miserable warts is that they are helping me understand what Jesus meant when He said I should love others as I love myself. I love myself enough to know these warts don't make *me* unattractive; they are, instead, something unattractive that has happened *to* me. And because of them, I now find myself looking differently at people with other kinds of defects. I am beginning to see them as people who, like me, are made in the image of God, except for a few flaws that don't really matter.

Lord, I don't like my defects, but I thank You for them. Through them You are teaching me more about love. —P.H.S.

19

...MEN ought always to pray, and not to faint.

—LUKE 18:1

Some years ago while touring Quebec, Canada, I visited the church of St. Anne de Beaupré where there is a staircase called the *Scala Santa* (Holy Stairway). It is a copy of a staircase in the Basilica of St. John Lateran in Rome, and that, in turn, is said to be a replica of the stairway Jesus ascended on His way to meet Pilate before His trial.

A guide told me that many pilgrims climb this stairway on their hands and knees, pausing for prayer at each step. "A form of penance," he said. I began to wonder what it would mean to me, a Protestant, if I did the same as those pilgrims. On impulse, I decided to try.

I knelt down on the first step. There I prayed for a safe journey for my parents who were going on vacation the next week. I moved up to the second step. I prayed for a cousin in the hospital. By the 10th step my knees were getting sore. I prayed for two friends who were having marital difficulties. By the 20th step my hands were red and hurting a little from the slippery hardwood, but now I was praying for all unemployed people who couldn't find work.

At last I reached the top. By now I was praying for world peace. I sat down on the 28th step and thought about the experience, and how the scope of my prayers seemed to have expanded. I hadn't climbed the staircase to put myself in the shoes of Jesus, as some people had, or to share His pain. I wasn't in pain, or tired. I felt exhilarated.

Ever since, the memory of those 28 steps has helped me to expand and deepen my prayer life. Perhaps you, too, might benefit from trying this discipline from time to time: Picture yourself on a staircase, praying at each step, letting your prayers grow as you ask the Lord to be with specific people, and eventually, whole groups — even whole governments of people. Maybe you won't make it to the 28th step (I seldom do) but I can tell you this: The higher you climb, the closer you'll feel to God!

Oh, Lord, keep me open to all the exciting ways of drawing closer to You! —E.V.S.

20

'MID all the traffic of the ways —
Turmoils without, within —
Make in my heart a quiet place,
And come and dwell therein. —JOHN OXENHAM, HYMN

Routine chores had piled up so high I was overwhelmed. As a result, I didn't even know where to start. "How am I going to get going today?" I asked myself.

An idea came to me. I began listing each chore on separate slips of paper: weed garden, letter to insurance company, call nursing-home friend, clean out refrigerator, put hem on brown skirt.

And then I had a little revelation. Why not give God a slip or two? So I wrote on one, "How about a few minutes of prayer?" And on another I wrote, "Why not stop and read a bit of Scripture?"

I folded each slip of paper and placed them inside a small box. After I shook the box up, I picked out a slip and set about doing what it said. I wrote the letter.

I know my chore box may sound a little silly, but from time to time it really does bring some excitement to my day, and it lends a little magic, too. When I pull out a prayer or a Bible slip, how welcome it is to have a sudden visit from a very special Friend!

Any day is made better, Lord, when I find a way to include You.

—S.P.W.

21

...SILVER and gold have I none; but such as I have give I thee...

—ACTS 3:6

One summer afternoon a small barefoot girl sat on the bank of a pond with her granddaddy, fishing. He wore a straw hat. She wore a dandelion behind her ear. A wind rustled in the pines. And there was not another sound — just her granddaddy's breathing. He had left work early to bring her fishing. She knew that was not easy. For he was a busy man. He was a judge.

For just a moment the girl forgot her pole. The end splattered into the water, sending the dragonflies scurrying off their lily pad. "Whoa, fishing pole," her granddaddy said, reaching over to steady the cane pole. She giggled.

"Watch that cork," he said, his finger pointing to the water. "When our fish comes nibbling, let him have a taste, then pull."

"Yessir," she said.

Shadows crept over the water. The sun sank low. But the old man sat as still as the pines, as if time were suspended and their minutes were as countless as summer berries.

She rested her cheek against his arm. "Granddaddy, are you sure there's a fish in this pond?" she asked.

He smiled at her, his eyes sparkling behind his glasses. Evening gathered around their shoulders like an old country quilt, pulling them together.

Suddenly the cork zinged under the water with such force the girl slid down the bank. "It's a whopper!" cried her granddaddy. She dug her toes in the mud and leaned back into his arms. They pulled. Breaking through the water, erupting into the last glimmer of daylight, burst the biggest fish she had ever seen. She held up the silver fish and sucked in her breath. Her granddaddy's face beamed down at her. And neither of them spoke. They only stared at one another over the dancing fish.

The gift of that afternoon was just about the best present the child ever got. I know. For I was the little girl with the dandelion behind my ear. And the granddaddy who left work early was mine. And he taught me something priceless that day. That there are many wonderful gifts I can give those I love, but the one that lingers when all the others are gone, the one that knits the brightest threads into life, is the gift of my time — the gift of myself.

The moments I share with those I love are the really cherished ones. Don't let me be too busy today, Lord. —S.M.K.

22

...HE hath delivered them to trouble...

—II CHRONICLES 29:8

The other day I read about a man in Maine who raises dandelions, yes, actually cultivates the gardener's peskiest foe. Apparently there's a good market for edible dandelion greens.

But growing dandelions isn't as easy for this farmer as you might think. His plants, pampered with fertilizer and tender care, are delicate and susceptible to blight. Cultivated dandelions tend to wither and die. To be strong, they need the competition from grass and other weeds.

As I thought of their brawny brothers marching victoriously across my lawn — despite my every effort to do them in — I felt better about the troubles in my life. Without them I too might become a delicate thing, and I know God doesn't want that.

Lord, my troubles are as much a part of me as my joys. Teach me to draw strength from both. —R.S.

23

FOR the eyes of the Lord run to and fro throughout the whole earth... —II CHRONICLES 16:9

The first time I ever flew in an airplane I looked down at the earth below and was awed by the patchwork quilt spread below me. Tiny houses, like those in the game Monopoly, stood in neat little rows. *When God looks down on His world,* I thought, *it must look something like this*. I tried to imagine that from certain homes prayers were being offered up to God. In my mind the prayers looked like what people say in the funny papers, surrounded by a heavy line with a white background. Then I remembered that my pastor once said, "Never think that God doesn't have time for your prayers, even if they are little ones."

Now when I'm driving on the highway and find myself almost out of gas, or my son is going to take an important test, or my husband and I simply can't find time to be together, I quickly remember my first view from a plane. And I see Georgia and our little community of Lilburn and our streets. Then I see my little prayers rising up: "Lord, get me to the filling station." "Please help Jeremy with his test." "Father, I need to spend a little time with my Jerry." And I just know that God hears me.

When I'm feeling awfully small, Lord, I need to know that I am large in Your eyes. —M.B.W.

---

24 *...BUT we glory in tribulations also: knowing that tribulation worketh patience; and patience, experience...* —ROMANS 5:3, 4

If someone is looking for me on a Saturday morning during July and August, it's a safe bet he'll find me on a tennis court doing battle with the wily and resourceful Larry Uhlick.

We're dogged opponents. I decide to rush the net after a strong forehand, and Larry's already decided to lob his return over my head. He's expecting a sizzler back from me after his weak second serve, but I send him a floater that upsets his timing and he smashes into the net. I run down his dropshot and slice a return back at impossible angle... right into a spot where he appears as if by miracle. And so it goes.

"You know, Larry," I told him last summer after we had cut and slashed our way to near-exhaustion, "we ought to find new opponents. We're too hard on each other."

"But that's the beauty of our games together," Larry said. "Neither of us wins without a struggle. I have to use everything I've got to beat you, and our games bring out the best in both of us. The pro told me that since we've started playing together, both our games have improved dramatically."

Larry was right. Without a struggle no game is worth playing. After all, struggles are a gift from God; they give us an opportunity to better ourselves.

From now on, Lord, I'm going to try to see each obstacle as an opportunity for growing. —J. McD.

---

25 *THEREFORE if thou bring thy gift to the altar, and there rememberest that thy brother hath aught against thee; Leave there thy gift before the altar, and go thy way; first be reconciled to thy brother, and then come and offer thy gift.* —MATTHEW 5:23, 24

A short item in a recent edition of *The New York Times* says that the Vatican in Rome is reviewing, and is likely to reverse, the heresy conviction of a noted astronomer. The man is Galileo, and he's been dead for nearly 350 years.

My first thought was *Why bother?* It happened so long ago. What difference would the review really make to anybody?

As I've thought more, though, I've begun to sense the importance of this act. The Church wants to, *needs* to right the wrong it has done Galileo, because even if Galileo has died, the wrong lives on. God knows this. And cares.

As the recent days have passed, this need to clear the conscience has gathered force in me, too. There are many wrongs, big ones and little ones, that I've made in my life. I, too, need to find them and do something about them.

"It's no use trying to forget wrongs," I hear God saying. Wrongs never die. So don't forget them, right them!

Forgive me, Father. —E.B.P.

---

26 *IT is an honor to receive a frank reply.*

—PROVERBS 24:26 (LB)

It's not always easy to be honest. Last week a good friend told me how her family had been going to a lake on Sundays instead of church. "Since I have a job, I feel that our family time together is important, don't you?"

I didn't know what to say. I wanted to take hold of her and say, "Don't get out of the habit of worshiping together in God's church!" But how would that come across — critical, judgmental, self-righteous? Instead, I simply nodded.

It bothered me. Finally I asked my minister, "What should I have done? I didn't want to offend her. But not saying anything gave her the impression that I thought it was all right."

"Karen," he answered quickly, "your friend would have benefited from knowing how you felt. Telling the truth is harder than avoiding it."

"How would you have handled it?" I asked.

"Always be gentle when giving people honest answers. Let them know you've been through the same thing. Perhaps you might have said, 'I've found that, for our family, we feel lost if we don't worship together.'"

In the future, when a friend asks me about something important, I'll care enough to answer honestly, gently. Because that's a sign of true friendship.

We're all seeking truth, Lord. Let me not mislead myself or others along the way. —K.B.

27

"FORWARD!" be our watchword,
Steps and voices joined,
Seek the things before us,
Not a look behind. —HENRY ALFORD, HYMN

We floated there, half a mile from shore, two insignificant human specks in the mighty Pacific. It was to be my first attempt to ride the surf at Waikiki. I had expected it to be exciting. Actually, I was scared stiff.

Enormous mounds of water traveling at racehorse speed surged under our surfboards. From the trough, they looked like onrushing mountains. From the crest, they looked like green avalanches. I was no surfing expert. I wished I had stayed home.

But the time had come to try it. I paddled over to the brown-skinned beachboy who had come with me as guide and protector. "What's the most important thing to remember?" I quavered.

He gave me a pitying glance — and three laconic words: "Don't look back!"

Well, I survived that day somehow, but I never forgot that advice. Why focus on things that can frighten or overwhelm you? Why glance over your shoulder at past regrets or mistakes? Christ Himself, on His way to Jerusalem where He knew death awaited Him, did not hesitate or look back. "He set His face to go to Jerusalem," says St. Luke. "He *steadfastly* set His face to go to Jerusalem." (Luke 9:51)

Surely that is the way to live. Not looking back. Looking forward. Steadfastly.

Lord, let me face the dangers and difficulties of life as You did. Without flinching. Steadfastly. —A.G.

---

28 *NO man can come to Me, except the Father Which hath sent Me draw him...* —JOHN 6:44

When our children were younger, their grandmother gave them a small incubator and two fertilized eggs from the local hatchery. The children devoted themselves to those eggs, gently turning them every few hours, checking temperature, counting the days. What a thrilling moment it was when we began to hear pecking sounds from inside the shells! But when Day 21 (hatching day) arrived, the chicks had not yet made any cracks in their shells. I called the hatchery. "Should we help the chicks out a little by breaking through from the outside?"

"Absolutely not," replied the man. "Hatching has to happen from the inside out. If you broke through from the outside, the chicks would probably not be strong enough to live. The best thing you can do is to just keep providing warmth."

I thought of that incident today, as I was trying to help a friend break through her resistance to Jesus. It helped me to realize that I can't break through that shell from the outside; but I *can* surround her with the warmth of Christian love and ask Jesus to enter into her heart. If I can provide the warmth, He will provide the inner strength for my friend's new birth.

You've taught me, Lord, that love is patient, love is kind.
—M.M.H.

29

O GOD, in restless living
We lose our spirits' peace,
Calm our unwise confusion,
Bid Thou our clamor cease.

—HARRY EMERSON FOSDICK, HYMN

We hadn't seen our friends, the Barts, for many years, and our yard was a mess. My husband and I were working furiously in the hot sun to clean it up before they arrived.

I should stop and make lemonade, I told myself. But, no, my watch told me. I wasn't going to finish as it was... The doorbell! Surely they couldn't be *this* early.

It was Mrs. Worthington from next door. "Thought you'd like some roses."

I thanked the older woman, hoping she wouldn't linger.

"You both look tuckered out," she observed.

"And more to do. We have company coming." I put meaning behind the words.

But Mrs. Worthington was not to be hurried. "Looks awful nice to me. And, anyway, your company is coming to see you, not your house. There's no need to be troubled about many things, June."

'Troubled about many things!' How could I have forgotten Jesus' admonition to Martha regarding her bustling about the household while Mary visited with Him?

Mrs. Worthington was right, you know. It's easy to become so troubled with the many things of our lives that we miss the good things Christ has in store each day. Like a visit. Like roses. Like lemonade!

And let me remember that, Lord. —J.M.B.

30

...FOR the Lord seeth not as man seeth; for man looketh on the outward appearance, but the Lord looketh on the heart. —I SAMUEL 16:7

One summer morning long ago a young Mexican-American girl who lived near our farm came up the lane to see my mother.

She was carrying some exquisite material and a dress pattern. Although she could speak no English, we understood by her gestures that she wanted my mother to make her wedding dress.

My mother nodded her approval and started measuring the pattern to her.

A few days later when the dress was finished, the young girl came for her final fitting. She looked beautiful. She turned from the mirror, gave my mother a hug and went into a lengthy speech in Spanish.

Mother heard her out, nodding now and then, even though she didn't know a word of Spanish. When the girl had left I asked, "Why did you let her go on when you didn't understand her?"

Mother simply said, "No, I don't know Spanish, dear. But when someone speaks from the heart, no matter what the language, I can understand the meaning."

Father, help me to speak from my heart, so that other people will understand my meanings. —F.F.

31

OUR hearts are restless until they find a home in Thee. —ST. AUGUSTINE

As we waited in the airport line to check our bags, I began to chat with the woman ahead of me. She said that both she and her husband had been raised in Japan as missionary children.

"We don't always feel like Americans," she said.

"Do you ever think of going back there?" I asked.

She shook her head. "No, because we don't feel like Japanese either."

I felt sorry for her. *How awful,* I thought, *to belong nowhere.* But then, just as I was thinking that, a marvelous grin lit her face. "Haven't we been lucky? We feel at home everywhere!" Then she went on: "Ever since I was a little girl I've loved the psalm that begins, 'Lord, thou hast been our dwelling place in all generations.'" (Psalm 90:1)

So that was her secret! Wherever she was, she could always feel at home — in Him.

Oh, Lord, give me a faith so strong that I too will never feel a stranger on this earth.

—P.H.S.

S	M	T	W	T	F	S
1	2	3	4	5	6	7
8	9	10	11	12	13	14
15	16	17	18	19	20	21
22	23	24	25	26	27	28
29	30	31				

The Eighth Commandment

Thou shalt not steal. —EXODUS 20:15

ME steal, Lord?
Surely You don't mean me,
For I do believe I've never
consciously
taken property
unlawfully.

Ashtrays?
Well, perhaps some little things
like that, but never many,
and anyway, that's common practice.
It's always seemed appropriate
for ashtrays to be "appropriated."

Late?
Yes, I *was* late yesterday,
but that's hardly highway robbery.
No, I hadn't thought of
someone else's time as
something priceless gone to waste,
Never, ever, to be replaced.

Yes, Lord, yes,
I'm beginning now to see
the different things that I
can steal, unwittingly.
Teach me now,
before I go astray again;
that larceny's not just
black and white —
It also comes in gray.

1 *...LOVE thy neighbour...* —MATTHEW 5:43

I stood in a small group with some of my neighbors, watching the bright orange flames lick at the ceiling of our local doughnut shop. Firefighters were everywhere, chopping holes in the roof, pouring water through what had been the front window, hanging on long extension ladders, trying to drown the fire from above. Smoke billowed from the shop, often hiding the firemen behind a wall of gray.

"How awful!" one person said.

"We must pray that no firemen are injured, and for the owners of the store," another offered.

"I just wish there was something more we could do," I added.

At that moment, a man and woman came through the crowd. She carried a small folding table and a shopping bag; he held two large jugs. And before anyone could wonder what was happening, the two were offering coffee and cookies to the beleaguered firefighters, policemen, and the store owner and his family.

Sometimes "loving my neighbor" means more than just caring. Sometimes it takes a little initiative — and imagination, too.

Save me from the guilt of being an innocent bystander, Lord.

—J.J.

2 *FOR with the same measure that ye mete withal it shall be measured to you again.* —LUKE 6:38

My grandpapa was a huge man who loved to sit on his front porch after he retired. He wasn't in good health, but he never complained. He smiled a lot with his eyes, before the smile reached his mouth. One summer afternoon he and I were sitting on his sagging front porch in the intense northern Florida heat. We gazed out at my grandmother's assortment of colorful flowers in the front yard. Then Grandpapa got that smile in his eyes that meant something good was surely going to happen.

"Mannie, what do you say you and I walk over to the store and pick out the biggest, coldest watermelon there and have us a watermelon cutting? Just you and me."

He got up slowly, painfully. We walked the half block to the store, and I watched as he selected a huge watermelon and paid the man 35 cents for it. Back in the kitchen he sliced it in two and did something I'll never forget. He scooped out the middle and put all the choicest red fruit in a large mixing bowl. This he handed to me, after tasting and approving it. We went back out on the front porch, and he watched me eating the melon.

"How come you gave me all the very best center part, Papa? I never had just the middle before," I asked, with juice running down my chin and onto my shorts.

His eyes smiled. "Cause I've found that when I give the very best away that's when the very best comes back to me."

If the gratitude and love of a little girl count, then my grandpapa got the very best back from me. That was 35 years ago, but I've never cut into a watermelon since without remembering that golden afternoon on Grandpapa's porch and his wonderful lesson in abundant living. Grandpapa said it his way; Jesus said it like this: "Give, and it shall be given unto you; good measure, pressed down, and shaken together, and running over..." (Luke 6:38)

Lord, I've already received. Let me be a giver. —M.B.W.

3 *...AND another book was opened, which is the book of life...* —REVELATION 20:12

Browsing through a gift book my young daughter received, *The Guinness Book of World Records*, I soon became absorbed in its lists of record-breaking feats: the fastest-run mile, the longest fingernails grown, the biggest ship built. But as I read on — the record for hairsplitting, 16 strands; the record for nonstop talking, 150 hours; the record for Ferris-wheel riding, 37 days — my mind began to wander.

How silly, I thought, as I read about the six people who set the record for playing the longest game of tiddlywinks (240 hours). But then I began to wonder if I could set a record for anything. What would it be that could be meaningful? How many times can I be first to say "I'm sorry"? How long can I listen to my child share her problems without making a critical comment?

There are all kinds of records I could set, so why don't I begin?

Dear Lord, the record I want to present to You is a record for loving. —N.S.S.

4 *AND immediately Jesus stretched forth His hand and caught him, and said unto him, O thou of little faith, wherefore didst thou doubt?* —MATTHEW 14:31

I'm not exactly a mermaid, but I'm a confident swimmer. I try to get to the pool every day, and I can do the crawl for 35 minutes without stopping. It wasn't always so.

I remember years ago, after I had learned the basic strokes at the local "Y," my instructor was encouraging me to swim the length of the pool and back. This meant going through the 12-feet-deep section and I was terrified. I was certain I'd forget everything I'd been taught, and sink to the bottom of the pool.

Sensing my fear my instructor, who was also a Sunday-school teacher at my church, said, "Look here, Eleanor, if my presence isn't enough for you, try to imagine Jesus standing beside the pool. As you swim through the deep water, remember that He has His eyes on you. Do the strokes to the rhythm of these words: 'Fear not, I am with thee... Fear not, I am with thee...'"

I followed her suggestion and, as I concentrated on Jesus and my strokes, I forgot about the deep water. And, you know, the day came when my fear was gone — sunk to the bottom of the pool!

Dear Jesus, today I may have to swim through deep waters, but I will swim unafraid, knowing that You are with me. —E.V.S.

5

HAVE thine own way, Lord,
Have thine own way,
Thou art the potter,
I am the clay. —ADELAIDE POLLARD, HYMN

One summer not long ago I worked on a freight dock. The work was hard and hot, but I didn't mind it. It was great exercise. What I did mind was the dock master, Don.

Don did his work well, but he could be a royal pain if he felt I wasn't doing my work well. When I put certain goods on the wrong pallets, misplaced bills of lading, or heaved things a little too casually, Don always took me to task, but good.

One day I said to a co-worker, Steve, "This dock isn't for me. Don just rubs me too much the wrong way."

Steve pulled down an empty pallet from the stack, and as we

loaded it with peach crates, he said to me, "Don isn't rubbing you the wrong way, Ed. He's just rubbing you smooth."

That seemed an odd thing to say, so I asked him what he meant.

"Face it," he explained, "you're new here. Don knows his job, and he knows when you're not doing yours right. He's just smoothing you out, so why fight him?"

He's just rubbing you smooth... I think about that phrase often. Sometimes when things aren't going my way, when I have troubles that I think I don't deserve, I find I want to lash out at somebody... even at God. It's then that that phrase comes back to me, *He's just rubbing you smooth*.

And maybe that's the way God is turning me into the kind of person that He wants me to be.

I know I'm not what You want me to be, Lord, but I'll keep trying. I promise.

—E.B.P.

---

6 ...*FOLLOW Me, and I will make you fishers of men.*

—MATTHEW 4:19

I can still remember the Friday morning, years and years ago, when I caught a dawn train in Chicago bound for northern Wisconsin. Somewhere along the way, a young man in his 20s boarded the train and took the seat facing mine. He was wearing a sailor's cap, the brim turned down and festooned with fishing lures. He was carrying a fishing rod. His luggage was a duffel bag and a wicker creel full of fishing tackle.

From time to time, the train would cross over a river or run alongside a lake and, in the early morning sunshine, we would see a fish leap up out of the water at a hovering fly. Each time, the young man would gasp and exclaim, "Look at that! Look at that!"

Eventually we came to a small town and the young man got off.

Awaiting him on the platform was his family: a husband and wife and two teenagers, a boy and a girl. They greeted the young man with hugs and laughter, and the boy teased: "Look who thinks he's going to catch all the trout!"

There was no more to the scene than that, and I don't know why it has remained with me over all these years or why I think of it so often. Perhaps it was because of the unabashed love I sensed in it, the sheer joy of being home, the simple pleasure of wading thigh-deep into a cold stream to challenge a trout.

These days when I read the papers or watch the television news, I seem to be bombarded by threatening crises of all kinds. But I don't think life is really like that. I think that life can be a cascade of happiness, the happiness of being alive, of being with loved ones, of doing something together that is just plain fun. And I think this is God's way of telling us that faith need not be built on major miracles, but on our gratitude for those simple joys He gives us.

Dear Lord, I thank You for Your small blessings — reminders of Your steadfast concern for my happiness. Through them, I become happier in You. —G.K.

7

GREAT wide, beautiful, wonderful world,
With the wonderful waters round you curled,
And the wonderful grass upon your breast,
World, you are beautifully dressed. —MATTHEW BROWNE

She was a friend of mine in college. Young and healthy. Yet she never went anywhere without a hot-water bottle and an umbrella. Evelyn was one of those people who seemed to hold the world at arm's length.

One summer day she went with me to a lake party. We arrived as the sun sprinkled its shining light onto the water like bobbing diamonds. I stood at the water's edge, taking it all in, wanting to embrace it somehow. Ribbons of blue water curled onto the sand between my toes. Behind me the grass rippled in whispers. Above clouds floated in silence. The whole world seemed like a big, bright invitation from God.

Then I noticed Evelyn. She had plopped down on a towel, put up her umbrella against the sun, draped a scarf over her shoulders, a shield over her nose and was rubbing protective lotion on her legs. "You got any bug spray?" she asked.

"Come on," I said. "Let's swim."

"The water looks murky to me," she replied. "Besides, I'd hate to risk my sinuses flaring up."

So I went without her. I plunged deep into those cool, dark waters, then burst up into the hot, dazzling light. As I did, I saw Evelyn huddled on her little towel, slapping bugs, not really seeing or feeling the world. Not really involved with life.

My father had a name for this. He called it "surface living." And there have been times when I, too, have fallen into its subtle trap. I gave in to inertia. I let the wonder dim and my awareness slip away. And instead of seeing a lake I began seeing a hazard to my sinuses.

But Jesus spoke of abundant living. He said, "I am come that they might have life, and that they might have it more abundantly." Maybe, in part, He was saying that He came to wake us up to the joys of existence, to coax us off our towels and from beneath our umbrellas into a new sensitivity and involvement with life where we see all the world as God's miracle, and enter in.

But in the end, it's all up to us — whether we float on the surface of life, or whether we dive deep.

Lord, help me take the plunge. —S.M.K.

8

DEAR Lord and Father of mankind...

—JOHN G. WHITTIER, HYMN

"Our Father Who art in Heaven..." To most of us, these words seem absolutely true and natural. They state so clearly our relation to God. But when my friend Bilquis Sheikh became a Christian those words troubled her.

Born in Pakistan, Bilquis grew up believing that God was a distant and impersonal power. Even when she later came to know and love Jesus Christ she still couldn't believe that God was someone she could think of as her father.

Trying to help Bilquis, a friend said, "Talk to God in the same way you always talked to your father, your dad."

This technique didn't work right away, but it got Bilquis thinking of her father. "When I was a little girl," she told me, "and would have to ask my father something, I was at first afraid. He worked in an office at home and I'd peek in, not wanting to interrupt. When he saw me, though, he'd put down his pen and call out his pet name for me. 'Keecha,' he'd say, 'come, my darling.' Then he'd put his arm around me and ask me about my troubles."

The more Bilquis thought of these fatherly moments, the more she saw that being a father meant always listening lovingly to a troubled child.

Kneeling in her room, now a grown-up woman, Bilquis looked up to heaven and cried out, "Oh Father, Father God." And as she prayed a wonderful warmth filled her. That warmth told her that God is our Father, always listening for us.

Our Father, my Father, Who art in heaven... —R.S.

9 *SO we belong to each other, and each needs all the others.* —ROMANS 12:5 (LB)

During my small-town childhood almost every family had a strawberry bed, and most kids really liked to pick them. Darting toward the patch with a pan was almost like hunting Easter eggs.

To me, strawberries were like little people hiding under their delicate umbrella of leaves. Plump ruddy dads and pinky-rouged mothers and aunts, and flocks of rosy-cheeked children. Were they playing games, having a picnic or gathered in a big jolly family reunion? I sensed even then their nature — that strawberries are companionable things.

"And this is true," says a friend who raises them now. "Whenever I plant two touching each other they grow twice as big and have twice as many runners and berries." She also tells me strawberries are of the rose family. Once, when she accidentally set out two rose bushes in their bed, "The roses smelled like strawberries, and the berries tasted like roses!"

How beautiful, I thought. God so loves the world that He has planted that love in all living things. The need to reach out, touch, become entwined with other lives. Even when those who appear in our midst seem different, how much we often find we have in common. And how often, like the strawberries and the roses, we can sweeten one another's lives.

Lord, if I am to grow and bear your richest fruit, I must keep close to others. —M.H.

10

IT ain't no use to grumble and complain,
It's jest as easy to rejoice;
When God sorts out weather and sends rain,
Why rain's my choice. —JAMES WHITCOMB RILEY

It was a gloomy, foggy, rain-drizzled morning when Plaford and I sat down for breakfast. Flowers outside the windows were bowed down and dripping; yellow tassels of the oaks were falling limp and soggy on the balcony and sidewalks; squirrels were drying their slicked coats with vigorous shaking; no birds were singing.

We bowed our heads for the morning prayer and Plaford said, "We thank You, God, for this food, and for this beautiful day..."

"What beautiful day?" I asked when he'd finished.

Smiling, he answered, "Never judge a day by its weather."

Thank You, God, for a wise and wonderful husband.—Z.B.D.

11

...YEA, I will uphold thee... —ISAIAH 41:10

Every marathon runner knows that there is a point in the 26.2 mile race called "the wall." It lies somewhere between the 18th and 22nd mile; and you know you've hit it when your muscles start aching unbearably, your legs feel like rubber, and you get depressed and begin to feel like a bathtub being drained. Physiologically, this is when your muscles have used up their store of glycogen, the type of sugar that produces energy. Until your body makes a rather painful transition to fat as fuel, you are literally running on empty.

A lot of runners drop out at "the wall." But a lot of others run through it. What are they running on? Guts. Sheer fortitude. A spirit that has yet to be reduced to a scientific formula. Just as scientists don't know, aerodynamically, how a bee can fly, neither do they know how a human being can run 26.2 miles.

I happen to believe that the principles of running can be transferred to my own life. I have to be ready to make the transition from running on my own steam to running on God's fuel — faith. With God's help, I can finish the race.

Thank You, Lord, that I can run and not be weary. —C.C.

12

WALK Thou beside us lest the tempting byways
Lure us away from Thee. —GEORGIA HARKNESS, HYMN

My husband and I had been climbing in the White Mountains and were now hiking back to the car. We came to a railroad and decided that following it would provide a quicker way out of the woods than the winding trail we were on. A sign said no one was allowed on the tracks.

But we were tired, and anyway, we couldn't see any danger in taking them.

A half mile later, after rounding a bend, we saw how foolish and reckless we'd been. The tracks now ran over a terrifyingly high trestle, with no refuge for us if a train came. And the track both ahead and behind was curved, so we wouldn't see an onrushing train until it was too late.

Scared and humbled, we ran back to the original trail and took the safe way home. Later, I made sure our children knew how senseless their parents had been.

"The makers of that sign knew what they were doing," I told

them. "They knew about dangers we couldn't see; we should have trusted them."

There are signs everywhere in life that we ignore at our peril. When I was even younger than my children I was shown ten very important ones — and so were you: The Ten Commandments.

When will I learn, Father, that You do *know best!* —P.B.H.

---

13 *JUDGE not according to the appearance...* —JOHN 7:24

Legend has it that when master painter and sculptor Michelangelo bought a piece of low-grade marble and lugged it home, everyone from his stone dealer to his neighbors chided him. "What good is that ugly rock? Why waste your time?" they asked.

Michelangelo answered all of them the same way. "There is an angel trapped in that stone, and I must set it free."

And gradually, as he worked, carefully and patiently, under his magical chisel the stone's imperfections were transformed into a beautiful angel.

I find that it helps me to remember Michelangelo's "trapped angel" whenever I'm annoyed by someone who is rude or selfish. Isn't it true that, with a little patience and careful handling, you can release angels from "human clay" too?

Lord, give me the vision and patience to set an "angel" free today. —M.G.W.

14 *HE hath put down the mighty from their seats, and exalted them of low degree.* —LUKE 1:52

Uncle Jake, who helped me each Saturday with yard work, and I were taking a break one summer afternoon, sipping lemonade. We both were silent, and I was turning over a frustrating week at the office in my mind. Involuntarily, I heaved a sigh.

"Doesn't sound good," Uncle Jake offered. "What's wrong?"

"Oh, I don't know, Jake. When I was younger I thought I was going to make a name for myself in the advertising business. But lately it seems I've been going down a lot of blind alleys."

Uncle Jake snorted. "What's so biggety about a name? Did you ever think there's some mighty great folks in the Bible who ain't got names?"

"No," I confessed. "Who do you mean?"

"I'll bet you can't tell me the name of the Good Samaritan. Or the little fellow who had the five loaves and fishes. What about the healed leper who came back to thank Jesus? Or the man on the cross by the Lord, who defended Him? There's lots of no-names in the Book, and many of 'em helped Jesus do His work. They didn't make a name for themselves, but they each helped glorify the name of our Saviour."

How right Jake was! Whenever I've been more interested in doing a good job than in making a name for myself, I've found those old blind alleys widening into bright, broad avenues.

Lord Jesus, may my work glorify Your name, not mine.

—C.M.D.

15 *THE Lord is good, a strong hold in the day of trouble; and He knoweth them that trust in Him.* —NAHUM 1:7

After a week of enervating tests at New York City's Lenox Hill Hospital, my elusive ailment was finally diagnosed, and now I was being wheeled into the operating room for gallbladder surgery. Even though I had received a sedative injection, I was agitated.

Obviously it showed because a smiling nurse came over, took my hand, and said kindly, "Hello, I'm Corinne. You're a little nervous, aren't you?"

I smiled weakly. "More than a little nervous," I told her.

Still clasping my hand, she said, "Well, no need to be because, in just a few minutes, we're going to make you better than new."

Another weak smile from me, the reluctant patient.

Then Corinne said, "You know there are two ways to approach an operation. You can worry yourself half to death, or you can trust us. Our surgical team is the best. You have nothing to fear." Then she winked, gave my hand a firm squeeze and whispered conspiratorially, "Especially since I'll be in there with you making sure they do everything right."

With these words, finally I was able to relax.

Just as Corinne had said, everything went well. And, perhaps not so curiously, what I remember most about my whole hospital experience is Corinne's message. I can approach life two ways. I can worry myself to death. Or I can trust. And what's the point of calling myself a Christian if I don't put my trust in Jesus?

If I could only trust in You as fervently as I worry, Lord, then I'd never have to worry at all. —J. McD.

16

I WILL never leave thee, nor forsake thee.

—HEBREWS 13:5

Last summer, my husband and I went sailing with some friends. There was a good wind when we set out but, in the middle of the lake, the wind died down. Not being seasoned sailors, my husband and I got a little nervous about getting home in time to have a supper we'd planned with our neighbors. "Don't worry," said our host, "the wind will come again. You have to learn to accept the rhythm of the wind and relax." He was right. Before long, we were moving again, smoothly and swiftly.

Sometimes I am propelled into a spiritual high by a weekend retreat, or a personal message that seems to rise off the pages of my Bible, or a deep prayer experience. But, inevitably, there comes a time when I feel a lull. I hope I can remember, the next time I hit the spiritual doldrums, that, if I'll just keep my sail raised by praying daily, I can count on the Holy Spirit to fill it and start me moving forward again.

My sails are unfurled and waiting, Lord. —M.M.H.

17

HAVING then gifts differing according to the grace that is given to us...

—ROMANS 12:6

Duty to God. To me, those words had always had a heavy sound, making me picture unpleasant tasks being performed by pinch-faced Puritans. *Still,* I thought, *that's what serving God is all about — "bearing the yoke," "passing the test."* That's why, when the head of the women's committee asked me to bake a cake for the annual church bazaar, I wearily said yes. Even though I hate baking cakes and am not good at it. Dreading the ordeal, I put it off until the night before the bazaar. Everything went wrong. The first cake scorched. The second one fell. At 2:00 a.m., exhausted and angry, I finally managed to piece together one cake from two. Duty to God was a drag, I decided. I became convinced of that the next day when mine was the only cake which didn't sell. Resentfully, I surveyed the poorly lettered bazaar posters above the various tables along the walls. As a commercial artist, I would have enjoyed doing those.

Later, when I apologized to the head of the committee for my cake, she sighed as she replied, "I love baking cakes, but I had to stay up all night to make those posters."

Now, whenever I'm asked to bake, I volunteer to do the posters, instead. God gave me artistic ability, just as He has given each of us some special talent. Looking around our church and community, I've noticed an interesting thing: For those people who use their special talents to serve God, duty is not an ordeal—it's a joy.

Dear, Lord, today I will do the task for which You have prepared me. —M.F.H.

18 *When the Bible Speaks to Me*

THE BOOK OF JOHN

Miss Ellen, bidding her former students good-bye at the close of a reception in her honor, stood as arrow-straight as when

I'd been in her second-grade class. I extended my hand to her, saying, "It was a nice day, Miss Ellen."

"No, June," she said, "It *is* a nice day!"

How like Miss Ellen, I thought, *always living in the present, and savoring it.*

That evening when I took out my Bible and started to read the eighth chapter of John, I could still hear Miss Ellen saying, "It *is* a nice day." Her words continued to echo in my head as I read, "I am the light of the world" (John 8:12); and then, at that moment, I somehow made the connection. This was Jesus talking, and He, too, was using the present tense: "I *am* the light" (John 8:12). The more I read, the more excited I became. "I *am* the door..." (John 10:9); "I *am* the Good Shepherd." (John 10:14); "I *am* the way..." (John 14:6). The *I ams* placed Jesus there beside me as He had never been before.

I thrilled that evening to this little personal discovery that I'd made — the presence of Jesus in the here-and-now. It's a discovery I use to this day, thanks to my old teacher who goes right on teaching me (in the present tense, of course!).

— JUNE MASTERS BACHER

19

TWO men looked out through prison bars,
One saw mud, the other stars. —FREDERICK LANGBRIDGE

It was evening, the benediction time of a hot summer day, and as my husband and I walked across the large parking lot at the mall, a cool breeze played about catching bits of paper, frisking through island plantings and shrubs.

"Isn't this breeze great!" Plaford said. "It reminds me of hot summer days when I was a kid helping Dad in the field, and a good breeze would stir up, cooling our tired horses and giving us new breath. And I remember evenings when my folks would take kitchen chairs out of our hot house, and we'd sit on the back lawn. A little wind would whip up bringing the fresh smells of the garden and Mom would say, 'Isn't that a wonderful breeze!'"

As we walked into the grocery, a woman was saying to her friend, "I know this wind is going to ruin my new hairdo, and it'll probably blow dust all over my clean car."

One wind — two ways of looking at it.

Help me, Lord, to see the goodness in everything. It's there to be found. —Z.B.D.

---

20 *IF at first you don't succeed,*
Try, try again.
That's the lesson you should heed,
Try, try again. —WILLIAM E. HICKSON

Quick! Name the most famous baseball player in history.

If you're like me, you named Babe Ruth — and for good reason. During his career, the Babe hit 714 home runs, at a time when baseballs were a lot less lively than they are today.

But he held another record, too. The Babe struck out 1330 times. Despite those strikeouts, his lifetime batting average was a phenomenal .342. I think Babe's success is rooted in a comment he once made to a sportswriter: "I just keep goin' up there and swingin' at 'em."

No one bats 1000. We are human, and we're going to fail — in career achievements, in personal relationships, in service to Christ, sometimes even in common decency. But Babe's method remains the best one when you've tried and failed. You never have lost as long as you keep swinging.

Come to think of it, Babe was in the same league with another philosopher, St. Paul, who also believed in taking another swing. He said, "...forgetting those things which are behind...I press toward the mark for the prize of the high calling of God in Christ Jesus." (Philippians 3:13, 14)

Remind me, Lord, that when I fail, I'm only practicing for my next success.

—P.V.S.

21

HE brought me up also out of an horrible pit...

—PSALM 40:2

During a drought year, when I was a child, my grandmother's well failed, so my cousin Ted and a friend hand dug a new one. Every day I watched in fascination, and, when the well was completed, I asked to go down in it. To this day I'll never forget the experience.

Ted looped a rope around me and lowered me slowly to the bottom. It was cold and damp in that dark hole, and I had a horrible feeling of being trapped — doomed almost. I looked up at the small circle of light 60 feet above me. I signaled Ted by a sharp jerk of the rope, and soon — very thankfully — was standing again in brilliant sunshine.

In the half century since that time, I've often been "down in the well," as sorrow and misfortune took the sunshine from my life. But I've never had to remain there. I could always look up and see a circle of light. I could always signal God by praying to pull me out. Time and again I've felt, as the psalmist said, that I'd been brought up out of a pit and had my feet set upon a rock, a song of rejoicing on my lips.

Through prayer, Lord, I can always ascend to You. —J.E.

---

22 *LET us draw near with a true heart in full assurance of faith, having our hearts sprinkled from an evil conscience, and our bodies washed with pure water.* —HEBREWS 10:22

Do you, like me, sometimes find yourself carrying around unnecessary burdens of guilt? I find that I really need to receive God's forgiveness, anew, every single day. And one way that I've found to do it is through a symbolic washing — the same kind of cleansing that is a recurring theme throughout the Bible.

Before my bath I confess my sins to the Lord, repent and ask His forgiveness. Then I ask Jesus to wash away my guilt, clean my thoughts and purify my motives. When I step out of my bath, I feel doubly clean.

Thank You, Lord, for Your cleansing forgiveness. —M.M.H.

---

23 *...MARTHA, Martha, thou art careful and troubled about many things: But one thing is needful: and Mary hath chosen that good part...* —LUKE 10:41, 42

The day was finally done. The house was spotless. All of the curtains had been laundered and the windows washed. The best silver was polished, and already the table was laid with Mama's treasured china. Edna, an old school friend, was coming the next day, and I wanted the house to be perfect.

I crept out of the bathtub and into bed, my body aching with fatigue. I would have to skip my Bible reading tonight; I was just too tired. I'd pray a short, quiet prayer. That would do.

I closed my eyes and from the depths of my memory came the words, not of a prayer, but of a childhood grace said at mealtime: "Come, Lord Jesus, be our Guest. Let all we do this day be blest."

Though I only whispered the words, they seemed to reverberate throughout my bedroom. "Be our Guest," I had said. I had just invited my Lord to a house that was polished and scrubbed for Edna's arrival. But I was inviting Him into a heart where no preparations had been made.

I got up, turned on the light, and reached for my glasses and my Bible.

Quietly I prepared the way for the Lord.

Forgive me, Father, when I let the mundane things of daily life take precedence over You. —D. D.

---

24 *ABIDE in Me and I in you...* —JOHN 15:4

One morning I sat at my desk feeling as if I didn't have an ounce of faith or energy in me. I picked up my paperweight and rolled it idly between my hands. It was just a simple black rock.

Absently I brushed the rock against my lip. I drew back. The rock tasted salty. I touched my tongue to it. It was like dipping into a saltshaker. Why was this little rock so salty?

I thought back to when I'd found it: the year before, while

wading in Israel's Dead Sea, the saltiest body of water on earth. The rock had soaked up a salty flavor simply by being in the water.

Thinking so intently of salt brought to mind the words of Jesus: "Ye are the salt of the earth," He says to us in Beatitudes. You are the strength and flavor of My kingdom. But if we lose our flavor, He goes on to say, we are of no use to anyone.

Being so lifeless, I was of no use to anyone. Feeling lackluster and defeated was a waste of His time and mine. It became clear that to become His "salt" again, to recapture strength, I'd have to immerse myself in His wisdom, just as that rock had immersed itself in the water of the Holy Land.

I got out my Bible and began to soak myself in its richness.

Let me be close to You, Lord, so that I can be useful to You — and others too. —S.M.K.

25

...PUT on love, which binds everything together in perfect harmony. —COLOSSIANS 3:14 (RSV)

"How do you make that banana dessert that Dick raves about?" a young wife asked her mother-in-law. "He keeps talking about a sweet banana dessert you made when he was a child. All he can tell me is that the bananas must be cut in very small pieces."

Her mother-in-law smiled. "I know what Dick is talking about. When the boys were young, we had to skimp along on a very tight budget. But I found that a little imagination could make a big difference in our supper. On rare occasions when we had a couple of bananas I'd dice them, sprinkle them lightly with sugar and serve them in my prettiest glass dishes. This became our very special banana dessert."

"Just diced bananas sprinkled with sugar?" asked the young wife incredulously. "Was that *all*?"

No, that wasn't all. There was imagination, yes, but there was also love.

Lord, teach me the difference that love can make. —D.E.

26

THE Lord is my shepherd; I shall not want. —PSALM 23:1

Lately I've been watching Sarah, a black-and-white feline who is the newest member of our cat clan of four. At the moment, in some obscure way known only to cats, she's treated pretty much as an outsider. She is not permitted to sip her milk with the other cats.

I've taken to feeding Sarah in her own special dish atop the clothes dryer. But even with me standing by on guard, she seems oblivious to my protective presence. She eats in a frenzy of haste, darting nervous glances over her shoulder, even though with me there she has nothing to fear.

Last week I caught myself worrying over an upcoming interview with a sports star known to have a chip on his shoulder, even though I had prayed about it. Just like Sarah the cat! When will I learn that, just as Sarah has me to protect her, I have God?

I don't want to look over my shoulder, Lord; I want to look up to You. —W.D.

27

. . .AND they believed the scripture, and the word which Jesus had said. —JOHN 2:22

My close friend Beth and I are also neighbors, so we often meet at our mailboxes which are side by side.

Because our rural carrier stops at 10:00 each morning, it wasn't long before she and I developed the habit of dropping into each others' homes for coffee. Too often, we also had something to eat.

We used to call these visits our "CC times" together. CC stood for coffee and cake.

Soon we both started putting on weight. One day we wondered aloud to one another, other than the friendship we enjoyed, what good, really, was coming from our CC times together?

"Let's," Beth said, "change our CC times into 'CB times'!"

"Huh?" I said.

"Coffee and Bible times," Beth said. "Let's start with the Gospel verses, read a chapter a day, and then discuss it."

We've done just that. Now we've both lost weight, and we're better nourished at that!

I've learned to talk to You, Lord. Now I'm beginning to see how rewarding it can be to talk about You. —I.C.

28

PRAISE God from Whom all blessings flow. . . —OLD HUNDREDTH

As I was trying to hang a picture, my hammer missed a slender nail and landed squarely on my left thumb. Loud exclamations, swinging the hand, anointing it with various salves and lotions did not prevent its swelling and turning black.

"Oh, that's too bad," a friend sympathized, spotting the thumb.

"In a way it's a kind of blessing," I told her. And I really meant it. I've used my thumbs all my life without really appreciating them, without giving them a thought. I've found it takes two thumbs to remove a jar lid — one to help hold the jar, one to twist the lid. It takes two thumbs to tie a shoe, two thumbs to fold clothes. There must be hundreds of things I use that thumb for and don't realize it. The injury to my thumb makes me aware of blessings I nearly ignore.

God, Your wisdom in creating all things is beyond comprehension. For everything You've given me, I thank You. —Z.B.D.

---

29 *. . .BUT the greatest of these is charity* [*love*].

—I CORINTHIANS 13:13

Yesterday I ran into an old friend who had some good news to tell me. After two years of constant rebellion, her teenage daughter was once again enthusiastic about school and church activities.

"Do you have any idea why she rebelled?" I asked.

"No," she answered, "I really haven't. But I do think I know what brought her out of it.

"You see," she went on, "no matter how many problems Monica caused me during the day, I never allowed myself to end my day without thanking God for her, that she was my child and that I had been given the privilege of raising her. Then, every morning, I'd pray again. I'd ask the Lord to help me love Monica more than I ever had before. My prayers kept me free from the whirlwind of her rebellion. And when she quieted and began to reach out for love, I felt no grudges or bitterness; my love was there."

Driving home, later that afternoon, I reflected on what my friend had told me. Her prayers were not only appropriate for a rebellious child, but for any human relationship — husband, parent, neighbor, friend. To love, to love without condition, that's the important thing.

Keeping faith in You, Lord, means keeping faith in love. Let me love and love and love. —B.H.

30

THOUGH I speak with the tongues of men and of angels, and have not charity... —I CORINTHIANS 13:1

One night deep in the dark days of the Depression, New York's famous Mayor Fiorello La Guardia was presiding in night court when a man was found guilty of stealing a loaf of bread. The man said he needed the bread to feed his starving family.

"The law is the law," said La Guardia, "I must fine you ten dollars."

"I don't have any money," the accused said.

La Guardia took $10 out of his pocket and tossed it into the huge hat he used to wear.

"Mr. Bailiff," La Guardia announced, "here's the fine. Now I am fining everybody in this courtroom fifty cents for living in a city where a poor man must steal bread in order to feed his family. Collect the fines and give them to this man!"

The bread thief left La Guardia's night court with more than $40 in his hands, walking like a man in a dream.

Was strict justice done? Perhaps not. And yet doesn't Paul say in Galatians 5:14 "For all the law is fulfilled in one word, even in this; Thou shalt love thy neighbour as thyself."

Love — that's the key word here.

The more I follow You, dear Jesus, the more I see that charity is only disguised justice. —M.A.

31

...PRAY one for another, that ye may be healed...

—JAMES 5:16

For six weeks, I'd been praying with — and for — Lori, a young woman who was going through a time of deep spiritual depression. She felt cut off from God and was unable to accept His healing forgiveness. "I can't even pray any more," she said. "I'd just feel like a hypocrite if I tried."

I did a lot of listening, shared some of the things that had helped me to get through spiritual deserts in my own life, and I prayed aloud for Lori when we were together and silently when I was alone. Still, nothing seemed to help. Then a few days before our family was to leave on a trip, Lori called to say goodbye. "*Please* have a safe trip," she pleaded. "I need you back!"

"Then, Lori, will you do something for me?" I asked. "Will you pray for a safe trip for us?"

She hesitated. Then she said, "I'll do it. I promise!"

When we got home, Lori could hardly wait to tell me about her breakthrough. At last, she was able to pray again, and to feel the healing power of the Holy Spirit.

Are there people on your prayer list who seem to be at a standstill? Why not try reversing things, and asking *them* to pray for one of *your* very real needs? It may be the most valuable gift you can give them.

Lord, help me to remember that prayer heals not only the one who is prayed for, but also the one who prays. —M.M.H.

September

S	M	T	W	T	F	S
			1	2	3	4
5	6	7	8	9	10	11
12	13	14	15	16	17	18
19	20	21	22	23	24	25
26	27	28	29	30		

The Ninth Commandment

Thou shalt not bear false witness against thy neighbour. —EXODUS 20:16

ONE day in court
I placed my hand upon the Bible
And swore to tell the truth
The whole truth
So help me God.

Then I sat and proceeded to tell the court
Partial truths
Twisted truths
Anything to make my case look good.

And so it went
Closer and closer to outright lying
Until suddenly — this is hard to believe —
My hand began to hurt,
The same hand I'd rested on the Bible.

I knew what it was telling me.
It was saying: Don't ever say
To your neighbors
Words you'd never dare say to God.

Now I place my hand on Your Word
Once more, Lord.
Help me be a true witness.
Help me, please.

1

WHEN the time was come that He should be received up, He stedfastly set his face to go to Jerusalem.

—LUKE 9:51

You don't have to be a tennis nut like me to admire the cool precision and stunning power of Bjorn Borg. But something else always impresses me about this superb athlete when I watch him play. Virtually alone among his competitors, Borg never disputes a call, never complains, never glares at a rude spectator.

And this has been his hallmark for all the years he has played professionally. No matter what goes on around him, Bjorn Borg plays on, steadfastly. I have seen him wince at a bad call, but then approach the next point with renewed resolve and concentration. If a fan heckles, Bjorn doesn't heckle him back. Instead, his concentration deepens.

At the beginning of Jesus' final journey to Jerusalem, His disciples advised Him to get even with a Samaritan village that snubbed Him by calling "fire to come down from heaven" on it. Jesus chided these disciples — saying that He was in the business of saving lives, not destroying them — and led them to another village to spend the night.

Jesus continued steadfastly on.

Bjorn plays steadfastly on.

When I have a task that's important to me, shouldn't I do the same?

Lord, help me to treat life's little frustrations for what they are: little.

—J. Mc D.

2 *A NEW heart also will I give you, and a new spirit will I put within you . . .* —EZEKIEL 36:26

The summer that hurricane Agnes struck our area in Virginia my husband and I were on a trip West. Phone calls warned us that the flood had swept through the lower floor of our summer home on Lake Jackson. "And all those beautiful roses you set out are gone!"

It was a sorry sight to which we returned. Inside — mud, ruined furniture, water-soaked books, papers, clothes. Outside — stone walls collapsed, trees uprooted, the float torn free and leaning drunkenly halfway up the opposite bank. Heartsick, we plunged into cleaning up the mess. But as we worked, aided by wonderful neighbors, we heard the stories of devastation elsewhere. Even so, we could hardly bear to look toward that ravished rose garden.

Bald in places, buried by debris in others, it looked utterly hopeless. "It's pretty late to get bushes, Marjorie," my husband said as we finally trudged sadly down the hill. "Probably the best thing is just to plow it up and put in some grass." He dragged a log aside, began to rake. Then suddenly exclaimed, "Hey, look! They didn't *all* give up." And sure enough, here and there a bush still clung to the ravaged ground. Bowed, soiled, well-nigh rent apart, they not only held fast, a few were actually putting forth tiny new green leaves. And one a brave pink bloom!

"Oh, you brave little thing," I cried, kneeling to prop it up. And doing so, I smelled its fragrance. And a thrill of wonder and joy ran through me at the fierce will to survive that God puts into all living things, even the will to bloom and be beautiful again.

My husband and I looked at each other, smiling. We were both thinking the same thing. We'd start over, this whole garden would bloom again.

Lord, when life gets rough, when I too get bowed and beaten by the storm, help me to remember those fearless roses. —M.H.

3 *...LORD, teach us to pray...* —LUKE 11:1

I used to have trouble praying for others in certain difficult situations. I never knew quite what to say. Then my friend Pat suggested, "Why not try praying the psalms?"

"How's that?" I asked.

"First pick out a psalm that fits a person's problem and then put that person's name in the psalm. For instance, yesterday, my brother-in-law Rick was deeply discouraged so I prayed him into the 23rd Psalm:

> "The Lord is Rick's shepherd; he shall not want.
> He maketh Rick to lie down in green pastures:
> He leadeth Rick beside the still waters.
> He restoreth Rick's soul."

Got a troubled friend? Here are some other psalms that Pat suggested to me: Psalm 46 for a loved one in trouble; Psalm 37 for one who needs patience; Psalm 27 for a friend who is worried; Psalm 119 for one who seeks to be closer to the Lord.

Thank You, Lord, for giving me the just-right words.—S.P.W.

4 *THE eternal God is thy refuge...* —DEUTERONOMY 33:27

For ten years my small transistor radio has given me good service, but now in its old age it has developed a slight idiosyncrasy. Once in a while it is sweet and clear, but mostly it sounds fuzzy. But if I put my hand on it, the radio performs sweetly.

Well, I'm getting older, too, and, frequently, get a little fuzzy. I forget where I've put things — that "safe place I'll be sure to remember"; I tire easily, and my bad knee complains on the stairs.

The radio and I have found the same remedy — the touch of a hand. I, for one, need the strength of God's hand.

Lord, why haven't I always known that I could live my life better with the touch of Your sure hand? —J.E.

5

...I CONTINUE unto this day, witnessing both to small and great... —ACTS 26:22

To be honest with you, I've always found it difficult to "witness" to my faith. Though I have never wanted to hide it, for some reason the thought of talking about it to others makes my knees shake. It took me awhile to find out that God can be honored in quiet, unexpected ways.

A few weekends back I drove into the country to visit an old friend Brian, who has a cabin by a stream. He loves living there, and after a day of swimming, hill climbing and helping an elderly neighbor gather her blueberry crop, I was in awe of Brian's energy and good, generous spirit.

Just before I left I asked Brian where he got all of his vitality and love of life. He shrugged at first, but he finally said, "Well, I guess it comes from God. Yeah, I'm sure it does."

I'd never heard Brian speak of God before, and as I drove home a thought dawned on me: What a great way of witnessing Brian had! Without making a big deal of it, he simply and exuberantly lived out God's will. And yet God didn't go unmentioned, because sooner or later I — and probably other people, too — asked Brian where he got all his wonderful spirit from.

Would this method of witnessing work for me? Well, from now on I'm going to live out God's teachings as fully as I can, with verve, and when someone asks me where I get my spirit, I bet I'll feel very free in saying, "From God, of course."

In my own life, I know that it's deeds, not words, that matter, Lord. Let my witness be quiet, but unmistakable. —E.B.P.

6

WORK is love made visible. —KAHLIL GIBRAN

I'm sure you've seen the famous painting, "The Praying Hands," done by the German Renaissance painter, Albrecht Durer. It's a portrait of rough, beaten hands gently clasped in prayer. It wonderfully symbolizes the peace and quiet power of prayer. Would you ever choose it as a symbol for Labor Day, as well? I would, but that's because I've heard the story behind the painting.

Around the year 1490 Durer and a friend were both trying to establish themselves as painters, but meeting only hardship. Finally, Durer's friend decided he'd better go to work as a laborer. But he wasn't forsaking painting altogether. Until Durer broke through as an artist, the friend would give Durer all the money he could spare.

Durer's breakthrough took time. The friend labored hard — as a sawyer or as a bargeman on the rivers of Europe — and he sent money to Durer whenever he could.

Years later, Durer and the friend were united once again. They sat down to dinner one evening, and as they said grace, Durer saw his friend's work-worn hands held together in prayer. All the unselfish perseverance and love in those hands became transcendently clear to Durer at that moment. His friend's goodness took him by the heart.

It's no wonder that the painting of those hands has endured. The hands symbolize so well two of God's greatest gifts to us: *prayer* and *work*. Through prayer God comes into our lives and gives us His love. And then, through work, we create the places where God's love can flourish. We build great industries and small peaceful homes, we give children the chance to learn life's lessons, and we give artists the chance to express life's truths.

On this Labor Day, Lord, I owe You a prayer of thanks. I hold my hands together and thank You for the gift of labor, for the chance to make Your love real in the world. —R.S.

---

7 *...LIVE peaceably with all men.* —ROMANS 12:18

Fresh out of high school in Effingham, Illinois, I was employed as a reporter for the *Daily Record*. During my first week I was assigned to cover a trial at the courthouse.

I'd learned that the attorneys Piper and Bauer, who opposed each other in the case, were known as the best lawyers in the area. But I was entirely unprepared for the fierce, fiery declarations that they hurled at one another. They became the angriest men I'd ever seen. I truly feared they would get into a fight.

Finally, the courtroom hushed, the judge pronounced sentence. Attorneys Piper and Bauer left the room just ahead of me.To my utter amazement they walked arm and arm down the circular stairs, talking quietly. I couldn't believe my eyes.

Hurrying to the office I told the editor this unbelievable thing: that after their shouting, clawing, verbal battle those lawyers were just hunky-dory! Hypocrites, they were!

The editor smiled. "Zona B., these men don't hate each other," he explained. "They're not enemies. It's their job to win in court; to influence the jury. They must hold a difference of opinion and still remain friends. In fact," he added, "it would be well if all of us copied that characteristic."

How right he was! People should not be considered enemies because they differ with us, or have opposing beliefs, opinions, politics. I hate to think of all the friends I'd lose if they decided they didn't like my opinions. St. Paul admonishes us to live peaceably with all men. I can love my neighbor without loving every word he says.

Lord, sometimes I need to overlook what is in people's minds so that I can love them for the goodness in their hearts.—Z.B.D.

8

TRUST no Future, howe'er pleasant!
Let the dead Past bury its dead!
Act — act in the living Present!
Heart within, and God o'erhead!

—HENRY WADSWORTH LONGFELLOW

I had looked forward to getting together with my fellow teachers in the faculty room following our first day of classes last September. But something troubled me about our conversations. "Bill and I plan a much longer vacation next summer," one colleague told me. Another said, "I'm going to take an even longer one! George and I are retiring at the end of the school year. We can't wait." To all this I added my plans for a long-awaited cruise to Alaska.

But I left the faculty room strangely depressed — not really knowing why. All our futures seemed so exciting. What was the matter with me? I looked up, and suddenly I knew. It was a stunningly beautiful, crisp September day. It was a wonderful day right then, but all of us had been missing it by pinning our hopes to the future. And then a favorite saying of my father's came floating back to me: "Today is the tomorrow I looked forward to yesterday, and I'm enjoying every minute of it."

Isn't this at least partially what Jesus had in mind when He warned us to "take therefore no thought for the morrow: for the morrow shall take thought for the things of itself"? (Matthew 6:34)

I think so.

Dear Jesus, I'm grateful for the glory of this day. —J.M.B.

---

9 *...WHOSO putteth his trust in the Lord shall be safe.*

—PROVERBS 29:25

"Today I want to walk by myself." Tom looked up at me, his face solemn and determined. "All right," I said, leaning down to kiss him, "I'll watch you from the window." It was the third day of kindergarten for Tom, our youngest child.

From the front window of our corner house, I could see down the long, winding street almost the whole distance to the school. As I watched, Tom's already small figure grew smaller and smaller as he trudged down the road. He reached a curve in the street and for a brief moment disappeared from my view. Then he reappeared and suddenly turned and waved. My eyes filled with tears. I knew he could not see me standing at the window, but was waving because he was sure I was there.

That little episode happened many years ago. But each time I reflect on that memory, I experience again how much Tom's simple trust meant to me that day. And I think once more about how that little act of faith was a picture of the way God would like us to trust in Him. How He must long for us — His children — to step out to face all of life's challenges and problems with a child-like confidence that He is watching over us even though we cannot see Him.

Tom is 18 now and making plans to go to college. I realize that someday soon I will stand by the window again and watch him leave. And I know that my prayer then will be that he will always have the same kind of faith and trust in his Heavenly Father that he had in his earthly mother on that day years ago.

We are all Your children, Father, trusting in Your watchful care.

—C.M.C.

10

OUR Lord has written the promise of the resurrection not in books alone, but in every leaf in springtime.

—MARTIN LUTHER

This is a peculiar little story I'm about to tell you. Yet, it is true.

My father-in-law died on September 10, a sudden death at the age of 60. He was a devout Christian and a church deacon. But something about the untimeliness of his death left my mother-in-law without much comfort.

She bravely carried her grief through winter's bleakness, through all those barren, dead weeks. Even as spring came and waked the world, her burden seemed locked within her. The jonquils pushed up like tiny breaths of life from beneath the earth. And the lone dogwood tree in Mom's front yard burst into new life. It opened its delicate pink buds, crowning the yard like an Easter bonnet. Mom watched the little tree from the window; it had always been a favorite of hers, as well as my father-in-law's.

Summer withered away, children walked back to school and a leaf or two drifted off the trees in the yard. Still, Mom's grief lingered. On September 10 it became quietly intense. But something almost magical was about to happen.

As she wandered to the mailbox that day, her eyes lighted on the dogwood tree in a moment of wonder. For there in the center of the browning yard, under a golden, almost autumn sun, the little tree had burst into bloom. It shimmered in new pink blossoms. *Spring* blossoms right there on the doorstep of autumn. And for Mom there was no doubt. The reality of resurrection was written in the petals that had come back to life on that day, of all days.

Later that day as I stared in bewilderment at the flowering tree, I felt drawn into the tiny miracle, too. For through a dogwood, God had sent a message of comfort in His own special handwriting: "Let not your heart be troubled, for he who believes in Me, though he die, yet shall he live."

Thank You for the promise of resurrection Lord, that keeps popping up everywhere around me, like the bulbs of springtime. —S.M.K.

11

...A THREEFOLD cord is not quickly broken.

—ECCLESIASTES 4:12

My brother Neil and I were driving along the countryside near his home deep in the heart of Pennsylvania's Amish country. Neil explained some of the Amish customs to me and said that they do without electricity, cars, and many other modern conveniences.

"They're very self-sufficient, aren't they?" I said.

"Well, yes, if you mean going without electricity and so on. But, no, in that they're very dependent on one another. Recently they had a barn-raising nearby. Hundreds of Amish came from all over and built a huge barn for a man. In one day, for free. The women cooked huge amounts of food and, when the barn was finished, they all celebrated. They were celebrating their togetherness, not their independence."

Sometimes I think I'm independent, but I'm really not. I need others, but most of all I need the closeness of the Lord.

Father, why should I want to be sufficient unto myself, when You have so much I need?

—C.C.

12

O WATCH, and fight, and pray;
The battle ne'er give o'er. —GEORGE HEATH, HYMN

"I need you to pray for me," my friend Ginger whispered as we came alongside each other in a store aisle. "We're going to Texas by plane for a week's vacation."

At first it seemed as though she were asking simply that I pray for a safe and happy journey, but she was asking for much more than that.

"I'm afraid of flying," Ginger told me, "but I'm tired of being bullied by that fear. I'm going to face up to it and ask Jesus to help me defeat it. Please," she said, asking again for my prayers, "I need all the help I can get."

Of course I prayed for her, and so did a lot of other people.

Ginger made that trip to Texas, flying both ways, and came home triumphant.

Maybe her fear doesn't seem all that meaningful to you or me, but it was very real to her. Has some fear been holding *you* hostage? Why not try doing what Ginger did? Admit what your fear is. Ask God to help you face up to it. Get your friends to bolster you with their prayers. And then do battle!

In Your name, Jesus, I will vanquish my fears. —P.B.H.

13

LOOKING unto Jesus the author and finisher of our faith... —HEBREWS 12:2

My writer's dream had finally come true. My novel was being filmed for television. Because of family responsibilities, I was not able to go to Hollywood to watch the whole filming, but I did get to fly out for the final day.

How proud I was as the director led me around the set. How proud, that is, until he introduced me to the actress who was playing my heroine, Rachel.

"Rachel," the director said (during filming all the actors went by their character names), "this is Lois Duncan. She wrote the book."

I don't know what I expected. Congratulations, perhaps? An admiring smile?

Instead, the actress stared at me blankly.

"Oh," she said in surprise, "you mean there was a *book*?"

I tried not to show it, but her remark hurt. After all, I had *made* Rachel! I had thought her up, given her features and personality, and sweated to make her come alive for my readers. Yes, it did hurt.

I was still thinking about the incident that evening as I started to say my prayers. And then it hit me. How much credit had I given God for having created me?

Lord, You are the Author of us all. Help me to remember that—and to praise You for it—always. —L. D.

---

14 *THEY helped every one his neighbour...* —ISAIAH 41:6

One morning I was leaving our bank, which was then in the process of being remodeled. Near the door there was a lot of debris, jagged planks, nails protruding from short pieces of lumber, and loose gravel all over.

I looked up to see an elderly woman approaching.

I had better wait and help her get past this mess, I said to myself.

I moved a little to see if I could push trash away to make a better path for her. When I did this, my sleeve caught on a carpenter's horse and it caused me to stumble and fall to the ground.

Now the lady came to my rescue. She helped me up and, as I stood there a bit dazed, she brushed the dirt from my knees and from my dress.

It's important, isn't it, to live in a climate of helpfulness? After all, as the old adage says, "The life you save may be your own."

Thank You, God, that help is a two-way street. —F. F.

15 *When the Bible Speaks to Me*

JOHN 7:37,38

The water at our summer cabin in the Rocky Mountains is often filled with sediment and has a peculiar taste. But within about ten minutes' hiking distance from the cabin is a little spring of perfectly pure, sparkling fresh water. I've gone to the cabin nearly every summer since I was a child, and every time I visit that spring, I think of the living water in the Bible.

When I was seven years old, I knelt by the altar in a little brown church in McCook, Nebraska, and gave my life to Jesus. In return, He gave me a spring of living water just as He promised when He said, "If anyone thirst let him come to Me and drink. He who believes in Me, as the Scripture has said, 'out of his heart shall flow rivers of living water.'" (RSV)

How many times I have gone to that spring within me. Though it's a spiritual spring, I like to visualize actual water bubbling forth within my heart. When I'm burdened with guilt, I go to that spring asking forgiveness, and its pristine waters wash away the ugly stains, making me fresh and new.

When I feel hurt or rejected or lonely, I go there as an empty vessel asking to be filled. As I wait there, the One Who *is* Love fills me to overflowing, and I go away with water to spare and to share. When I'm in physical pain, I let the living waters flow over the area that hurts, soothing, comforting, restoring.

When I'm going through a dry period in my prayer life, I know I have to find my way to the spring within. But I never have to wander in that spiritual desert for long because there is always the seventh chapter of John:

"If anyone thirst, let him come to Me," and He is always there.

— MARILYN MORGAN HELLEBERG

16 *THE Lord lifts up the downtrodden...*

—PSALM 147:6 (RSV)

My three-year-old son and I set out on a four-mile hike. Seth brought along a canteen of water, and though I tried to convince him he didn't need the extra burden, he was adamant.

As we marched through the wooded glens, Seth shifted the canteen from one shoulder to the other. At the two-mile mark I offered to carry it. Absolutely not, he said.

At the three-mile mark Seth began to tire and stumble. As tears welled up in his eyes, I said, "Do you want me to carry it now?"

"No!" he blurted. "But will you please carry *me*, Daddy?"

And so onto my shoulders he went. At the end I put Seth down and he said, "See, Dad, I carried the canteen all the way."

"I guess you did," I said, holding back a laugh, not wanting to ruin his feeling that he'd proven himself. On our way home I thought how Seth would outgrow such willful beliefs soon enough. But wait! *Even in middle age*, I thought, *I still suffer from the same sort of false pride.*

So often when I make it through a difficult time, I take pride in my fortitude. But all along Someone else was holding me up.

Next time I have a burden to carry, I'll remember Who that Someone is. And I'll give thanks to Him.

I fight weakness all I can, Lord, but it's Your strength I really depend on.

—D.L.

17

BE ye doers of the word, and not hearers only . . .

—JAMES 1:22

When a visitor to an outpost in the wilds of South America saw the neat compound that a missionary had hacked out of the jungle, he said, "God has really been at work here."

But then he noticed the missionary's calloused, work-hardened hands and added, "But He didn't work alone, did He?"

Sometimes it's awfully easy to praise God piously for everything, forgetting that the Lord doesn't do everything. His way is to use people — to use *me.*

Lord, let me be a doer. —B. M.

18

FOR as he thinketh in his heart, so is he . . .

—PROVERBS 23:7

When I was a little girl, my best friend was named Josie. One day a new girl moved onto the block and, very soon after, Josie dropped me. "I'll never speak to Josie again," I stormed to Mother. I was angry and heartbroken.

"Of course you will," Mother said. "Keep on loving Josie. Act as if you were sure she still loves you. She'll come back; you'll see."

It was difficult. Pride and hurt feelings got in the way, but I kept acting as if Josie were still my friend. And, after a while, I had two best friends — Josie *and* the new girl.

Acting "as if" sounds like a child's game, but it isn't. Some of the deepest religious thinkers deal with simple ideas. For instance, I believe that William James was telling people like me to act "as if" when he said: "Be not afraid of life. Believe that life *is* worth living, and your belief will help create the fact."

When I stumble, Lord, remind me to use the "as if" principle to keep me from falling.

—D.E.

19

CHRISTIANITY is either a dull habit or an acute fever.

—WILLIAM JAMES

Do you think of yourself as an average Christian? Let me tell you something a wise and perceptive minister once told me. "Be careful about being average, son," he said. "If a man stands with one foot on a block of ice and the other on a red-hot stove, then, on the average, he should be feeling pretty good, right?"

Wrong, of course; I got the point. And I still think about that old minister every time I read what God says in Revelation 3:15, 16. "... thou art neither cold nor hot: I would thou wert cold or hot. So then because thou art lukewarm, and neither cold nor hot, I will spue thee out of My mouth."

I have learned that one can't be a lukewarm Christian. One either believes in Christ and His message or he doesn't. He endeavors to follow Him or he doesn't. There is no "on the average" or wishy-washy in-betweens about it. God wants us hot.

I am Yours, Lord, no ifs, ands or buts.

—R.S.

20 *O WHAT peace we often forfeit,*
O what needless pain we bear,
All because we do not carry
Everything to God in prayer. —JOSEPH SCRIVEN, HYMN

Do you ever have one of those "I just don't know" days when you feel like crawling into your shell? Those days when you say to yourself: "I just don't know if my life has meaning"; "I don't know why John's getting on my nerves lately"; "I don't even know what we'll have for dinner..."?

When these sorts of stalemates began getting me down all too often, I sat myself down and asked myself a few questions: *If you call yourself a Christian and believe in the inherent goodness of God and His wonderful plan for all He has created, what's all this fretting about? Don't you trust God enough to let Him help you?*

Now whenever I feel small and insecure I take a moment to turn to Him, the Source of all good. And my grand dilemmas melt down to little problems I can deal with. My life will have more meaning if I volunteer at the hospital. Maybe John would be more agreeable if I served his favorite dinner... Hey, that's what to serve tonight, pork chops and hashed brown potatoes!

The next time you "just don't know," it's time to have a little visit with Someone Who knows everything you don't.

Thank You, Lord, that when I "just don't know," You do.

—P.B.H.

21 *. . .IT is more blessed to give than to receive.* —ACTS 20:35

It was one of those gentle Georgia days on Granddaddy's farm, when the sun played behind the clouds, casting hazy orange shadows across the fields. I was picking cotton. I was only seven and the burlap sack I pulled was lots bigger than I was. But I'd begged Granddaddy for the chance to pick and he'd given in.

The cotton field stretched out ahead of me shiny and green and freckled with white. There were lots of pickers in the field. They were paid by the pound, so their hands moved fast. They could skin a bush of its fluffy white balls before I could scratch my nose. Their sacks were growing fat. Mine was unmistakably thin. I wanted to quit. That's when an old black woman idled up beside me, her hair tied in a faded red bandana. "Mind if I pick with you?" she asked.

"No ma'am," I said. "I don't guess so."

Her fingers worked like music down the row. But she did a curious thing. Every time she dropped a handful of cotton in her sack, she dropped one in mine as well. "One for you and one for me," she said.

My bag grew plump. I began to smile. But I was puzzled. So when we got to the plum tree shade at the fence, I said, "Why are you putting a handful in my sack each time you put one in yours?"

Her crinkled face smoothed out into a wide smile. "Child, don't you know your Bible? Don't you know the place where it says, 'Freely ye have received, freely give'? (Matthew 10:8) Remember this and don't forget — for every handful you take in life, that means you've got one to give."

And the child didn't forget. For sometimes when the taking in my life outweighs the giving, I remember, and I try to balance it up. . .a handful of giving for every handful of taking.

Lord, as I pull my little sack of need through this day, let me remember: One for You and one for me. —S.M.K.

22 *HE with earthly cares entwineth*
Hope and comfort from above;
Everywhere His glory shineth:
God is wisdom, God is love. —JOHN BOWRING, HYMN

I was shopping for a birthday card for my daughter. As I scanned the rows of cards words leaped out at me: "Happy Birthday, Sweetheart." "To my beloved wife." "Happy Anniversary, Husband."

My happy mood was gone and familiar traces of depression settled on me. I was alone with no husband or sweetheart.

Then I glanced at a row of cards with different captions. "Thinking of you." "Just to say hello!" "To someone all alone." No, I wasn't the only lonely person in the world.

When I went home I started writing letters to people that I thought might be lonely. I told them I was thinking of them, that God loved them and I would be praying for them.

I was no longer alone and, suddenly, I no longer felt depressed. I felt God's love all around me.

Now, whenever I get lonely I write people to remind them that God loves them — and me, too.

How can I be lonely, Lord, when I can reach out to others and to You. —B.H.D.

23

O LORD, support us all the day long of this troublous life, until the shadows lengthen, and the evening comes, and the busy world is hushed...

—CARDINAL NEWMAN, PRAYER

When I first started writing, someone said to me, "Know the ending of your story before you start it. Plan that first and aim everything else toward it."

I don't always live up to this rule in my writing, but over the years I've found it to be a great way to plan each day. First thing in the morning, I say (preferably aloud), "This is the day which the Lord hath made; we will rejoice and be glad in it." (Psalm 118:24) Then I think of the evening when the day will end. I picture the family at home, together again after a full, busy day. I feel the peace and love that fills the air.

If I hold this picture in my mind, it's a lot easier for me to sidestep situations during the day that might make the evening more difficult. Angry or spiteful words that would blemish the evening's peaceful scene are left unsaid. I guard against jealousy and fear, and I find smiles are easier to come by when I know that peace and quiet awaits me.

It can await you, too.

Let the peace I create during the day extend into the night, sweet Jesus.

—D.D.

24 *NOW faith is the substance of things hoped for, the evidence of things not seen.* —HEBREWS 11:1

When our 11-year-old son Jeremy asked the blessing one evening, he surprised us by praying, "And God, I want to thank You that You are going to help me get a go-cart... somehow."

We explained to Jeremy that we were not about to give him the money for a go-cart. I even explained that I didn't want him on one, much less buying one. He listened politely, nodding.

The next night he prayed, "Thank You, God, that You will work it out so my mother will change her mind and I can somehow get the money for a go-cart. Show me a good one."

For months he prayed this. He even got his daddy to take him to look at used go-carts he'd read about in the paper. He got a job cutting a neighbor's grass for five dollars a week. It was sometimes 100 degrees that summer, but Jeremy faithfully cut the grass while his twin brother Jon played ball or sat in the shade. He saved his money methodically in a large plastic container. He also began to save tin cans to earn money. And he kept thanking God for the go-cart.

Then fall came. Both boys usually played football. However, I didn't want Jeremy to play this year. He was too small to play in unlimited weight. Jon outweighed him by 20 pounds. On the spur of the moment one day I offered to give Jeremy the exact amount of money that it would cost Jon to play ball, if he could be happy not playing.

He nodded and said enthusiastically, "You got a deal." The money went into the go-cart fund. His daddy thought the go-cart was a good idea. Well, I reasoned, if I have to choose between football or a go-cart, I'll have to go with the go-cart.

After nearly a year of saving, working and praying the day came that Jeremy, Jeremy's daddy, Jon and I drove to Hamilton Brothers go-cart store in Atlanta. Jeremy had decided that God wanted him to have the very best — no used, cheap model. Jeremy dumped all his money out on the counter and the manager patiently, matter-of-factly counted through it all. He had enough to buy the blue go-cart in the window. Jeremy "rode" it home, joyfully sitting in his go-cart that we'd loaded in the back of our station wagon.

Now, when I want something really big that seems out of the question, I am reminded how my son, with confident determination, thanked God for his go-cart *before* he even had a dime, or a job, or my blessings about buying one.

Father, give me the stubborn faith of a child. —M.B.W.

25

YOU shall not make gods of silver to be with Me...

—EXODUS 20:23 (RSV)

Money, money, money. Sometimes it seems to dominate my life. How much do I need? Where's it going to come from? How much do I dare borrow? At times I seem to be thinking of nothing else. But last week I heard an old legend that clarified a few things for me. It went like this:

Once there was a rich, arrogant king whose only concern was getting richer. His people could've starved, and he wouldn't have noticed. But this didn't mean he completely ignored God. Once a year this king summoned all the bishops and archbishops of the realm to his castle. He wanted them to tell him he was a good man in God's eyes, piling up riches in heaven as well as on earth.

Most of the churchmen told the king the untruths he wanted to hear, but one young friar was different. He took the monarch to the throne room window and said, "Your Majesty, please look out this window and tell me what you see."

"I see people," the king said, looking down into the busy street. "There's the miller with his grain, and the shoemaker, and the goldsmith." Then the friar held a mirror up before the king.

"What do you see now?" he asked.

"Myself," the perplexed king answered.

"Yes," said the friar, "that's exactly how it is. When you look through a clear glass, you see others, know who they are, perhaps even come to love them. But when your glass is covered with silver, as a mirror is, you see only yourself. God has given your majesty riches, but they aren't what you see in silver. Your true riches are out there. Your people."

Lord, help me never to let money come between me and my love for others. —E.B.P.

---

26 *JOY to the world! the Lord is come:*
Let earth receive her King:
Let every heart prepare Him room...

—ISAAC WATTS, CAROL

Today's the day that I go to my date book and take out that note I wrote to myself away back in September, 1963:

> "It may be September, but I'm listening to Christmas carols, really listening to the joyous words. Why? Because Christmas was lost to me last year. Too many presents to buy, too much food to cook, too many cards to address. Christmas began in a frenzy and ended in frustration.
>
> "So that's why, on this beautiful September day, I baked my Christmas cake for dinner. I'll surprise the family with it—a gift straight from

> the heart. In a few minutes, I'll pick up my Bible and read the story of the Nativity in St. Luke."

Yes, today's the day that I celebrate my mini-Christmas. Every year this little celebration reminds me not to let the details of Christmas obscure its real meaning. I want to make sure, starting now, that the birth of Christ stays front and center in my mind.

Christmas will never be far off, dear Jesus, as long as I remember that You are always near. —M.W.

27

HUMBLE yourselves in the sight of the Lord, and He shall lift you up. —JAMES 4:10

When I opened my front door there was a Fuller Brush lady. I was annoyed because she'd interrupted me in the busiest part of the morning. "No!" I said curtly. "Absolutely no!" Then I closed the door on her.

Seconds later I was sorry for what I had done. I opened the door to call after her and apologize, but she had gone. "Oh, Lord," I prayed, "forgive me; I've done wrong. If only I had the chance to make amends..."

Late that afternoon the doorbell rang again. It was a young girl collecting money for the American Diabetes Association. She looked awfully hot and tired so I invited her in and gave her a glass of iced tea. Then, just before I made a small contribution, I discovered that she was heading home, a three-mile walk.

I drove her home in my car. In my heart I knew I'd been given my chance to make amends. I could do nothing to salve the Fuller

Brush lady's feelings, but I could do something for another of God's children. It was a form of penance for me, but perhaps I had made the first link in a chain of good that might one day reach all the way round to that very same Fuller Brush lady.

When I deprive the world of goodness, Lord, help me to find ways to replenish it. —G.N.

---

28 *...MY mouth shall shew forth Thy praise.* —PSALM 51:15

During my first year of teaching, two boys, each named Ted, were in my class. One was a happy child, an excellent student and a fine school citizen. The second Ted spent much of his time goofing off and making a nuisance of himself. I was convinced that he would be a problem all year.

Then, toward the end of September, the PTA held its first meeting, and a mother came up to me and asked, "How is my son Ted getting along?"

For some reason I assumed she was the "good Ted's" mother and exclaimed, "I can't tell you how much I enjoy him. I'm so glad he's in my class!"

"That's wonderful," she said.

The following morning, Ted, my problem child, came up to me. "Mom told me what you said last night. I don't think any teacher's ever wanted me before."

That day Ted's work was done neatly and correctly. I had several opportunities to offer him sincere praise, and each time he glowed with pride. Before long my problem child became one of my best students.

I sometimes wonder if God didn't arrange that case of mistaken identity to teach an inexperienced teacher a valuable lesson: the investment of praise and trust can pay remarkable dividends. And by enriching the lives of others, we enrich our own as well.

I praise Your holy name, Lord. In You I place my trust.—A.J.L.

29

...HIS waters shall be sure. —ISAIAH 33:16

I stood in the warm Mexican sunshine in Acapulco and watched the divers hurling themselves off the high, rocky point to plummet into the foaming sea far below. How daring those divers are! They hurl themselves out into the air on faith, literally on faith, for when they leave the cliff there isn't enough water below to break the dive. The wave that will bring the necessary swell of water into the cove is still out in the ocean. Those divers have to have faith that the wave will be there when they need it.

Isn't that the kind of faith I need? The feeling of assurance that God — like the wave — will be there when I hurl myself into the unknown.

You are there, Lord, always there. —B.H.D.

30

WHOEVER...notices that his brother is in need and then locks his heart against him, how is the love of God in him? —I JOHN 3:17 (ML)

Sometimes God talks to me in odd ways. Take for instance the day the telephone rang just as the kids and I were about to leave the house to go shopping. A friend was calling to ask if she could come to see me. I knew why. She and her husband had just separated; she wanted to talk.

At that time my own life was just as difficult as hers, and far busier. "I'm sorry," I lied. "We won't be home until supper-time."

We hadn't driven more than three miles when a tire on our dilapidated car went flat. I maneuvered the vehicle to the shoulder of the highway, told the kids to stay inside, took the jack out of the trunk and bent down to the tire as cars and trucks whizzed by, inches from my back. But the jack was broken. Now I stood on the highway in desperation. No one would stop.

No one, that is, until an elderly man and woman in a Cadillac pulled up across the highway. Carefully the man crossed over, assessed my situation, went back and got his own jack and returned to change my tire.

I thanked him profusely. Then I said, "I do hope we didn't spoil your outing."

"We're not on an outing," he replied gently. "I'm taking my wife to the hospital where she is to be admitted today. But we just couldn't drive by and leave you stranded, could we?" He wished me luck and was gone.

"Now *there* was a Good Samaritan," I said to the kids as I got behind the wheel again. And at that moment I started thinking. As it turned out, we didn't go shopping that day. I took the kids home and then I went over to my friend's house.

Didn't I tell you that God has His odd ways of talking to me?

I know I'm slow to learn, Lord, but please keep telling me that the more love I give to others, the more room I make for Your love. —F.R.

S	M	T	W	T	F	S
					1	2
3	4	5	6	7	8	9
10	11	12	13	14	15	16
17	18	19	20	21	22	23
24	25	26	27	28	29	30
31						

The Tenth Commandment

Thou shalt not covet... —EXODUS 20:17

MY neighbor Sam had all the goods.
A fine house, fancy car, blue-chip stocks
And an inheritance in the offing.
Aha! But he sold his soul
In the reaping, no?
No. Sam was gentle, kind and generous.

I should've felt lucky to have a friend
Whom fortune had smiled so sweetly on.
Should've given thanks for a friend
Who shared so fully — but I didn't.
Didn't give one single
Thing in return.
Because I was poor — wretchedly so
In the spite-filled way those who
Covet always are.

And so the day came, of course it came,
When I couldn't bear Sam's riches
Any more. And so I hid,
Hid in my painful envy.
But then, one lonely afternoon,
There Sam was again, at my door,
Offering me a gift I hadn't earned.
Offering me the one thing I hadn't coveted:
His friendship. His greatest wealth.

That day I too became rich,
For at last I'd come to know
That there are things
More valuable than things.

1

WHEN the woes of life o'ertake me,
Hopes deceive and fears annoy,
Never shall the cross forsake me:
Lo! it glows with peace and joy. —JOHN BOWRING, HYMN

Did you ever think of the power that symbols have for us?

Not long ago I heard an unusual story about a man who turned a piece of rope into a tangible symbol that actually helped him recover from a grave illness. He was bedridden for a long period of time and had reached his lowest point when it came to him that he was waging not one, but two battles. One was a battle with pain, and the other with self-pity. "I'm almost at the end of my rope," he confided to a visitor one day.

"Well, you know what you do at that point, don't you?" the visitor said. "Tie a knot in the rope and hang on."

Those words were like medicine to him. Sure, the future seemed uncertain, even intolerable, if he thought of it in terms of weeks and months. But if he could just find a way to hang on...

That afternoon he asked his wife to find him a short piece of rope. He took the rope, tied a knot in one end, and hung it over the railing of his bed. When the pain came, when self-pity took over, he'd grab hold and say to himself, "I can hold on, I can hold on,..." And holding on for just five minutes at a time helped him fight his way back to health again.

The idea of using a symbol that way sounds odd at first, but it really isn't. Symbols have always played powerful roles in our lives. Think of the pride and courage we feel when we catch sight of The Stars and Stripes fluttering in the breeze; think of the sense of triumph we gain from the most magnificent of all symbols — the cross!

Your cross is my *symbol, Lord. I thank You for it.* —N.V.P.

2 *AND seeing the multitudes, He went up into a mountain.... And He opened His mouth, and taught them....* —MATTHEW 5:1, 2

Whenever I read a certain portion of the Sermon on the Mount a conversation I once had with our five-year-old comes back to me. I was annoyed because it was bedtime and her room was a shambles. "What's the matter with you?" I demanded. "You know you're not supposed to leave your things all over the floor. Why can't you be good?"

She surveyed the jumble of books, toys, dolls and stuffed animals with a sad little face. "I don't know," she said. "I try. Doesn't it even count if you try?"

Well, of course it counts! In His great Sermon Jesus didn't say, "Blessed are the righteous." What He said, in effect, was "Blessed are those who *want* to be righteous." There's a vast difference...and consider how reassuring this difference is. Perfection isn't being required of us by the Master. We're simply being told that the important thing is to *want* very much to be good — and that this is within the power of each of us.

And I think He was telling us something more. If you want very much to be a certain way, you will struggle and strive until you begin to approach that goal. "Blessed are those who hunger and thirst after righteousness, *for they shall be filled*."

Two thousand years ago the clearest Thinker of all time knew the power of the deeply desired wish — and urged us to use it.

Thank You, Lord, for understanding us so well. —A.G.

3 *...COMMUNE with your own heart upon your bed, and be still.* —PSALM 4:4

The church service had been lovely, but driving home I was already a bundle of nerves. Guests were coming that afternoon. As I thought through my dinner plans out loud, my husband drove silently.

"Why are you so quiet?" I asked him.

"I'm just feeling good about my party," he said, smiling.

That probably sounds strange to you, but I knew right away what George meant.

What he said went back to our son Bryce's fourth birthday. The moment the party ended, I began cleaning the house like a madwoman. As I pounced on the party favors and half-eaten cupcakes, I noticed Bryce lying on the floor, in a bed of ribbons and wrappings.

Just as I was about to tell Bryce to get up and give me a hand, I saw my husband looking fondly at him. I then took a good look, too, and what we both saw was sheer joy and contentment. Then our blissful son said to us, without looking up, "I'm just feeling good about my party."

So often, after a peaceful prayer or church service, I rush right back into the hurly-burly. Then I later wonder why life has to always be so hectic. It doesn't. Now and then I should just sit back and feel good about God's generous love.

Let me not drive through life so swiftly, Lord, that I fail to see the beauty along the way. —J.M.B.

4 *AND be ye kind one to another...* —EPHESIANS 4:32

6:50 a.m. — The alarm buzzes through the air like a chain saw. I hit the snooze button and moan. "Lord, I hate Mondays."
7:15 a.m. — My husband cries out, "Aren't any of my shirts ironed?" My son cries out, "Where's my spelling book?" And the scrambled eggs stick to the pan.
7:20 a.m. — "The dog ate my science project!" yells my son Bob. His project is five molding slices of bread.
7:25 a.m. — The dog cowers under the table. My daughter bends over for a look and spills a glass of orange juice in her lap. Bob snickers and she cries. I mop. "Got my shirt ironed?" calls my husband.
8:05 a.m. — Bob goes off to school without his lunch money. My husband backs over Ann's tricycle in the driveway. I step on the dog's tail, he yelps. I break a teacup my mother-in-law gave me.
8:20 a.m. — I sink onto the sofa, wanting to tie a deadweight around the day and drop it off a bridge.
8:30 a.m. — The doorbell rings. In comes a dear friend carrying a pound cake, all warm and golden. "Surprise!" she says, handing me the cake. "Th-thanks," I stammer. "But it's not my birthday."
"Oh, I know," she says. "But it's Monday."
8:35 a.m. — My day has lifted like a hot-air balloon. "Thanks, Lord."

"Be ye kind one to another," the Bible says. Well, there are all sorts of ways to be kind, but if you want to see a sudden surge of joy, try *surprising* someone!

Father, show me the little ways that I can salvage other people's days. —S.M.K.

5 *SEEK the one whose hand has helped you,*
Seek him out and tell him so. —AUTHOR UNKNOWN

Five mornings a week I pack a noon meal for my working son who has a short lunch hour and a long appetite. Whether it is tuna-fish sandwiches, ham on rye, or a hot meat-loaf meal in a wide-mouthed thermos, he is unfailingly grateful for my efforts. I can't remember a morning when he hasn't called back to me as he left for work, "Thanks, Mom, for putting up my lunch."

It's surprising how good those thank-yous of his have made me feel. But it wasn't until this very morning that I suddenly realized how lucky I am to have a son to pack lunches for. I thought of all the lonely people in the world, people with no one to need them. And I turned to God and said, "Thank You."

Lord, my loved ones' needs are one of Your greatest gifts to me. Help me fill them with gratitude and love. —P.B.H.

6 *...LET us run with patience the race that is set before us.* —HEBREWS 12:1

I had wandered on my lunch hour to New York City's Battery Park and was sitting on a bench, brooding. Two hours before I had been told that I would have to take on burdensome new responsibilities as a part of my job as editor of a corporate magazine. There was so much to do that I didn't know where to start, and my future stretched out before me in a dismal parade of endless tasks.

Woolgathering, I watched some bright orange-and-black

butterflies hovering over some nearby shrubs.

"Pretty, aren't they?" an elderly man on the same bench asked.

"Yes," I agreed. "And they've really got it made. Nothing to do but flutter around all day," I added a little enviously.

"Well, not quite," he said. "They have to flutter around quite a bit each day. They're Monarchs, and they've got at least 2000 miles to travel before they complete their migratory pattern."

"Two thousand miles!" I repeated to myself as I returned to my office. "How do they do it?"

And the answer seemed to come right out of the air: "One day at a time."

One day at a time. *That* was how I would handle my new responsibilities. That was the only way.

What did Jesus say? "Don't worry about tomorrow. Today's problems are enough to keep you busy." In other words, like the butterflies, take them one day at a time.

Father God, give me the patience and persistence I need to reach my goal. —J. McD.

7

HE will deliver his soul from going into the pit, and his life shall see the light. —JOB 33:28

My two-year-old niece doesn't try to hide her fear of the dark. Yet, the other day, when her mother and I were rummaging through a dark cellar that gave even me the creeps, she was perfectly serene.

"I thought you were afraid of the dark," I said to her.

"No dark. Mommy's here," she answered promptly.

"Oh," I teased, "the light depends on who's around?"

She just smiled, as if she knew a secret truth.

Which indeed she did: The light *does* depend on Whom you stay close to, doesn't it?

When I truly trust myself to You, Father, my darkness becomes light. —M.A.

8

LET all bitterness . . . be put away from you, with all malice. —EPHESIANS 4:31

My prayer group had split up into pairs. Mary X confessed to me, "I've been praying for ten years that my husband will come back to me. He divorced me when our children were teenagers. Our children are grown and married now, and I'm so lonely. Why won't God answer my prayer?"

Mary and I prayed about her problem intensively, and gradually we began to see the problem for what it was. She wrongly believed that only her ex-husband could end the pain she felt, and by believing this she was keeping God from carrying out His plans for her.

Finally Mary was able to pray these words: "Father, at this moment I let go, freeing both Joe and me into Your care, opening a place for Your perfect wisdom. Only You can bring good into our lives." Mary cried tears of release, heaved a great sigh and said, "I feel as if a terrible weight is being lifted from me."

As I drove home that night I realized that Mary had taught me a great lesson. I, too, tend to hold onto hurts, selfishly thinking that the person who hurt me must come and end my pain. Now I see that a hurt not given up to God is a hurt that might never heal.

Father, why should I keep myself in a prison of pain, when You can set me free? —M.M.H.

9 *HE that loveth his brother abideth in the light, and there is none occasion of stumbling in him.* —I JOHN 2:10

My father sawed down the trees. My brother Tom and I hauled the cordwood back to the house.

The hauling started out as a simple job, but Tom and I, each with a tractor and a trailer, quickly turned the job into a contest. I was going to shag more wood out of that forest than Tom — no matter what.

My father had barely cut up the trees when we'd pounce on them. At one point, after topping off a load, I tore off for the house. I was looking back to check on Tom's pace when a trailer wheel hit a stump. I bounced off my seat and the whole load of wood pitched off.

"You've got to be more careful, Ed," my dad said.

"I was trying to do the best job I could," I protested.

"You were *not* trying for the best," my dad said. "You were just trying to go faster than Tom. Listen, it's a good thing if you boys can make each other do good work, but right now all you're making is a mess. Being 'better' than each other doesn't mean you guys are being your best. Not by any means."

My father was right, and Tom and I learned a lesson about working together. When I fall prey to the urge to be better than someone else, I remember that afternoon in the woods. The only person God wants me to be "better than," is the person *I* was yesterday.

Father, there is work to do. Teach me how to do it right — for You. —E.B.P.

10 *...THE charity of every one of you all toward each other aboundeth.* —II THESSALONIANS 1:3

Years ago, a church business meeting I was attending began to get out of hand with a lot of petty arguing. Then one of the members stood up and told a little story. It ran something like this:

Once there was a Chinese prince who died and was given a glimpse of both heaven and hell. First he was escorted to hell, where he found tables laden with various foods and delicacies, but the people were sitting there angry and frustrated, quarreling with each other. They were not permitted to pick up the food with their fingers, and they couldn't feed themselves because the chopsticks they were given were ten feet long.

Then the prince was taken to heaven. Again he found a bountiful banquet, and again only ten-foot-long chopsticks. But here the people were happy and content, for they sat on opposite sides of the table, each one feeding the person across from him!

When the storyteller sat down, the room was quiet. And from that moment on, we began to accomplish what we'd come for!

Lord, grant us a spirit of caring and cooperation, especially in those organizations formed to give service to others. —A.F.

11 *IN the world ye shall have tribulation: but be of good cheer; I have overcome the world.* —JOHN 16:33

The rain started early that morning. My children quickly got restless. "Why don't you read?" I said, wishing they'd be quiet.

But no, they wanted to play house. They pushed aside the

dining table, then draped blankets over the dining chairs. They went about filling their wool mansion with stray saucers, silverware and pictures hastily cut from magazines.

The hectic messiness of the room quickly got on my nerves. Just as I was about to condemn and shut down their house, I heard a wee voice beneath the quilts.

"John," the voice said, "isn't this fun?"

I kept quiet and I listened to the pure happiness of that voice linger, and draw up memories. On long-ago rainy days my brother and sister and I would take over our mother's great porch. We'd lean old oak rockers against the house, then cover them with quilts. Under those blankets we'd make our own little world, free of troubles and full of warmth.

My life is not free of troubles these days. It often gets as messy as that topsy-turvy dining room but, if I listen closely, even in the most difficult situations, I'll find that God always sends me a note of grace. I can still hear that child's voice saying, "Isn't this fun?"

How easy it is to pass Your beauty by, Lord. Teach me to know when it is there. —I.B.

12

BLESSED is he who speaks a kindness;
Thrice blessed he who passes it on. —ARABIAN PROVERB

It was a letter from a man in Indiana. A man I'd never met. It said: "Dear Mrs. Kidd, every week I write a letter of thanks to someone who has helped me in the past week. I learned long ago that gratitude, like perfume, is of no real value unless it's released. So today I write to you. I want to say thank you..."

I hadn't done much. He was expressing thanks for some small published piece I'd written. But as I held his letter in my hand, his gratitude filtered through the air with its lovely fragrance. A warm and special feeling spread through me. The stranger from Indiana was so right. Gratitude should not only be felt but expressed in order to do the most good.

I walked to my desk and pulled out a sheet of stationery. "Dear Mrs. Jones," I wrote, "I just began a practice of writing a weekly letter of thanks. Well, what you said when you spoke at the meeting yesterday helped me a lot. I want to say thank you..."

Help me not to bottle up thank-yous in my heart, Lord, but release them to spread their warm, sweet aroma to others. And to You, too. —S.M.K.

13 When the Bible Speaks to Me

EXODUS 19:4

Often when I take my Bible in hand it has a way of falling open at a chapter of Exodus where a long time ago I underlined a favorite verse. I never see that verse that I don't pause and think of old Mr. Dunwoodie. He was a neighbor and my companion and confidant when I was very young. Those were the days when my mother had to go back to work and I was uneasy about coming home from school to an empty house. Often Mr. Dunwoodie was waiting for me, and the two of us would sit together and talk.

Mr. Dunwoodie liked to tell me stories from the Bible, and one hazy autumn afternoon, sitting on the back-porch steps, he told me about the flight of the Israelites from Egypt and how they spent

40 years in the wilderness before reaching the promised land. And then he read Exodus 19:4 to me about how the Lord carried those Israelites out of Egypt on eagles' wings.

I was much impressed. Especially about the eagles.

"Funny thing about those birds," Mr. Dunwoodie went on. "They build their nests on the uppermost mountaintops, and when it's time for the baby eagles to learn to fly, the mother eagle spreads her wings and urges her youngsters to come aboard for a ride." Mr. Dunwoodie stretched out his arms in big circles to show me how the mother would soar into the atmosphere, and then, with a swift burst, she'd dive so fast that her passengers would tumble off. Startled, the eaglets would flap their wings frantically — and fly. "But should one of the little ones start to fall, the mother is always there below, circling, ready to catch it on her wing. Not one eaglet is ever lost."

After that day I was never uneasy again about being alone while my mother was at work. Mr. Dunwoodie's story comforted me then, and still does, for isn't the covenant God made with the Israelites that He'd carry them on eagles' wings the same He makes with me today? I know that if I fall, He is there beneath me, ready to lift me up and carry me safely home.

— MARILYN CONNELL JENSEN

14

TO be what we are, and to become what we are capable of becoming, is the only end of life.

—ROBERT LOUIS STEVENSON

When I first married, I dreaded social gatherings. I thought that I was uninteresting and that people would ignore me. So it was with dread that I approached a diplomatic reception that I had to attend with my husband, then a young foreign service officer.

When I walked into the glittering room, my worst fears were confirmed. Everyone looked very sophisticated. I was just a hometown Jane in a dress I'd made myself. My husband vanished, and I found myself in the midst of some diplomats' wives. To my astonishment, one of them complimented me on my dress. I hesitated, then blurted out that I had made it myself. It turned out that she did embroidery work, and soon our whole group was talking about our favorite projects. I had a wonderful time. Those people might have been sophisticated, but they were without any pretensions.

I believe that's the key to getting along with others — whether it be at a church supper or a diplomatic reception. Don't try to be someone you're not. To this day I'm grateful I admitted that I had made my dress because it started a conversation that banished my fears and reconfirmed a timeless lesson. God has made me what I am, a person of value in His unerring judgment, and He loves me. If I can be this me, without pretensions, then others will come to love me too.

Father, keep me from hiding or pretending; I like the way You made me.

—B.R.G.

---

15 *....WITHOUT ceasing I have remembrance of thee in my prayers night and day.*

—II TIMOTHY 1:3

I worked next to a woman at the office a while back who had the habit of answering just about every question or comment with the word "whatever."

Someone would say, "Ethel, do you want to go out for lunch today, or eat in the office?"

"Whatever."

It's hard to explain how and why she managed to use this blasé word so many times a day, but believe me, she found ways.

She nearly drove me crazy in the process. One day, after the fourth or fifth "Whatever," I said under my breath, "Lord, if she says that word again, I'm going to scream!" But no sooner had I said my peevish little prayer than I realized that prayer was what had been missing from this situation all along. Instead of being irritated by it, I would use Ethel's "whatever" habit as a reminder for me to pray.

Someone's habits bugging you? Why not find out for yourself that they need not be irritants? Instead, use them as reminders for a little quiet time with God.

Nothing — even the tiniest irritants — need separate me from Your peace, Lord. —E.J.

---

16 *...WHATSOEVER things are true, whatsoever things are honest, whatsoever things are just, whatsoever things are pure, whatsoever things are lovely, whatsoever things are of good report; if there be any virtue, and if there be any praise, think on these things.* —PHILIPPIANS 4:8

Before me on my desk is a leaf. It is beautiful — perfectly formed and a rich golden color. When I picked it up this morning, I thought I had never seen a leaf so lovely. But since then I have noticed a flaw, a tiny jagged hole no bigger than a pinprick in one side. And it bothers me. The more I look at it, the more it seems to destroy the beauty of the leaf for me.

Before me in my life are people. Family, friends, people. They, too, are beautiful, formed by the same Creator Who made the leaf. Yet in all of these people there are flaws — attitudes and habits that make it hard for me to enjoy them as much as I'd like. Should I dwell on the things that are lovely and good about them, or shall I concentrate on their flaws?

My Lord mingled with lepers and prostitutes and tax collectors, and saw the goodness that lay behind their flaws. He chose temperamental, selfish, doubting men as disciples and loved them into being the people God created them to be.

Before me is a leaf. Before me are people. Both are flawed, both are beautiful. Shall I dwell on the flaws, or rejoice in their beauty?

Before me, Lord, are people. Let me magnify their goodness.

—P. H. S.

17

...AND when he saw him, he had compassion on him.

—LUKE 10:33

How small and frail Lisa looked in the hospital crib. As we stood beside her, we scarcely noticed the man who came and stood with us. "Would you mind," he asked, "if I said a prayer for your baby?"

Dully we shook our heads, and he prayed aloud for our little one. *But why would this man pray for a child he didn't even know?* I wondered. *Was he a minister or a priest?*

Then he explained that his little girl was just leaving the hospital after successful heart surgery, and that many people had prayed for her recovery. "I'd like to pass on those prayers."

Our baby's surgery was successful too and now, as I watch her grow and run and play, I think often of that unknown father. I cannot thank him for his prayers any more than I can repay the kind people who took care of our other children, who cooked meals and washed clothes while our baby was sick. Often we're not able to repay kindnesses, but we can pass them on.

Now each time I send soup to a sick friend, or run an errand for an elderly neighbor or say a prayer for someone who is suffering, I know that I am passing on the love that was shown to us when Lisa was sick. Since I no longer worry about being able to repay kindness directly, I find I am able to accept help more graciously. I no longer use phrases like, "You shouldn't have," or "How can I ever repay you?"

I doubt that the man left beaten on the road to Jericho was able to repay the good Samaritan directly, but I like to think that he passed the Samaritan's kindness on to someone else. Perhaps when the unknown father prayed for our Lisa, he was actually passing along the concern shown by the Samaritan long ago.

Lord, help me to be a link in the chain of kindness that connects us all to You. —E.A.J.

18

REPENT...that your sins may be blotted out...

—ACTS 3:19

An old man recently told me about an incident from his school days. A group of boys had been making life miserable for their young teacher — tacks on her chair, frogs in the wastebasket, spitwads shooting across the room, graffiti scratched into desks. So one day, the teacher listed all of the offenses on the blackboard and said, "Now, I already know who did each one of these, but for *your* sakes, it's important that you confess and apologize. I'm going to be in the classroom during both recesses today and also after school. If anyone wants to admit anything and apologize for it, I'll simply erase that offense from the board and forget about it. Any items still on the board tomorrow will be reported to your parents." By the end of the day the board was wiped clean, and a better relationship between students and teacher had begun.

Like that teacher, Jesus already knows what my sins are. It's just that it's sometimes hard for me to believe that He really does *erase* them, once I've repented and asked His forgiveness.

If you have trouble accepting His total forgiveness, this visualization may help to convince your heart. Write your sins on a blackboard in your mind's eye. Then go down the list and, as you ask Jesus to forgive you for each one, see Him erasing that offense from your soul's blackboard. Then give thanks and start afresh.

I accept Your forgiveness, Lord Jesus. —M.M.H.

19

BUT let him ask in faith, nothing wavering...

—JAMES 1:6

Many years ago a friend of mine started a small neighborhood grocery store. The dear fellow had stocked only one shelf when I first visited him. It was lined with cans of pork and beans, all sporting bright red-and-yellow wrappers.

I knew that he was short of money, but I was appalled by the rows of empty shelves.

"Are beans all you have yet?" I asked.

He gave me a radiant smile and said, "Beans and a prayer is all that I need to get a start."

He was right! Before long his friendly store was the best stocked, busiest in our whole countryside.

Dear God, though my means may be meager, let me have enough faith in You to go ahead with any endeavor. —F.F.

---

20 *WE are not divided,*
All one body we,
One in hope and doctrine,
One in charity. —SABINE BARING-GOULD, HYMN

It's odd, but it didn't seem unusual when an elderly lady sitting in the corner of the intensive care waiting room spoke out loud to the rest of us: "None of us seems a stranger here even though we're all quite different and don't know one another at all."

It was true. There was an immediate bond of sympathy and trust in that room. Suspicion or aloofness quickly melted away in the warm climate of shared concern for our loved ones who lay beyond in the hospital's intensive care room.

And why not? After all, weren't we all children of God — all dependent on our Heavenly Father and each other?

Will any of us ever be the same after what we experienced in that room? I hope not. I'm going to try to be a more open, caring, approachable person — a child of God, unafraid to act like one.

Lord, help me to keep in mind that people I meet today are only strangers if I treat them that way. —T.B.

21

MY grace is sufficient for thee: for My strength is made perfect in weakness. —II CORINTHIANS 12:9

When my son Jeff called long distance on my birthday, he announced, "Dad, I've got a great present for you!"

"Yes, Jeff?"

"I quit smoking!"

"You what?" I said, recalling that he alone among my five children had smoked since mid-teens. "Why? How, Jeff?"

"At my annual physical, my doctor said if I quit now my lungs would suffer no permanent damage. But no guarantees if I continued." I recalled Jeff's three-pack-a-day habit and wondered aloud how he was able to conquer it.

"I prayed, Dad."

"You prayed?"

"I knew it would be rough, so I made a vow to God that I would stop. I figured that I could let myself down, but I couldn't let God down. Every time I started to weaken and reach for a cigarette, I'd say the Lord's Prayer. Sometimes I'd say it forty times a day."

Jeff's vow worked. He stopped smoking.

And, not only that, but by ridding himself of his old, destructive habit, Jeff has strengthened his faith. Now he still says the Lord's Prayer every night — "just to thank Him."

With You, Lord, I can keep on turning weakness into strength.

—S.J.

22 *THIS is the day which the Lord hath made; we will rejoice and be glad in it.* —PSALM 118:24

Early one morning I slumped half-asleep at the breakfast table. "Another day," I muttered into my orange juice.

"Which day do you think's the greatest day of your life?" my husband asked.

"The greatest day?" I said. "Let's see, the day I was born. No, that's not it. How about the day we got married? Or the day I was baptized? Or the days the children were born?" I sank my chin into my hands. "Oh, I give up. It's too early in the morning for this."

"No, it's not," he replied. "It's perfect timing. You see, you're looking for the greatest day of your life in the wrong direction. The greatest day of your life is today."

Today? I gazed at him in surprise. And suddenly I saw that he was right. This was not just "another day." It was *the* day, the only day I had. The only day in which I could actually touch reality. A day to fill with more love than yesterday. A day to grow closer to God in. Why, it was a day bursting with marvelous possibilities.

I will always remember that particular day. For viewing it as the greatest day of my life was like putting a freshly polished pair of glasses on the face of my humdrum, nearsighted existence. That day was very special. But it was not the greatest day of life. No, today is.

Lord, help me make this day the best ever. —S.M.K.

23 *IF I take the wings of the morning, and dwell in the uttermost parts of the sea; Even there shall Thy hand lead me...* —PSALM 139:9, 10

From time to time New York magazine editors can get to feeling jaded and city-bound. Yes, even Guideposts editors — like me. Then along comes a manuscript that sends the spirits soaring, and the imagination sailing like kites in a bracing wind. Then editors thank God for writers, just as I did one gray morning when this poem came in from Myrtle Sparks of Auburn, Washington:

Free Spirits

High on mountain slopes,
Deep in hidden valleys,
Unseen by any man
Wild lilies flaunt
Their perfumed glory
On cresting winds.
Not wasted riches, theirs,
As some might suppose.
Joyously, they give their all,
Not for praise, not to be admired,
Rather a love offering
To the Lord Who gives all life.
Can we give more —
Or less?

Indeed, Lord, I do thank You for writers, and the wonderful new worlds that they help me find. —V.V.

24 *I WILL therefore that men pray every where...*

—I TIMOTHY 2:8

I read of a traveling salesman who pauses as he leaves each motel room where he has stayed to pray for its next occupant.

My traveling is pretty much limited to warm-weather camping. But this year my husband Bob and I are putting that man's habit into practice each time we prepare to leave a campsite.

Maybe you don't travel. But when you eat out how about saying a grace for the people who'll next sit at your restaurant table? Or, when you return a library book, what about saying a prayer for its next reader?

Dear Lord, please bless the reader of this book. —D.D.

25 *SET a watch, O Lord, before my mouth; keep the door of my lips.*

—PSALM 141:3

I came home from the committee meeting thoroughly out of sorts.

"The whole afternoon was wasted," I fumed. "Helen Anderson was there, and nothing pleased her. She didn't have a kind word for anything or anybody. All she did was find fault and criticize. That's a dreadful habit!"

"Yes," said my sister quietly, "and a very contagious one."

That's all she said, but I got the message.

Lord, as the doorkeeper of my lips, let me be ever vigilant.

—D.E.

26

...WHAT doth the Lord require of thee, but to do justly, and to love mercy, and to walk humbly with thy God. —MICAH 6:8

Emerson once said, "What we need most is someone to make us do what we can." I discovered the truth of this when I moved from full-time to part-time teaching. Within a few weeks, I found that I was accomplishing less than when I had a full schedule at school. "What I need," I grumbled to a friend one day, "is a good boss to make me shape up."

"You have a boss," she said. "You have God. You are responsible to Him for everything you do."

That night I confided my problem to God and asked Him for guidance. The next morning, with His help, I planned my day. Since then I no longer feel that I am working alone. God and I make long-range and daily plans. I write them down and carry them out. I *have* to. He is God.

How about you? Do you need a good boss to help you meet your goals? Why not try my Boss? He's the world's best Employer.

I thank You, Lord, for bringing out the best in me. —A.J.L.

27

WALK in the light! and thine shall be
A path, though thorny, bright:
For God, by grace shall dwell in thee,
And God Himself is light. —BERNARD D. BARTON, HYMN

Here is the truth. When you look at me, you won't see the light of God shining through me like a beacon, rays sharp and unbroken.

I am not a vivid, clear window; I'm nowhere near being that free of imperfections.

I'm more like the blue blown glass of Hebron that I bought on a trip to the Holy Land, a glass pitcher that broke into pieces on my way home. The glass was too special to throw away, though, and so one day my daughter took the pieces and painstakingly made a mosaic by gluing them to a clear cup.

The mosaic is beautiful. I place candles in the cup these days, and I spend hours watching the flame flicker and play in the broken bits of blue glass. The light from this is not a beacon; it works through the glass in soft, surprising ways.

And that's the way I believe God's light shines through me. Look at me closely and you'll see that I've been through losses, dislocations and painful breaks. But in all those pieces of my life, you'll also see the flicker and play of God's light. That light is there mending and healing me, illuminating the presence of God in all of my life, all through the good and the bad.

God's light is shining through you, too.

You've known me at my best, and at my worst, Lord, and You've loved me always. Thank You. —B.H.D

28

WHOSOEVER therefore shall confess Me before men, him will I confess also before My Father Which is in heaven. —MATTHEW 10:32

Sermons are sometimes preached in the most unlikely places. For instance, the night I saw the Broadway production of *Annie* in New York City, Betty Hutton was just joining the cast. I'd read in the newspaper that Miss Hutton had experienced a spiritual awakening and was making a comeback after many years of failure, family breakdown, bankruptcy and bouts with alcohol.

Waiting for the overture that night at the Alvin Theatre, I glanced through the program. There were extensive biographical sketches about members of the cast. All except Betty Hutton. Her biography consisted of five words, but those words preached a sermon to everyone in the audience. And when Betty finally appeared on stage, the theatre burst into a joyful applause. No one minded that the production was held up for several minutes as she stood in the spotlight, eyes glistening with tears. What were the five words Betty Hutton had written? "I'm back. THANKS TO GOD."

Ever since that night, I've tried not to cheat myself out of the special joy that comes from speaking openly about the Lord. We may not have a Broadway stage and a platform to inspire others with what the Lord is doing in our lives, but we *can* find ways that are right for us.

Thank You, Jesus. And thank you, Betty Hutton. God bless you.

—B.H.

29

...FOR I shall yet praise Him for the help of His countenance. —PSALM 42:5

Irritable and sleepless, I thrashed under the covers, rehashing the same old problem over and over. I pulled my pillow over my head to shut out the faint strains of someone practicing the piano in the apartment next door. *Tinkle, tinkle, tinkle.* Suddenly I remembered my first piano recital.

The teacher had tried to sugarcoat the ordeal of performing by turning the recital into a Halloween party. But I knew full well that wearing my bunny suit was not going to help me play — without sheet music — Beethoven's "For Elise," the piano exercise I had been assigned. When the dreaded moment came I was clammy and trembling inside my costume. I plunged in hoping sheer momentum would carry me through, but the worst happened. I went blank at the halfway point. Desperately, I began again only to stop dead at the same place. I began again. And again. At last, a hand under my elbow lifted me from the piano bench and the teacher's voice delivered me, "Thank you, Nancy," she said, gently. "*Thank* you."

I sat up on the edge of my bed. Wasn't I doing the same thing — obsessively repeating what I already knew because I didn't know what to do next? Why not ask my Teacher to rescue me?

You always know what my problems are, Lord. You'll show me what to do with them — in Your good time. —N.S.S.

30

GOD moves in a mysterious way
His wonders to perform . . . —WILLIAM COWPER, HYMN

We had just purchased a new car. My parents bought nothing without paying cash and for years we had saved for it. Dad, a carpenter, worked long hours. Mother sold butter and cottage cheese and bushels of cucumbers and gallons of blackberries . . . berries we picked and carried from Walker's woods a mile away. Finally, we bought the car. How proud we were; how it gleamed as we drove it down the road.

But Dad was against women driving.

One evening, however, Mother had to attend a meeting in Effingham six miles away; Dad was so busy that I was permitted to drive her. By the time the meeting was over, a big storm with slashing rain was raging outside.

Two ladies asked me to drive them home. As they directed me I drove east on National, parallel with the Pennsylvania Railroad, and turned right on Third. But I didn't know that Third became a one-lane street at the crossing. In my confusion I accidentally drove the car onto the railroad tracks.

Mother and the ladies scrambled out and stood wailing on the corner while I tried to back off the tracks. Suddenly I saw a huge headlight come around a curve from the east, not a block away. I ran from the car and stood wailing with the ladies as we watched the train bump, crumple and roll the car into a ball.

Roget's Thesaurus wouldn't hold the words Dad said when we got home, but during the settlement the insurance representative asked him to become a salesman for the company. He signed up, realizing he would soon be too old to labor as a carpenter. He became a top salesman. When he retired he drew Social Security, which wouldn't have happened had he not changed jobs. When he died, Mother received a Social Security check until her death — something most helpful.

Sometimes we ask, "Why, God?"

Then one day, we see.

For all things, Lord, I thank You. —Z.B.D.

31

TO cover up the kind of men they really are, they pretend to be pious . . . —MARK 12:40 (LB)

As a child I loved going trick-or-treating on Halloween because it gave me an opportunity to make-believe. Masked and disguised as a Roaring Twenties dancer, or a cowgirl, or a gypsy, I acted out my part with a bravado that I didn't really possess, buoyed by the thought that people wouldn't recognize me. Most of them probably didn't. But when I went to the house next door, our neighbor — old Mr. Hancock — knew me right away, even though he gave no sign.

Now, in later life, sometimes I'm tempted to put on various disguises, pretending to be more generous, or more honorable, or more truly Christian than I am. It wouldn't be hard to fool most of the people most of the time. But God, like old Mr. Hancock, knows exactly who I really am — and exactly what I'm really like. When I stop to think of that, all the disguises I'm tempted to use seem like the fantasies of a foolish child.

Oh, Lord, I can never fool You, so why should I try to fool others?

—E.V.S.

S	M	T	W	T	F	S
	1	2	3	4	5	6
7	8	9	10	11	12	13
14	15	16	17	18	19	20
21	22	23	24	25	26	27
28	29	30				

The Great Commandment

Thou shalt love the Lord thy God with all thy heart, and with all thy soul, and with all thy mind. —MATTHEW 22:37

I USED to wonder why
You wanted me to love You, Lord,
And love You so completely.
It did seem strange to me,
For I knew You had
    no human vanity
    or need for reassurance,
And the love I had to offer
    must have seemed so small,
    just one more gift
    among so many.

However,
As I've grown older
    and wiser through experience,
I've come upon this one
    illuminating truth:
By loving, we open ourselves
    to being loved.

Now,
As I give my love to You
With all my heart and soul and mind,
I see You as You'd have me see You,
A God of awe and majesty
Who cannot be outgiven.
And so, my God, at last
I stand before You,
Heart defenseless,
Arms outstretched,
Waiting to receive the love You want
    to squander on me!

1

SUN of my soul, Thou Saviour dear,
It is not night if Thou be near.
Oh, may no earth-born cloud arise
To hide Thee from Thy servant's eyes.

—JOHN KEBLE, HYMN

There once was a little girl who delighted in staying the night at the home of her grandparents and sleeping in their big, wide bed.

Above the bed was a picture of Jesus carrying a little lost lamb, and the mother sheep walking beside them, looking up, as if to say, "Thank You." By looking into a mirror at the foot of the bed, the little girl could see Jesus, so long as she was lying flat. However, when she sat up, Jesus would disappear, and she could only see herself.

Not understanding that her own body obstructed her view of the Saviour, she called her grandmother.

"Grandma," she said, "when I see myself, I can't see Jesus."

And when I grew up I realized what a profound statement I had made.

Lord, stay in my sight always. Never let me lose You.—Z.B.D.

2

BEHOLD My servant, whom I have chosen;
My beloved, in whom My soul is well pleased;
I will put My spirit upon him... —MATTHEW 12:18

Sometimes I wonder what it would be like if I had to be "elected" a Christian. I'd have to put myself before Jesus and ask for His vote the way candidates put themselves before the electorate.

But what would I tell Him?

Would I boast about my successes?

Would I attack others in an effort to make myself look good?

Would I make promises that I knew I wouldn't be able to keep?

It's a humbling prospect, for the thought of not being elected — or re-elected — is a grim one, indeed.

Beloved Jesus, thank You for Your vote. I'm going to do everything in my power to be worthy of it. —J. McD.

3

FOR it is not ye that speak, but the Spirit of your Father which speaketh in you. —MATTHEW 10:20

The woman had been searching through the crowded rows of greeting cards. "I want a special thank-you card," she said. "But none of these seems quite right."

The salesgirl handed her a plain white card, with only two words — Thank You — engraved on it in gold. "You could write your own message on this card," she said.

"But that's the trouble," said the woman. "I never know what to say! It's for a complete stranger, a man who came to the hospital twice and gave blood for our son. We are so grateful to him. We'll never forget his kindness."

"Then just write that," urged the salesgirl. "People know when words come from the heart."

On my way home I kept thinking about the times I had fumbled, awkward and silent, because I didn't know what to say. Maybe all that was necessary was a heartfelt, "Sorry!" There had been times when I could have lightened another person's day by simply saying what was in my heart: "I think you're wonderful!" Why is it so hard to listen to the promptings of one's heart?

I turned back to the greeting card shop. Maybe the salesgirl would be surprised when I thanked her for the insight she had shared, but I knew she would understand. The words would be straight from my heart.

With You in my heart, Lord, I can always find the right words.

—D.E.

4

MY faith looks up to Thee,
Thou Lamb of Calvary,
Saviour divine!

—RAY PALMER, HYMN

When I worked at the soda fountain of a Walgreen drugstore, I could never serve a cup of coffee without spilling it. Stare as I might at the swirling dark fluid in the china cup, some of it always spilled out in the saucer before I set it down for a customer.

Then the fountain manager, Elsie Kroeger, gave me some advice: "Don't look down at the coffee," she said; "it will throw you off balance. Keep your eye on your destination."

It worked. And it works in life, too. If I look down at myself, if I get too self-absorbed, I lose my spiritual balance. I need to keep my head up and my eye on Jesus.

Father, help me to forget myself and remember You. —R.S.

5 *AND Jesus, immediately knowing in Himself that virtue had gone out of Him, turned Him about in the press, and said, Who touched my clothes?*

—MARK 5:30

Ever since I was a child, whenever I prayed to Jesus I identified with the woman who touched the hem of His robe and believed — with utter faith in His divine power — that He would restore her health. Acting out that scene in my mind, kneeling at Jesus' feet, seeing His loving, compassionate face, had always brought peace of mind.

But tonight it wasn't working at all. I had just had an argument with my ten-year-old daughter, Becca, and I was feeling angry and resentful. I couldn't summon up the picture of Jesus in my mind for images of Becca's saucy, unremorseful face kept getting in the way. I felt so far from Him — and her. So alone.

My eyes strayed to the bookcase, to a shelf with a framed picture of Becca and me building sand castles together. And looking at that happy photograph, a new picture began to form in my mind. Instead of just me alone kneeling at Jesus' feet, I saw Becca and me there together, touching the cloth of His garment, looking up together at His forgiving face. Holding Becca's hand, I whispered, "Please, Jesus, there are some bad things between us, but we love each other very much and need Your help and healing. Thank You."

As the picture faded, so did the last traces of my anger.

Dear Jesus, I think You are especially glad to see me when I bring a friend along. —N.S.S.

6

FOR ye are bought with a price: therefore glorify God in your body, and in your spirit, which are God's.

—I CORINTHIANS 6:20

Over the years I've heard a variety of estimates of the human body's worth in dollars and cents — anywhere from 12¢ to $1.98. But recently I read that a Yale biochemist, Harold J. Morowitz, has made a new calculation based on the prices in a chemistry company's supply catalog. Some of the things we carry around with us every day without knowing it are pretty expensive these days. For instance, hemoglobin costs $285 a gram, insulin, $47.50 a gram, and bradykinin (amino acids), a whopping $12,000 a gram! All told, the average human being, if we could order him from a catalog, would cost exactly $6,000,015.44!

But really, what does it matter if our bodies are worth 12¢ or six million dollars? It is our souls that make us human, and our souls are priceless.

You created me out of Your love, Lord; let me never forget that Your love is infinite in its worth. —C.C.

7

LAY not up for yourselves treasures upon earth... For where your treasure is, there will your heart be also. —MATTHEW 6:19, 21

A number of years ago my husband and I were working in Egypt. One morning I was sitting at my desk in our home on the bank of the Nile when a valued servant, Ahmed, eased his way into the room, carrying a tray loaded with clean luncheon dishes. He knew I was busy and wanted to complete his task quickly, but in his haste he jarred the table on which he had placed the tray and...Crash! I watched in horror as my favorite dishes shattered on the cement floor.

I lost my temper and blasted Ahmed for his carelessness. Ahmed shrugged apologetically and shuffled to the pantry for a broom. That afternoon I overheard a conversation between Ahmed and Belie, our gardener, in which Ahmed told about the broken dishes.

"It must be very hard to be an American," Belie said.

"Why do you say that?" asked Ahmed.

Belie's answer really made me stop and think. "Because they have so many things to cry over when they get broken," he said.

Lord, keep reminding me about the real *treasures in life.*

—M.R.

---

8 *CHARITY* [*love*]*...seeketh not her own...*

—I CORINTHIANS 13:5

Not long ago I came across a little story written by Theodor Reik, the well-known psychologist. It was the true story of the courtship of Moses Mendelssohn, grandfather of the famous German composer.

Moses Mendelssohn, it seems, was a small and misshapen hunchback. One day he traveled to Hamburg and visited with a merchant who had a beautiful daughter named Frumtje. Moses fell deeply in love with Frumtje. But she avoided him and even seemed frightened by his grotesque hump.

On the last day of his visit he climbed the stairs to her room to say good-bye. She sat, busy with her needlework, her face glowing with an almost celestial beauty. At his appearance Frumtje looked down at the floor. Mendelssohn's heart ached. He tried to draw her into conversation and slowly led around to the subject that filled his mind. "Do you believe marriages are made in heaven?" he asked timidly.

"Yes," she replied. "And do you?"

"Yes, of course," he said. "You see, in heaven at the birth of each boy, the Lord calls out, 'This boy should get this girl for a wife, and that boy should marry that girl.' And when I was born, my future wife was thus announced. But in my case, the Lord also added, 'But alas, his wife will have a terrible hump.'

"At that moment I called, 'Oh Lord, a girl who is humpbacked would be a tragedy. Please, Lord, give the hump to me and let her be beautiful.' "

And the girl, deeply moved, stretched out her hand for Mendelssohn's and later became his faithful and loving wife.

When I read that story I began to think of my own relationships. How long had it been since I'd done some unselfish act — some loving, sacrificial act that seemed to whisper, "Give the hump to me and let her be beautiful." *Far too long*, I thought.

Oh Lord, help me to reach for the heights of unselfishness in my relationships.

—S.M.K.

9

COMMIT thy way unto the Lord; trust also in Him; and He shall bring it to pass. —PSALM 37:5

I placed my coat in the overhead rack, sat down, and buckled my seat belt. I hated to admit it, but I was apprehensive about flying.

"I don't know how these big planes get off the ground, much less fly across the continent," I said to the woman next to me.

"Nor I," she replied pleasantly, "I just figure that the pilot knows." She was thoughtful for a minute, and then said, "I guess flying is just another area where we have to put our trust to work, isn't it?"

I wasn't sure what she meant. "What other areas?" I asked.

"Well, we don't study medicine before letting a surgeon operate on us, do we? We have to trust that he can do it."

She was right. There were lots of things that I put my trust in each day. For instance, I never inspected a restaurant's kitchen before I ate its food. And there must be innumerable other ways in which I simply had faith — I believed — that things would be all right.

As the plane's motors roared alive I thought to myself: *If I put my trust in all these earthly things, how much more important it is for me to have faith in the God Who made all these things possible in the first place.*

As the plane rose in the air, my apprehension lifted, too. My trust was in Him.

Again and again You've told us to trust in You, Lord. I do. I shall. —P.B.H.

---

10 *. . . I AM come that they might have life, and that they might have it more abundantly.* —JOHN 10:10

The alarm buzzed this morning. I shot awake and resentfully pushed the button to silence. *No*, my mind protested, I don't *feel* like going to work. Why can't I just turn off the day and go back to sleep?

Suddenly I remembered something I had read recently about a peculiar gadget called a "shut-off machine."

It's a little wooden chest, about the size of a cigar box, with an electric switch on its side. When the switch is flipped on, there is a buzzing sound and the lid of the box opens. A few seconds later a mechanical hand appears, slowly reaches down, turns off the switch and disappears back into the box. The lid closes. The buzzing stops. That is the box's function. A machine whose sole purpose is to turn itself off.

Lying in bed I asked myself, "Am I going to be like that machine?" As if in answer, I heard the thud that announced my morning paper. A trash pickup rumbled by on early rounds. Early risers. Busy people. My curtains brightened with the dawn... and so did my heart. Another 24 hours of my life was about to begin. I threw back the covers. I'm not like that machine, I thought. *My* purpose isn't to turn myself off, but to turn myself *on* to the miracle of living.

That's something we *all* can do!

Lord, I will *make the most of this glorious gift You've given me — life.*

—D.H.

---

11 *FOR we are saved by hope...* —ROMANS 8:24

Whenever I read about famous people I'm always on the lookout for little clues in their early lives that hint at accomplishment that is to follow. Take the famous painter, James Whistler, for example. When he first married he was so poor that the only furniture he could afford was a bed. But throughout the modest Whistler home were chalked inscriptions on the floor with detailed description of the furniture that was to come.

At first I chuckled at the whimsical way that Whistler had been able to brush aside his poverty. That in itself was admirable. But I think there's another dimension to Whistler's chalkings. In his own unique, creative way, wasn't he really following the Bible's teaching about hope? Heeding St. Paul's advice of "But if we hope for that we see not, then do we with patience wait for it" (Romans 8:25), James Whistler went on to be a great painter.

Father God, help me to live with hope until I can turn dreams into realities. —M.A.

---

12 *...WHY beholdest thou the mote that is in thy brother's eye, but considerest not the beam that is in thine own eye?* —MATTHEW 7:3

The department store tea room was a welcome retreat after my long, pushy day of bargain hunting. Putting my packages on a chair next to me, I breathed a sigh of relief. What a chore it was trying to be first at all the bargain counters, but how proud I felt of all the money I had saved!

I noticed an overweight woman nearby happily eating her way through a gigantic banana split. *How gross*, I thought. *What a glutton she is!* I continued to watch her, fascinated by the mountainous mold of ice cream before her.

Suddenly she caught my staring eyes and, embarrassed, I turned quickly away, knocking my packages to the floor. As I picked them up, I began to see what a shopping binge I'd been on. A red blouse I didn't need. A gold chain, an extra wristwatch, another pair of shoes...

We all have our own gluttonies.

Father God, teach me to be as quick to spot my own frailties as I am to see the faults of others. —S.L.

13

REST in the Lord, and wait patiently for Him...

—PSALM 37:7

While I was in college a few years ago there was a Chicago Bears football game that I was dying to see. A friend had promised that he could get the tickets, but delayed doing it. One day he called me. "There aren't any tickets left for the game, but..."

I cut him off in mid-sentence — "But, nothing," I sputtered. He'd gotten my hopes up, but had let me down. I was angry that he had misled me, and I sure let him know about it, too.

"Jeff," he replied calmly, "if you had let me finish, I was going to say that we can work for NBC television, in the broadcast booth, and we'll get paid to see it."

I was embarrassed, and apologized profusely.

I've found I often put myself in the same position with God. Frustrated that a prayer has seemingly gone unanswered, I've worried, or worse, accused Him of not caring. But by the next day I often find my answer has come. At last I think I've learned to control my impatience with God, as well as with people.

No matter how long it takes, Lord, Your messages are always worth waiting for.

—J.J.

14

...AND His name shall be called Wonderful, Counsellor, The mighty God, The everlasting Father, The Prince of Peace.

—ISAIAH 9:6

Even though my given first name is Howard, I've been known to my family and friends by my nickname Jack ever since I was a young child. And I prefer to use that name.

As our children came along — three boys and finally a girl — each in turn eventually learned that my real name was Howard, because I signed my checks and legal papers that way.

One Sunday when our daughter was a first-grader my wife happened to overhear her saying the Lord's Prayer in unison with other children at the end of Sunday school. But Andrea's version was a bit different. She was saying, "Our Father, Who art in heaven, Howard be Thy name..."

When my wife told me about it, we both were amused, but we quickly set the child straight by showing her in the Bible that the word was "hallowed," not Howard. We also found out that, because the little girl was merely saying the prayer by rote, the words meant little to her. That made me re-examine my own performance on prayers, responses and hymns in church, for how often we adults mouth those words and never really take in what we are saying.

Father, help me to think about Your message in my worship of You.

—H.J.H.

---

15 *THY word have I hid in mine heart, that I might not sin against Thee.* —PSALM 119:11

I have a clipping taped inside my Bible's back cover. On the left half it lists a long line of "When-yous" such as "When you worry... When you fail... When you grieve..." Then on the right half is matched up a Scripture which concerns that particular problem, such as "... then read Psalm 55:22" or "Proverbs 29:25" or "Romans 8:38."

But one day my older son said, "Mom, what if you didn't have that Bible with you when you needed help?" Then he told about something he'd started doing — memorizing key verses. If he has a fear of failing on his job, he says to himself, "For God hath not given us the spirit of fear; but of power, and of love, and of a sound mind." (II Timothy 1:7) The important verse is embedded in his mind, ready for use.

Well, his idea sounded right. So I took the clipping and went to work on my most common failure, "When you doubt..." and memorized Luke 18:27, "The things which are impossible with men are possible with God."

And here are some of the verses I've memorized:

For illness — "And the prayer of faith shall save the sick, and the Lord shall raise him up; and if he have committed sins, they shall be forgiven him." (James 5:15)

For fearfulness — "And the peace of God, which passeth all understanding, shall keep your hearts and minds through Christ Jesus." (Philippians 4:7)

For discouragement — "Behold, what manner of love the Father hath bestowed upon us, that we should be called the sons of God..." (I John 3:1)

Father, knowing Your words by heart puts my mind at ease.

—I.C.

16

PRAYER should be the key of the day and the lock of the night.

—THOMAS FULLER

The renowned pianist Artur Rubinstein once said that if he was to stay in top form, he had to practice every day. "If I don't," Rubinstein said, "I know it. If I don't practice for two days, my family knows it. If I don't practice for three days, my public knows it."

In an odd way I think I can apply Rubinstein's statements to my prayer habits. If I go a day without praying, I feel vaguely empty. If I go two days, I'm sure some of my good friends notice a change in me. And, if I go a third day without prayer, there are bound to be people I meet who will find me less warm and responsive than I want to be.

Practice might not make me a perfect Christian, Lord, but it will make me a better one. —C.C.

17 When the Bible Speaks to Me
JOHN 21:1-7

The Bible is full of great deeds I'd like to have done: Moses' journey out of Egypt; Rahab risking her life for Joshua and his men; David's slaying of Goliath. But there's a deed in the 21st chapter of John, a simple deed, that for me stands out from all the rest.

More than a week had passed since Christ's crucifixion. The disciple Simon Peter, defeated by his denial of Christ, decided that he must return to his old life. "I go a fishing," he said to a few other disciples.

They joined him and together they all went out in a boat. All night they fished quietly, but without luck. At dawn a voice called to them from the beach asking if they'd caught any fish. No, they answered. Then came the words: "Cast the net on the right side of the ship, and ye shall find."

They did as they'd been instructed and instantly the net filled with fish. "It is the Lord!" one of them cried out and with this Simon Peter leaped into the sea. He swam to shore, overcome with the desire to be at his Lord's side.

These verses in the gospel of John stand out for me because so often I'm like Simon Peter: lost and defeated, sure that the Lord has given up on me. But then, without fail, the Lord calls out to me. He instructs me, calms my fears and fulfills my needs.

It's at this point that I must follow Simon Peter's example to its fullest. I must leap into the sea that stretches between the Lord and me. It won't matter how far off the shore is. When I truly believe, I can brave anything! — RICHARD SCHNEIDER

18

...HELP of the helpless, O abide with me.

—HENRY F. LYTE, HYMN

I'd been worried about my friend Joyce. Her husband's work had transferred them across the country, away from family and close friends. Then, out of the blue, his job was discontinued. I knew what a hard time they must be having.

Then a letter arrived.

"About Tom's work," Joyce wrote. "We are not so upset now as we were. Oddly enough we became encouraged from an episode we saw in our city's park. A little boy was sailing a toy boat on a pond when the wind pushed it beyond his reach. A big boy standing nearby began throwing rocks into the pond, splashing near the boat. The little boy cried loudly until he realized that the rocks caused ripples that sent his boat back to shore.

"Tom and I are still adrift," Joyce concluded, "but I am certain that Someone bigger than we are will help us safely to the shore."

And that is exactly what happened.

Through prayer, through faith, through friends, You give us strength, our Great Protector. —D.D.

19

UNTO Him be glory in the church...throughout all ages, world without end. —EPHESIANS 3:21

Every now and then a person stumbles upon something that reaches down and stirs awake an old sleeping memory. That's what happened to me not long ago when I picked up the newspaper. It was just an ordinary headline, yet it roused the memory of an afternoon in North Carolina...

It was raining. I sat on the front porch of a conference center with a woman who could have been my great-grandmother. She'd been a missionary to China until the Communists took over.

"I suppose it's sad now, knowing the church in China is extinct," I said, trying to make polite conversation.

"Extinct?" she exploded, her eyes snapping bright. "Let me tell you a story, young lady. One night the Communist Guard came through a little village where a Chinese pastor worked. They wrecked his church and made a great bonfire with all the Bibles in the village. When the flames were leaping hot and high, they left. Left the village in ruins. God's word burned to rubble and the church desecrated. The next morning the pastor stood over the charred remains, too heartbroken to cry. Hope gone. But do you know what he found there in the ashes?"

"What?" I asked, suddenly on the edge of my rocker.

Her eyes turned to the rain and her voice grew soft and

reverent. "The pastor noticed one page that had somehow escaped burning — part of the sixteenth chapter of Matthew. Most of the words had been singed away except for a fragment that said, 'Upon this rock I will build My church; and the gates of hell shall not prevail against it.' And we knew God had left that promise of hope in the rubble."

I must have registered disbelief, for she stopped. "Wait and see, young lady," she said. "God and His Church will not die out in China. Not there. Not anywhere."

"I hope you're right," I said with the doubt of youth.

As the memory of that rainy afternoon faded, I looked down at the newspaper that had brought it all tumbling back. The headline read, "The Church Shows New Life in China." I smiled to myself. The old woman was right.

Now, when I hear doomsayers predict the decline of faith or the demise of religion, I have a story to tell them. Why don't you remember it and tell it too?

Lord, let me take heart this day in knowing that even in the worst of times, You will prevail. —S.M.K.

---

20 *GIVING thanks always for all things . . .* —EPHESIANS 5:20

When I was a child, we wrote thank-you notes to God in church school on the Sunday before Thanksgiving. Maybe you did that, too. But when I was in the high-school class, our teacher took this idea a step further and had us write *next year's* letter, thanking God for the blessings we expected to receive between now and next Thanksgiving. It was a tough assignment, but it forced us to take stock of our values and focus on the future with hope and faith.

Being shy, I felt a need for more friends, so I thanked God for the friends He would send me during the coming year. I liked dramatics, so I thanked Him for giving me challenging roles in the upcoming school plays. I wanted to maintain high grades, so I decided what my average should be and thanked Him for helping me to achieve it.

The list went on, and though all of the things may not have come to pass exactly as I'd written in my thank-you note, many of them did. I think it's because the letter made my prayers more specific. I could pray, *believing* that these goals were achievable.

There are some important things I'd like to see happen in my life between now and next Thanksgiving. I think I'll show the Lord I trust Him to answer my prayers by writing next year's thank-you now. You might want to try it, too. If you do, be sure to save the letter because I think you'll be in for a happy surprise when you read it next year.

Thank You, Lord, for Your continued blessings — past, present and future. —M.M.H.

21

I AM a stranger in the earth: hide not Thy commandments from me. —PSALM 119:19

A Prayer For Bible Week
(November 21-27)

Without a map I came, Lord,
A stranger on this earth.
At first I stopped to ask directions
From the natives, but grew confused
By what they told me.

At a tourist bureau,
I acquired a Guidebook
Written, I was told,
By *the* Authority in the field.
I read.
I read some more,
And though the maps were clear,
The highways well delineated,
I grew impatient,
And thinking I might do better
    on my own,
I cast the Book aside.
Then I started out again
And wandered miserably
    in a maze of
    detours and
    dead ends until,
By chance, I found once more
That tattered Guidebook.

Now I try, day by day,
To follow its directions.
And day by day
I walk in peace, at last.

O Lord, thank You for the guides Your Book sets forth.
I want, I truly mean, to follow them.

—V.V.

22 *DO noble things, not dream them*...—CHARLES KINGSLEY

One evening just before a church potluck dinner, our friend Ruth had her purse snatched. It contained, among other things, her car keys and all that remained of her week's pay. As Ruth stood bewildered in our midst, I went up to offer help.

"What can I do?" I asked.

She just shook her head. "Nothing, thanks."

So that's what I did. Beyond feeling sorry, I did nothing.

Later I learned that Jean and Pete took up a collection to replace the stolen money. Dave found a locksmith who came immediately to replace her car locks. John organized a search of alley garbage cans in case the purse had been discarded. While I had been feeling overwhelmed and sorry, these people had come up with practical ways to help.

Jesus said, "As ye would that men should do to you, do ye also to them." (Luke 6:31) Now, at last, I'm beginning to understand.

Teach me, Lord, that when someone is in trouble expressing sympathy is just the first *thing I should do.* —P. H. S.

23 *PRAY as if everything depended on God and work as if everything depended on you.* —ANONYMOUS

Two farmers bought adjoining orange groves at the same time. One of them immediately began praying for his grove. He asked the Lord to send the right amount of sunshine and rain, to protect the trees from early frost, to keep them from destructive insects.

When harvest time came, his trees yielded a sparse return, but the other farmer had a bumper crop. "Did you pray for your grove?" he asked the other farmer.

"Yes."

"So did I. Why wasn't my crop as good as yours?"

"Well," his friend replied, "when we had drought, I hauled bucket after bucket and watered the trees. When frost warnings came, I started my smudge pots. I sprayed to reduce the insect population. Oh, I prayed too, but I reckon the Lord gave me two hands and a brain to help Him out in this growing business."

I often ask God to bless my projects, but if there is one thing I've learned in life it is this: Prayers have a better chance of being answered if you help them along with your hands and feet.

Lord, help me to be a do-er, as I grow as a pray-er. —S.P.W.

24

FAITH of our fathers! living still....

—FREDERICK W. FABER, HYMN

When you think of the great journeys your ancestors had to make to get to America, when you think of the hardships they overcame, do you sometimes feel weak in comparison? I know that I do. Where did they get their courage? I've wondered. Will I ever know such strength? For a long time the answers to these questions wouldn't come, but one recent afternoon, I got a clue.

My parents were moving to a new house and Mom and I were packing books into cartons. We came upon a big, glorious Bible—gilt-edged, 1000 pictures and a concordance. The spine was ripped and pages were unsewn, but my mother handled it lovingly.

On the inside front cover were listed the birthplaces and dates of her family, all the way back to Ireland. On a blank endpaper was a prayer composed by a great-aunt. And someone had long ago drawn stars by favorite psalms.

"This Bible has always had such a hold on me," my mother said. "Think of it, Edward, our family has been sharing this Book for ages. You know, I remember so well my grandfather poring over these very passages. They gave him such hope. You may not have to go through the trials he had to, but it's awfully good to know you have the same source of help."

My mother opened up new vistas for me that afternoon. Whenever I pick up a Bible, no matter how old or new it is, I can feel the ageless words giving me the same strength they gave my forebears. No wonder the Bible is eternal!

Oh, Lord, help me pass on what I've been given. —E.B.P.

---

25 THANKSGIVING

FOR unto every one that hath shall be given, and he shall have abundance... —MATTHEW 25:29

For fun I was giving my husband a magazine quiz, one of those designed to point the way to a bright, contented life.

"Do you get enough sleep?" I read. "Do you have a hobby?" Then I asked the next question without thinking. "Are you happy?" I held my breath. How could his answer be "Yes"? He was bound to a wheelchair by multiple sclerosis, dependent on me for so many things he once had done effortlessly himself.

"Of course," he said. Then he laughed. "Surprised?" he asked. "I don't know why. You know I never dwell on what I can't do. I concentrate on what I can."

"You're great about that," I said. "You inspire others."

He waved my compliment aside but gave me a pleased smile. "I've always loved to drive a car. I can still do it with hand controls. With some help, I go to the office every day and get around nicely in my power chair. Like other couples, we go out, have dinner with friends, take trips."

Then his eyes became serious. "Being handicapped *is* frustrating. But God gives us all a great abundance; there's so much to choose from, so many choices. I'd be a fool not to take advantage of them."

I put down the magazine. We didn't need the quiz.

Lord, in this wide, wonderful world You've given me, happiness depends on my outlook. On this Thanksgiving Day, and every day, keep me looking out for it. —M.B.D.

26

OPEN my ears that I may hear
Voices of truth Thou sendest clear.

—CLARA H. SCOTT, HYMN

Joan of Arc was asked this question: "If your Lord speaks to you, why doesn't He speak to me?"

"He does. You aren't listening," the Maid of Orleans calmly replied.

What about you? Are you listening?

You say, Lord, that we have ears but hear not. May this never be true of me. —D.D.

27

...I SEEK not Mine own will, but the will of the Father Which hath sent Me. —JOHN 5:30

Sobbing bitterly, four-year-old Benny ran from the room. Pieces of a child-sized jigsaw puzzle littered the carpet. His mother looked weary as she tried to explain her son's behavior.

"It's exasperating," she said. "The puzzle's designed for small children. And Benny does quite well, actually — until he gets to the sky part. With all that blue, he has to go by shapes.

"His problem *is*," his mother continued, "that instead of making the piece fit into the puzzle, he tries to turn the puzzle around until it fits the piece. And, well, the whole picture falls apart."

I guess we've all tried that, I thought later as I walked back across the lawn to my own house. Almost daily, I find myself trying to fit a friend or a family member into my plans instead of adapting myself to theirs. And what about God? Do I try to fit Him into my life instead of allowing Him to use my life as a part of His plan?

Remembering the fragmented puzzle, I know what I must do.

Father, forgive me when I try to fit You into my life instead of letting You place me where I am needed to fit Your plan.—J. M. B.

28 THE FIRST SUNDAY OF ADVENT

The daylight is shrinking and the nights are growing longer. We shiver a little, feeling the first longings for the warmth and brightness of Christmas. Once more the first Sunday of Advent is upon us. Once more the time has come to make ready our homes and churches — and ourselves — for the celebration of Jesus' birth.

Now, as the early night falls on this quiet Sunday, we come together to light the first candle of our Advent Wreath. The wreath, four red candles in a circle of evergreen, is again in its customary place of holiday honor. We gather around it. The lights of the house are turned off. We stand in darkness.

Is this what the world was like before Jesus came, we ask ourselves, was it as dark as this? We try to picture our world, our lives, without Him.

No, comes the answer, not total darkness.

A match is struck, a sudden burst of flame.

Not total darkness, for over the centuries mankind had the distant light of hope. God's prophets — the Micahs and Jeremiahs and Isaiahs — they told the world about the Messiah Who was coming. "The people that walked in darkness have seen a great light," said Isaiah. And for 800 years after that the world watched, and waited.

The match touches the wick of the first candle. The fire takes hold, and we remember the Saviour's words: "I am the light of the world. He that followeth me shall not walk in darkness."

The first candle of Advent is burning. Our faces glow in its light. We are on our way to Christmas! — V.V.

29

LORD, speak to me, that I may speak
In living echoes of Thy tone.

—FRANCES R. HAVERGAL, HYMN

Now and then I like to wander through the pages of *Bartlett's Familiar Quotations.* You can meet most of the great men and women of history there, and you can hear them speak words of great wisdom and power.

These enduring words always inspire me, but they often intimidate me, too, because I know I never say anything that well.

But the other day I think I learned something about the mysterious thing that makes words memorable. My husband had come home from an exhausting day at work. Irritated and preoccupied, he joined me for a sitting spell on the back steps.

Struggling to find a way to comfort him, I said, "But, honey, you're home now."

He was quiet for a moment, then a smile began to play on his lips and he said to me, "Home now. You know, that's one of the loveliest phrases I've ever heard."

Memorable words — sometimes God puts them in our hearts. All we have to do is draw them up.

Let me speak the words of Your love, Lord. They are immortal. —P. B. H.

---

30 *THOU wilt keep him in perfect peace, whose mind is stayed on Thee...* —ISAIAH 26:3

I used to marvel at old Mrs. Johnson and wonder at the source of her strength. She had lost her husband and her son. Finances had forced her to sell the family home and move to a small house at the edge of town. Yet I never heard her complain.

When she was nearly 90, she was still caring for her little house, tending her own yard and taking great pride in the garden she loved and nurtured. She generously shared her vegetables and lovely flowers with neighbors and friends.

Then she broke her hip. No longer able to care for her home, she was forced to move to a small apartment. My heart ached for her. Surely leaving her little home and beloved garden would crush even her staunch spirit.

One afternoon, shortly after she'd moved to her apartment, I visited her. I expected to find her sad and withdrawn, grieving over all she had lost. But instead she greeted me with the same cheerful good humor. She talked enthusiastically about her new apartment. "It has lots of light," she said. "Just right for my plants and they're doing beautifully. And when I lie in bed I can look through a window at the stars. I never lived where I could do that before. Isn't God wonderful the way He takes care of things?"

Then I knew the source of her joy and strength. It lay in acceptance. In living in the present rather than grieving for the past. And in trusting her future to God.

Lord, teach me, too, the way of acceptance. —A.J.L.

December

S	M	T	W	T	F	S
			1	2	3	4
5	6	7	8	9	10	11
12	13	14	15	16	17	18
19	20	21	22	23	24	25
26	27	28	29	30	31	

And the Second Is Like Unto It...

Thou shalt love thy neighbour as thyself.

—MATTHEW 22:39

DEAR Jesus,
Why all this fuss about neighbors?
Neighborhoods have changed a lot,
You know.
People come and go,
And neighborhoods lack identity today.
Why, my last neighbor
Was here just three months,
And the one who moved in today
Said he gets transferred every year.
He isn't even an American citizen...
Do you expect me to believe
That a coincidence of time and place
Bonds me to this neighbor?
...You do, don't You?
Now that I think about it
The message I should get
From my new neighbor
Is that the world is getting smaller
And moving faster.
You didn't tell me to categorize
Neighbors, did You, Lord?
You said: "Love thy neighbor."
And loving this new and different neighbor
Is more important today
Than it has ever been,
Isn't it?
Lord, I'm going to love
This new neighbor of mine
Until he loves me, too.

1

AND Thy word was unto me the joy and rejoicing of mine heart . . . —JEREMIAH 15:16

"You keep telling us that we should read the Bible daily," I said rather piously one day to a minister friend of mine. "But I've already read it through three times. Sometimes I wonder what good it does me to keep reading."

"Hmm . . . I see your point," he said, leaning back in his chair. "After three readings you must have the Bible pretty well memorized. You must gain a lot of strength from the stories of the great Bible heroes. Like Zerubbabel — doesn't he really inspire you to keep going when you hit one of those frustrating days?"

"Ah, well . . ." I stammered, "I'm not familiar with him."

"Oh, I see. After the long years of exile in Babylon, Zerubbabel led the Jewish people back to Jerusalem and supervised the rebuilding of the temple, despite intense efforts by his adversaries to stop the operation. (Ezra, Chapters 2-6) He was successful, too. Of course, when I'm feeling sorry for myself, I think of Mephibosheth; (II Samuel, Chapter 9) and when I see an example of God working through an unlikely person, I remember Cornelius. (Acts 10) There are many more exciting characters, too, but then, I don't want to bore you with this."

"It's not boring," I said quickly, and then added, "I think maybe there are at least three stories I should be reviewing."

It was a humbling revelation that day, but one which changed my whole outlook on Bible reading. Now I make it my goal to specifically note one *new* insight or verse or story that I read each day. One day I'll underline my Bible in blue, the next in red, then orange. And now it is like a rainbow of color, a reminder that the wisdom of the Bible — like a rainbow — is never-ending.

There's much I don't know about You and Your Holy Word, Lord, but there's so much I can learn. —J.J.

2 *GIVE, and it shall be given unto you; good measure, pressed down, and shaken together, and running over, shall men give into your bosom...* —LUKE 6:38

A few years ago I bought a green lipstick plant because I was assured that even a "brown thumb" like me would be rewarded by its lush blossoms. I watered it, misted it and fed it. It thrived. But no blossoms. After two years of waiting, I gave up on the blossoms and settled for the greenery it provided.

Recently a new secretary was settling in next to the office where I work. She put out a call for plant cuttings from the staff to brighten up her office.

That night I eyed the lipstick plant. It would yield some splendid cuttings, I thought, but I remembered the fern that had turned brown and died, and the sick ivy plant I'd given up on. When a plant was growing as well as the lipstick was, the best policy seemed to be to leave it alone.

The next day at work I discovered the new secretary hadn't received a single cutting. So, when I walked into the house that evening, I grabbed the scissors and cut off a foot of leafy green tendrils. The job was done before I could change my mind.

A couple of months later, I came home to an astonishing sight. There in the late-day sun my lipstick plant was alive with a wealth of pink blossoms.

There it was again: God's law of abundance. The more you give, the richer you become.

Lord, help me to trust my loving impulses. —R.H.H.

3 *...AND, behold, it was very good...* —GENESIS 1:31

In the 1930s Richard Kerr, a petroleum engineer, was working in the Saudi Arabian desert. His operations were painfully slow because endless stretches of deep sand prevented any kind of wheeled exploration. Only camels could make a go of it.

One day Kerr had a flash of scientific imagination. The camel, he reasoned, had been correctly designed for desert travel. Why not study it? He measured an average camel's weight and the spread of its foot. Then he designed wide, low pressure tires whose treads bore the same weight to surface ratio as the camel's foot. Eventually, the first dune buggy was born! And so, too, was modern oil exploration, because of Kerr's simple insight.

Nature teaches many lessons. One of the most important is that the Creator carefully designs a purpose into everything He has made — from a majestic mountain range to a camel's foot. What has He designed me for? Since He has given me a mind, I believe He means for me to discover His wonders and show my gratitude.

Lord, thank You. —G.S.

4 *BE strong and of a good courage; be not afraid, neither be thou dismayed: for the Lord thy God is with thee whithersoever thou goest.* —JOSHUA 1:9

I used to be the world's champ when it came to feeling unqualified. I was forever thinking anyone could do a better job than I could — any job. But a number of years ago a good friend, who had raised four children, told me, "It's funny, when we're young and don't know the first thing about raising kids — we have them.

We blunder along trying to learn about life and kids at the same time. And somehow we can even get excited about it. I guess that just proves the old saying, 'The Lord doesn't call the qualified, He qualifies the called.'"

So now when I get in one of my I-can't-because-I'm-unqualified moods, I tell myself that I *can* teach that Sunday-school class, I *can* talk to the kids in the neighborhood about the Lord, I *can* give old Mr. Johnston some words of encouragement, I *can*..., not because I'm qualified, but because the Lord is with me.

Thank You, Lord, for including me in Your great work.—B.M.

5 THE SECOND SUNDAY OF ADVENT

"I love Christmas, but this year it couldn't come at a worse time."
"I love Christmas, but I have so little money to spend."
"I love Christmas, but I sometimes wonder if it's really worth all the effort."

Reasons, we all have reasons for approaching the holidays with mixed emotions. Now, however, as we light the first and then the second candle of our Advent Wreath, our thoughts take us back to the Galilean hillside village of Nazareth in the days preceding the first Christmas.

"It couldn't have come at a worse time," Joseph might have said, when told that he must return to his ancestral home for the official census taking. It was a long way to Judea, almost a hundred miles, and it would take several days. He worried about the effect of the rigorous journey on Mary who was heavy with child. But the good and honorable Joseph accepted still another responsibility with stolid grace.

"I am a poor man," Joseph might have thought to himself as he contemplated the trip ahead. The donkey, the lodging, the food along the way, all of these things would be costly and burdensome. But Joseph was confident that somehow God would provide.

"I am so very tired," Mary might have thought as she and Joseph neared the City of David. And to arrive, at last, only to find no one, and no place, to receive them — how discouraged she had reason to be. But Mary's spirits did not flag. Mary knew, she *knew*, that all the struggle of the past days and months, and all the pain that she was beginning now to feel, were worth the effort.

And that's the way it is for us who light our Advent candles and make our plans to celebrate the birth of Jesus Christ: We *know* that Christmas is always worth the effort. — V.V.

6

ART thou weary, art thou troubled,
Art thou sore distressed?
"Come to me," saith One,
"and coming, Be at rest." —JOHN M. NEALE, HYMN

A short time ago my sister-in-law and I went into our local bank to take care of some business. As we stood by the counter, we simultaneously glanced up at the wall facing us. There, in large black letters, was the question, "What were you worrying about at this time last year?" We looked at each other and smiled.

On the way home each of us tried to recall the particular worry that had plagued us then. "Seems to me," I said after considerable thought, "I might have been worrying about the pain in my side that turned out to be caused by stress because I was worried about the pain in my side."

We laughed. Both of us had had our ups and downs, our

uncertainties, but one thing was sure: We were still here, but our worries weren't. And the surest thing of all — God was watching over us.

I'll always lose my worries, Lord, if I never lose sight of You.

—A.J.L.

7 *...KNOCK, and it shall be opened unto you.*

—MATTHEW 7:7

One day my tabby kitten Delancey dropped a rubber ball into an empty watering can and then put his head inside to retrieve it. But he couldn't get his head out again. He was stuck.

What panic! He backed off the windowsill, batting futilely at the can with his front paws, falling on the floor in a clatter. Then he zigzagged around the room, his muffled meows emanating pitifully from inside the watering can. I tried to catch him, but he wriggled away from me in fear.

Finally, he came to a halt in the corner, his sides heaving. I picked him up and gently talked to him. Little by little I was able to free him.

Poor Delancey! He didn't know enough to come to me right away. *But how often,* I thought, *am I exactly the same — panicking in the face of some problem, and not letting my Master take me gently in His hands. No, I prefer to exhaust myself first.*

Delancey licked his paws and calmly helped himself to a few laps of water as if nothing had happened. I'm not sure whether he learned anything, but I know I did: When in trouble, don't zigzag, head straight for the Lord. He wants to help, and can.

Lord, how often I let my problems imprison me — needlessly. If only I could learn to take them to You first.

—C.C.

8 *HE who receives a benefit with gratitude repays the first installment on his debt.* —SENECA

"It is more blessed to give than to receive." I've always tried to make that my motto, but recently I learned that receiving can be also blessed.

A flu bug got me in its grip and wouldn't let go for weeks. Keeping up with the simplest household chores was getting to be too much, but when anyone offered help I'd proudly say "Thanks, but no."

Finally my friend Florence showed up at my door with a pot of stew, insisting that I take it. We chatted until Florence got up and said, "Let me do your dishes while we talk."

"Absolutely not," I said.

"Listen, Isabel," she said to me, "it's not easy to be a receiver, but give me the chance to be a giver. Don't you think it's a good idea for you to let me enjoy the blessing of being one?"

Florence was right. A giver needs a receiver.

Lord, help me to be a gracious receiver. —I.C.

9 *GO, labor on! spend and be spent;*
Thy joy to do the Father's will:
It is the way the Master went —
Should not the servant tread it still?

—HORATIUS BONAR, HYMN

Have you ever noticed how when you give yourself to your work, your work gives you peace of mind in return? You become oblivious to all kinds of irritations that would normally disturb you. I've noticed that if I don't keep my shoulder to the wheel, the office chatter distracts me, the heat stifles me and the pile in my in-box dismays me.

Cotton Mather, the Puritan divine, once wrote about my sort of problem in terms of bees. Mather noticed that every swarm of bees has its own distinctive scent, and when swarms collide, the different smells of the two groups trigger an all-out war. But when bees are busy with the work nature entrusts them with — pollinating plants — they all get covered with pollen nectar. For that time they all smell the same. Peace reigns. Work gets done.

God, Mather goes on to say, has entrusted each of us with work to do. Of course there may be times when I feel as though I'm caught in a warring swarm. But if I immerse myself in the task at hand, then peace reigns. Work gets done.

So many times I let the irritations of life trap me, Lord, and yet You always give me the chance to work myself free. Thank You for Your patience, Father. —E.B.P.

---

10 *NOW thank we all our God*
With heart and hands and voices...

—MARTIN RINKART, HYMN

Years ago, when Rudyard Kipling was one of the more popular writers of his time, it was reported that he received ten shillings for every word he wrote. Some students at Oxford University sent Kipling ten shillings with the request that he send them back "one of your very best words." He cabled back: "Thanks!"

That amusing story has a way of sticking in my mind. Ever since

I first heard it I've thought of "thanks" as being a ten-shilling word. And the story has turned me into a kind of philanthropist. Every day I try to share the wealth of thank-yous with all those I meet. Carnegie built libraries; I can build goodwill.

Father, now that I've learned my "thank-yous" have value, help me to find other words I can use to enrich the lives of others.

—J. D. P.

11

REJOICE in the Lord alway; and again I say, Rejoice.

—PHILLIPPIANS 4:4

The late comedian Jack Benny was once honored with a distinguished humanitarian award. "I don't really deserve this award," Benny said in his acceptance speech, "but then, I have arthritis, and I don't deserve that either. Thank you very much."

Benny was being funny, of course, but there was some truth in what he said. I feel I didn't "deserve" to have my car break down yesterday, but then I didn't "deserve" the basket of fruit that some kind neighbor left on my doorstep. I didn't "deserve" the downpour on last Saturday's picnic, but then I didn't "deserve" that heartwarming telephone call from an old college friend.

So, it's not a question of whether I really deserve these things. The important question is this: do I handle them with good grace? That grace comes from God. If I have it, I can endure, and enjoy, the expected ups and downs of life.

Help me to accept the events of each day, dear Lord, with a humble and thankful heart.

—J. J.

12 THE THIRD SUNDAY OF ADVENT

"How many days until Christmas?"
"Thirteen."
"Only thirteen! Why, that's less than two weeks. Hardly enough time to..."

The holiday pace is quickening, the pressure is mounting; the nerves are beginning to jangle.

Hush!

It's time to light our Advent Wreath. Once more we join together to watch in prayerful silence as first one candle, then another, then still another is lighted. This evening we recall the words of the prophet Isaiah as he foretold the birth of the Saviour. "Unto us a child is born..." Isaiah said, "and His name shall be called..."

Let's say the words out loud, together, resoundingly!

"...Wonderful
Counsellor,
The mighty God,
The everlasting Father,
The Prince of Peace."

The Prince of Peace—how those words linger soothingly in the mind. They remind us that Jesus came to bring us peace, and not just freedom from wars among nations. Jesus came to show us that peace in the world must begin with people, with individuals. He came to bring each one of us peace of mind.

Now, on this Advent Sunday evening, we stand in the light of three flickering candles. Our ruffled temperaments grow calm. We feel a new serenity, a tranquility of heart and mind that we will take with us throughout the busy week ahead. — V.V.

13

. . . VENGEANCE is mine; I will repay, saith the Lord.

—ROMANS 12:19

"Turn the other cheek." It's hard to do, but it's important, and practical, too, as I learned a number of winters ago.

One wet, cold day I was driving downtown with my youngest boy strapped into the car seat beside me, when a young vandal on the sidewalk hurled an ice ball. It smashed a side window of my car and showered the seat with glass.

At first I was terrified for my child but, as soon as I saw he was all right, I jumped out of the car and took off after the fleeing juvenile.

Before I'd gotten very far, though, a man stopped me. He explained that he taught at the school the ice-ball thrower attended. "I'll see that the boy is disciplined," he said. "You get home before your baby gets too cold."

When I got home I began to see how badly I'd acted. In my ugly rage, I left my baby all alone in a freezing car.

I couldn't believe how quickly I'd let that mischief-maker turn me into someone just as irresponsible as he. That's when I began to see that I really must turn the other cheek, or vengeance will consume me.

Vengeance is destructive, Lord; let me always turn the other cheek.

—P.B.H.

14 *...YOUR Father knoweth that ye have need of these things.* —LUKE 12:30

Last Christmas season, while doing my shopping, I stopped to rest near a store's Santa Claus booth. In the line of children were a young mother and her boy talking in sign language. As his mother urged the little deaf boy forward, I braced myself for the awkward moment to come.

"And what do you want for Christmas?" Santa asked the little boy when he took his place in Santa's lap. The child, unable to speak, hung his head. He looked toward his mother and made signs to her, probably saying "Please help me, Mom." To my complete amazement, Santa grinned and began talking to the boy with *his* fingers. Santa knew sign language! The boy was so overjoyed he could barely contain himself.

As I resumed my gift-hunting, I felt joyful, too. The moment seemed like a little miracle, and it reminded me of a time when, as a child, I too felt the joy of being heard.

My grandmother was trying to teach me to pray. "But God is so far away," I remember saying to her as she put me to bed one night. I looked doubtfully out at the dark sky. "How can He *hear* me way up there?"

"But He's not way up there," Grandmother insisted. "He's right here in this room. You could whisper and He'd hear you."

And from that moment to this, I've not forgotten that.

You hear me above life's roar, Lord; You see me in the dark. You're ever near. —D.H.

15 *When the Bible Speaks to Me*

1 KINGS 19:11, 12

For weeks everything had gone wrong for me. Work projects failed. Relationships went sour. Bills piled up. I knew I had to get away.

Early one morning I took a bus to the New Jersey coast and soon found myself wandering down to a long stretch of beach called Sandy Hook. In summer it is a bustling resort area, but now, in the deep of winter, I had the place to myself. I made up my mind that I was going to walk and walk and walk until I was so tired that I couldn't think of problems.

As I wandered along beside the sea, I became aware of a phrase, only four words, echoing in my mind: "A still, small voice...A still, small voice," over and over. And the more I walked the more my mind seemed to whisper those words to me. There was something comforting about them, soothing. I knew that they came from somewhere in the Bible, but where?

When I got home that night, with the help of a Bible concordance I found the phrase in 1 Kings 19, and it had to do with Elijah, the prophet who was in trouble and hiding from his enemies. This is what it said:

> "And, behold, the Lord passed by, and a great and strong wind rent the mountains, and brake in pieces the rocks before the Lord; but the Lord was not in the wind: and after the wind an earthquake; but the Lord was not in the earthquake: And after the earthquake a fire; but the Lord was not in the fire: and after the fire a still small voice."

In a Bible commentary I read that the real translation of this familiar phrase is "a sound of gentle stillness" — which makes it very clear that God comes to us in moments of quiet.

So that was my problem! I was so busy worrying about myself

that I hadn't given God a chance. I had prayed, of course, but I hadn't taken the time to listen.

Since then, I have not needed the desolation of a lonely beach in deep winter for the moments of quiet when the Bible can speak to me. I can prepare myself anywhere, anytime, simply by shutting off the loudspeakers of my self-concern and opening my heart to the whisperings of God. — GLENN KITTLER

16

ALL good gifts around us
Are sent from heaven above,
Then thank the Lord, O thank the Lord
For all His love. —MATTHIAS CLAUDIUS, HYMN

We visited recently in my nephew's home on his birthday. Dinner finished, his wife brought out the expected candle-flaming cake, but it didn't say the usual "Happy Birthday." His two children had written — painstakingly — with a pastry tube: "To the greatest daddy in the world."

We were in Tulsa, Oklahoma, a short time ago, having dinner with friends at a marvelous restaurant. I commented on the delicious food. "We eat at home most of the time," my host said, looking at his wife lovingly. "I'm used to delicious meals."

A few nights ago Plaford and I called at the home of his brother Glen and wife. We knew he'd be leaving early the next morning on a long business trip. While I was in the kitchen, I noticed a note propped against a vase of flowers on the breakfast table. It read, "The happiest moment of my week will be the sound of your step as you open the door and call, 'I'm home, Honey.'"

Little unimportant things?

Little? Yes.

Unimportant? Never.

Lord, remind me always that affection and gratitude are not much good unless they are expressed. —Z.B.D.

17

FOR thou shalt be His witness unto all men...

—ACTS 22:15

Some people can go up to strangers and witness for Christ. I've never been able to do that. But I'm finding that there is more than one way to proclaim my love of Jesus.

Last year I received a Christmas card with a little, cross-shaped gold lapel pin attached. I fastened it to the collar of my blouse and forgot about it. Later in the day, I was giving speech therapy to a deaf girl named Linda. Progress with her had been slow because she seemed to have built a wall around herself that she wouldn't allow me to penetrate. Suddenly Linda let out a little squeal. Her face lit up as she pointed to my collar and said, very slowly and carefully, "Jee-sus!"

I smiled back, looked down at my collar and said, "Yes, Jesus!" Linda reached out, grabbed my hands, and squeezed them.

"Jesus," we repeated in unison, and suddenly we were sisters. Breakthrough!

Now I've started wearing a little gold cross on a chain around my neck every day. Some people look at it and then look away. But some people brighten up immediately because of my gentle, unobtrusive way of saying, I love Jesus.

I do love You, Jesus, and I'm proud to declare it. —M.M.H.

18

WHEN thou hast eaten and art full, then thou shalt bless the Lord thy God... —DEUTERONOMY 8:10

Getting ready for Christmas? Want to bake a special cake? Here's a time-honored recipe for: Scripture cake, King James Version.

1 cup Judges 5:25 (last clause)
2 cups Jeremiah 6:20 (sugar)
2 cups I Samuel 30:12
1 cup Numbers 17:8
1 cup Judges 4:19 (last clause)
2 cups Nahum 3:12 may be added if desired
2 tablespoons I Samuel 14:25
Season to taste, II Chronicles 9:9
6 Jeremiah 17:11
Pinch of Leviticus 2:13
4½ cups I Kings 4:22
2 tablespoons Amos 4:5 (baking soda)

Follow Solomon's prescription for making a good boy (Proverbs 23:14, first clause), and make a good cake. Bake in a tube pan in moderate oven for 30 minutes. Oh, and one more thing — if you give this cake as a gift, be sure to include a copy of the recipe.

And bless this food, Lord. —B.H.

19

THE FOURTH SUNDAY OF ADVENT

One candle...
Two...
Three...
Four...

At last all the candles of our Advent Wreath are burning, and we stand in their glow, contemplating their meaning for us.

We see their blazing light, and know that it proclaims the coming of the Great Light, Jesus Christ.

We feel the heat of the candle flames, and know the warmth of Jesus in a cold world.

We watch the way the wax melts, diminishing each candle, symbolizing the deepest meaning of Christmas: for as these tapers give away their light, they also give away themselves.

Now, we prepare to celebrate the birth of the One Who came to give us light — and gave Himself as well.

The room this evening is alive with light; our eyes shine; our thoughts shimmer with visions of holiday merriment. Let us go forth, then, to greet the newborn King with the true spirit of Christmas — which is selfless giving. — V.V.

20

GO ye therefore, and teach all nations . . .

—MATTHEW 28:19

A visiting minister took over the pulpit in our church last Sunday. The moment he began his sermon I was disturbed, for the minister's voice was loud and grating. His gestures were exaggerated. I found myself wondering where he could've picked up such peculiar mannerisms. I didn't know I'd actually tuned the minister out, until I heard him talking about the passage in Matthew where Jesus was scorned for breaking bread with sinners.

By that time I didn't know what the minister was talking about, because I hadn't been listening. I felt deeply ashamed. The minister had come to bring us a message of Biblical truth, and yet I did not hear it because I was too busy picking on his voice and style. What if God didn't like *my* style? Would He not listen to my prayers?

From that moment on I vowed to always keep my ears open to the words of God in God's house!

You always listen to my *prayers, Lord. May I always listen to You.*
—R.S.

21

...God resisteth the proud, but giveth grace to the humble.
—JAMES 4:6

When my oldest daughter Julie was in her first year of junior high school, she decided to run for school president. Because she was new in the school and running against two boys, I didn't think her chances were very good. The morning of the election I made sure to tell her that when she lost, she should graciously congratulate the winner. She should be a good loser.

When Julie came home that afternoon, I said to her, "Well, how did it go?"

"Mom, you didn't tell me what to do if I *won*!"

She had won, and she was right — I hadn't prepared her. As we sat down together, I tried to think of what makes a good winner. Eventually we both decided that winning shouldn't be looked on as a chance to be selfish and proud. Because, in electing Julie, her classmates had given her something precious: their trust. She owed them her best in return, in thanks.

Our little talk about winning got me thinking about how I act when I enjoy good fortune. I have received so many blessings from God. Do I just accept them, or do I take on the responsibility that I've been entrusted with? Blessings are gifts from God, freely given. I'll try to be worthy of them.

For all the blessings you've given me, Lord, I give You my whole heart in return.
—M.B.W.

22 *BE thou prepared...* —EZEKIEL 38:7

A television interviewer once asked champion race-car driver Johnny Rutherford if he believed he had to have good luck to win.

Rutherford paused only a moment, smiled and replied, "There is an old saying I like: 'Luck is where opportunity meets preparation.'"

God provides the opportunity every day. Are you making the preparation?

Lord, teach me that leading a disciplined, Christian life doesn't happen by chance. Make me willing to work. —D. D.

23 *NEITHER shall they say, Lo here! or, lo there! for, behold, the kingdom of God is within you.* —LUKE 17:21

I grew up in the Midwest, and when I was done with my schooling, I grew very restless to leave home. My hometown in Illinois seemed completely empty of adventure. But I was torn; after all, the place was my home.

My father settled my confusion one day when he gave me a book about the great painter, Grant Wood. As I read, I found that Wood had also been a Midwestern farm boy.

He, too, had gotten very restless as he grew, and finally went off to Paris. Wood lived the life of an artist in Paris, but wasn't able to produce any work that he could call his own. Both his life and his art at this time were pale imitations of the European masters.

When Wood inevitably returned to the Midwest, he felt defeated, but nonetheless started painting the fields and barns of his boyhood. One particular painting brought everything together for him. Wood posed his dentist and his sister side by side, placed a pitchfork in the man's hand, and painted *American Gothic*. Wood had found a place he could call his own: home.

I think I saw in Grant Wood what my father wanted me to see: that though I might wander off, I should never forget that home is where the true treasures of my life lie.

Dear Lord, thank You for the wealth that lies all around me, right now, right where I am. —R.S.

---

24 *...THE Lord is in His holy temple: let all the earth keep silence before Him.* —HABAKKUK 2:20

Not long ago members of the Lutheran Church of Peace in Rochester, New York, received word that there was to be a "no excuse" Sunday. On this special day there would be cots for those who needed to rest, blankets for those who claimed the church was too cold, fans for those who felt the church was too hot, hypocrite scorecards for those who claimed there were too many hypocrites at worship, aspirin for those who had headaches, poinsettias on the altar for those who only worship at Christmas and lilies for those who only worship at Easter! The pastor said attendance went up 50 percent above the previous Sunday.

I laughed when I heard about this "way-out" way of emphasizing a point, but I stopped smiling as I began to think of all the excuses I had for not worshiping God — not just on Sunday — but in my *daily* life. My favorite excuse: "Too busy," followed by "too tired," etc....

Come to think of it — I need to have a "no excuse" worship service at least once a day!

Father, I have no reasons for neglecting a daily time with You — only excuses. Forgive me — and thank You for giving me another chance... —J.D.P.

25 CHRISTMAS

As we prepare Daily Guideposts *each year, it has become a custom to choose a much-loved Christmas story for you to read on this special day. This year we hope that you'll gather your family around you and read aloud "A Gift of the Heart." It's by Dr. Peale, and it's a story that really happened. And we hope that because of it, Christmas will happen to you.*

—THE EDITORS

New York City, where I live, is impressive at any time; but as Christmas approaches, it's overwhelming. Store windows blaze with lights and color, furs and jewels. Golden angels, 40 feet tall, hover over Fifth Avenue. Wealth, power, opulence... nothing in the world can match this fabulous display.

Through the gleaming canyons, people hurry to find last-minute gifts. Money seems to be no problem. If there's a problem, it's that the recipients so often have everything they need or want that it's hard to find anything suitable, anything that will really say, "I love you."

As Christ's birthday drew near several years ago, a stranger was faced with just that problem. A girl in her late teens, she had come from Switzerland to live in an American home and perfect her English. In return, she was willing to act as secretary, mind the grandchildren, do anything she was asked. Her name was Ursula.

One of the tasks her employers gave Ursula was keeping track of Christmas presents as they arrived and acknowledging them. Ursula kept a faithful record, but with a growing sense of concern. She was grateful to her American friends; she wanted to show her gratitude by giving them a Christmas present. But nothing that she could buy with her small allowance could compare with the gifts she was recording daily. Besides, it seemed that her employers already had everything.

Then, in the solitude of her little room a few days before Christmas, a marvelous idea came to Ursula. It was almost as if a voice spoke clearly, inside her head. "It's true," said the voice, "that many people in this city have much more than you do. But surely there are many who have far less. If you will think about this, you may find a solution to what's troubling you."

Ursula thought long and hard. Finally on her day off, which was Christmas Eve, she went to a large department store. She moved slowly along the crowded aisles, selecting and rejecting things in her mind. At last she bought something and had it wrapped in gaily colored paper. She went out into the gray twilight and looked helplessly around. Finally she went up to a doorman, resplendent in blue and gold. "Excuse, please," she said in her hesitant English, "can you tell me where to find a poor street?"

The doorman looked doubtful. "Well, you might try Harlem. Or down in the Village. Or the Lower East Side, maybe."

But these names meant nothing to Ursula.

Holding her package carefully, Ursula walked on, head bowed against the sharp wind. If a street looked poorer than the one she was on, she took it. But none seemed like the slums she had heard about. Once she stopped a woman. "Please, where do the very poor people live?" But the woman gave her a stare and hurried on.

Darkness came sifting from the sky. Ursula was cold and discouraged and afraid of becoming lost. She came to an intersection and stood forlornly on the corner. What she was trying to do suddenly seemed foolish, impulsive, absurd. Then, through the traffic's roar, she heard the cheerful tinkle of a Salvation Army bell.

At once Ursula felt better; the Salvation Army was part of life in Switzerland too. Hurrying up to the bell-ringer, she asked, "Can you help me? I'm looking for a baby. I have here a little present for the poorest baby I can find."

The Salvation Army man wrinkled his forehead, hesitating. Then with a smile he said, "It's almost six o'clock. My relief will show up then. If you want to wait, and if you can afford a dollar taxi ride, I'll take you up to a family in my own neighborhood who needs just about everything and they have a new baby."

"Wonderful!" said Ursula.

The substitute bell-ringer came, and a taxi was hailed. In its welcome warmth, Ursula told her new friend about herself, what she was trying to do. He listened in silence, and the taxi driver listened too. When they reached their destination, the driver said, "Take your time, Miss. I'll wait for you."

On the sidewalk, Ursula stared up at the forbidding tenement, dark, decaying, saturated with hopelessness. "Shall we go up?" the Salvation Army man asked.

But Ursula shook her head. "They would try to thank me, and this is not from me." She pressed the package into his hand. "Take it up for me, please. Say it's from...from someone who has everything."

Arriving back at the apartment house on Fifth Avenue where she lived, she fumbled in her purse. But the driver flicked the flag up. "No charge, Miss. I've already been paid."

Ursula was up early the next day. She set the table with special care. By the time she had finished, the family was awake, and there was all the excitement and laughter of Christmas morning. Soon the living room was a sea of gay discarded wrappings. Ursula thanked everyone for the presents she received. Finally, when there was a lull, she began to explain hesitantly why there seemed to be none from her. When she finished, there was a long silence. No one seemed to trust himself to speak. "So you see," said Ursula, "I try to do a kindness in your name. And this is my Christmas present to you."

How do I happen to know this? I know it because ours was the home where Ursula lived. Ours was the Christmas she shared. We were like many Americans, so richly blessed that to this child from across the sea there seemed to be nothing she could add to the material things we already had. And so she offered something of far greater value: an act of kindness carried out in our name, a gift of the heart.

26 *...TAKE no thought for your life, what ye shall eat, or what ye shall drink; nor yet for your body, what ye shall put on. Is not the life more than meat, and the body than raiment?* —MATTHEW 6:25

I remember one Christmas when I was a kid, my baby sister opened her present, threw away the toy, and played with the box. I thought it was so funny, I horselaughed until I was rolling on the floor. Since then I've found that many youngsters mistake the wrappings for the real present. But so do adults.

I try not to fall into the same trap. I am thankful to God for the house we live in. But I know that it is only the wrapping on the Lord's gift. He didn't just give us a house. It is a home, a sanctuary where my family learns the meaning of life, love and happiness in the will of the Lord.

I think of the job I have as a gift from God. But the important thing about it is not the money I make; that's only the wrapping. My job is where I can learn to deal with others, a challenging ministry where my Christian life can be a light to those around me.

My car isn't just a shining metal extension of my pride. It is a tool the Lord has given me so that I can make better use of my time for Him. He's letting me know my time is valuable to Him.

Part of my spiritual growth is learning where the values in life are. Can *you* list some of the gifts the Lord has given you? Do you see the real treasures concealed by the wrappings? Name them and discover with me the richness and largeness of life.

Lord, let me always be able to see the true wonders of Your grace. —B.M.

---

27 *JUDGE not, and ye shall not be judged: condemn not, and ye shall not be condemned...* —LUKE 6:37

I left church that sunshiny morning feeling a bit smug. The sermon had been a stern attack on the "big three" — alcohol, cigarettes and drugs. The pastor had dwelt on the bad effects these substances had on our bodies, our "temples of the Living Lord." I could be smug. I was a non smoker, non drinker, who had never touched hard drugs, and I felt a benign kind of pity for those who had.

And then the Lord, as He so frequently does, popped my balloon. He reminded me in clear "instant replays" of those times in my life when I had been: "drunk" with the pride of overcoming these awful temptations; "smoking" over the way I'd been slighted by a busy salesclerk; "high" over the misfortune of someone I had no use for because it served him right. He reminded me of the times when I had "hangovers" of depression when life didn't give me what I thought I deserved; when I'd "spaced out" trying to emulate a group I thought had the answers, but weren't God-centered; when I had been "burned up" over tasks my children had left undone after I had assigned them.

A quiet voice seemed to say, "Shall I go on?"

Contritely I replied, "No, thanks. I've got the message."

And the message was that I had no cause to be smug. I could do as much damage to myself by being consumed by pride, greed, envy, jealousy, hatred and fear, as I could by consuming harmful substances.

Thanks, Lord, for reminding me to review my own shortcomings before smugly pointing to those of others. —D.S.

---

28 *TAKE from our souls the strain and stress,*
And let our ordered lives confess
The beauty of Thy peace. —JOHN G. WHITTIER, HYMN

Do you ever have a word going through your mind, repeating itself for no reason you can think of? That happened to me the other day. A word I almost never have occasion to use, yet it kept echoing in my head: *relinquish.*

Off and on all day I tried to think why, but the answer didn't come until that night, as I said my evening prayers. For nearly a week they'd been the same: Lord, heal this friendship, gone sour because of a misunderstanding. And help me find time for daily reading of Your Word — how often I fail! And oh, Lord, these petty family squabbles that keep us from enjoying each other in love and kindness — take them away!

Then, there it was again, that word. *Relinquish.* And I recognized it now as the answer to my prayers. God, telling me what I must do:

Relinquish — the feelings of hurt pride. Take the first step — call my friend and apologize for my own thoughtlessness, which certainly played a part in our misunderstanding.

Relinquish — all the time-wasting rituals and routines that add up to "no time" for the really important things. Give Bible reading the priority it deserves!

Relinquish — the need to be right, the attempts to pull others'

strings, to run each family member's life to fit *my* convenience.
God speaks to me all the time, and often He uses just one word.

Lord, make me aware of the many ways You speak to me.—A. F.

---

29 *O ALL ye works of the Lord, bless ye the Lord,*
Praise Him and magnify Him for ever.

—THE BOOK OF COMMON PRAYER

One year my sister-in-law gave me a five-year-diary for Christmas. "Start on January first," she said, "and, since there isn't much room for each day's entry, wait till night and then fill in the most important things that happened that day — things you want most to remember."

On New Year's Eve the following December, I sat down and leafed through the pages I'd filled during the year. The entries threw a new light on the "important" things in my life. Of course I had noted parties, trips taken, and similar mundane things; but the entries that caught and held my attention surprised me.

I lingered pleasantly over such entries as a winter's walk along our snow-lined country road; a few minutes alone outside during an evening when frosty stars hung low; the pleasant smell of wood smoke on the night air; the joy of snuggling a new fuzzy puppy; a pleasant visit with a friend who stopped by and stayed for coffee; the wild, free call of redwings arriving ahead of schedule; clothes drying in the March breeze; a gift of dandelion blossoms from a little neighbor boy. Common, everyday things — not important at all. But how good to know that these are the real treasures.

Lord, thank You for showing me that, no matter how little there is in my bank account, I shall never be poor. —A. J. L.

30 *PERFECT submission, all is at rest,*
I in my Saviour am happy and blest.

—FANNY J. CROSBY, HYMN

I haven't reached what you'd call old age yet, but I've lived a long time and have plenty of scars to prove it. It doesn't bother me any more that I'm not the attractive young woman I once thought I was, for I feel *real*. You'd know what I meant by this if you'd ever read the children's classic "The Velveteen Rabbit" by Margery Williams. That book is all about what it takes for toys to become real — and the wise Skin Horse knows the secret:

"When a child loves you for a long, long time, not just to play with, but *really* loves you, then you become Real. It doesn't happen all at once. You become. It takes a long time," the Skin Horse says.

"Generally, by the time you are Real, most of your hair has been loved off, your eyes drop out and you get loose in the joints and very shabby. But these things don't matter at all, because once you are Real you can't be ugly, except to people who don't understand."

Well, nowadays I need glasses and my joints creak a bit, but I don't care. I have a Heavenly Father Who loves me, *really* loves me. I am secure in His love. To Him, I am beautiful. To Him I am very Real.

And thank You, Father, for the love I receive from others, too!

—J. D. P.

31 *I PRESS toward the mark for the prize of the high calling of God in Christ Jesus.* —PHILIPPIANS 3:14

It was New Year's Eve and I sat in church. All in all it had been a good year. I'd had a couple of successes in my new writing career — very small ones to be sure — but the taste of even tiny victories can linger with bewitching sweetness.

Someone nearby dropped a hymn book, jarring me back to the minister's voice.

"There was a boy who was painting a great picture," the minister said. "So great that his teacher exclaimed over its progress every day, calling the other students so that they would see the lessons being put to use.

"Weeks went by and finally the painting was done. The next day the boy would frame it, but that night a hot-water pipe burst and in the morning the painting was a mess of bleeding colors.

"The boy was heartbroken. He said to the teacher, 'My work is ruined.'

"But the teacher thought differently. 'No, it's not. The real work you did wasn't on the canvas. The real work was what you learned in your mind. Now use that learning to bring out the even better picture that's inside of you.'"

As the preacher finished his sermon, he said two words, two simple words to get us through the New Year. He said, "Press on."

So many times I'd been told to put my failures behind me, but now I was being told to leave my successes behind, too.

And that makes sense. Perseverance, not satisfaction, is what enables me to grow nearer to the person God wants me to be.

I approach this New Year eagerly, Lord, because it gives me the chance to bring out the very best You have put in me.—S.M.K.

The Guideposts Family of Contributors

The following devotional items were prepared by Guideposts editors.

Prayer/poems introducing each month: January, April, May, August, November—VAN VARNER. February, March—ELEANOR SASS. June, July, December—JAMES MCDERMOTT. September, October—EDWARD PITONIAK.

Lenten graces: First week—ARTHUR GORDON. Second week—JAMES MCDERMOTT. Third and fourth weeks—VAN VARNER. Fifth week—EDWARD PITONIAK.

M.A. (Manuel Almada) New Bedford, MA. Advertising copywriter. Business consultant. Author of over 500 magazine articles. pp. 122, 134, 198, 249, 291, 326.

J.M.B. (June Masters Bacher) Escondido, CA. Columnist, poet, teacher, inspirational writer. Latest book: *Quiet Moments*. pp. 33, 50, 89, 113, 135, 145, 176, 193, 218, 239, 260, 288, 341.

K.B. (Karen Barber) Columbia, SC. Freelance writer, Editor: Women's Aglow Newsletter. p. 215.

I.B. (Idella Bodie) Aiken, SC. High-school English teacher. Juvenile novelist. Latest book: *South Carolina Women: They Dared to Lead*. p. 294.

T.B. (Thelma Brisbine) Wenatchee, WA. Inspirational writer. pp. 85, 303.

T.C. (Terri Castillo) Queens, NY. Assistant book editor, *Guideposts* magazine. p. 59.

I.C. (Isabel Champ) Mulino, OR. Inspirational writer. Photojournalist. Newspaper columnist and freelance magazine contributor. pp. 52, 54, 74, 124, 139, 148, 206, 247, 329, 354.

A.C. (Annamae Cheney) Escondido, CA. Freelance magazine writer, inspirational writer. pp. 33, 77.

C.C. (Christine Conti) New York, NY. Assistant editor, *Guideposts* magazine. pp. 25, 83, 115, 142, 179, 233, 263, 322, 330, 353.

C.M.C. (Catherine M. Cox) Anoka, MN. Inspirational writer. p. 261.

D.C.C. (Doris C. Crandall) Amarillo, TX. Inspirational writer. p. 184.

C.M.D. (Charles M. Davis) Waverly, OH. Public relations and advertising consultant. Inspirational and business magazine writer. pp. 44, 88, 119, 207, 236.

M.B.D. (Mary Bouton Davis) Canoga Park, CA. Freelance writer. Columnist. Inspirational writer. p. 339.

Z.B.D. (Zona B. Davis) Effingham, IL. Newscaster. Inspirational writer, speaker. TV, radio and newswire correspondent. pp. 48, 168, 194, 233, 240, 247, 259, 311, 318, 361.

W.D. (William Deerfield) West Orange, NJ. Associate editor, *Guideposts* magazine. pp. 30, 55, 70, 177, 246.

B.H.D. (Barbara Hudson Dudley) Thousand Oaks, CA. Freelance writer. Former college drama professor. Latest book: *Henrietta Mears Story*. pp. 273, 280, 308.

D.D. (Drue Duke) Sheffield, AL. Inspirational writer, magazine writer. Poet and playwright. Certified lay speaker, Methodist Church. pp. 122, 133, 137, 141, 162, 243, 274, 307, 332, 340, 366.

L.D. (Lois Duncan) Albuquerque, NM. Author of 27 books for juveniles. Contributor to national magazines. Inspirational writer. Latest book: *How to Write and Sell Your Personal Experiences*. pp. 138, 265.

D.E. (Dorothy Enke) Emerson, NE. Inspirational writer. pp. 146, 245, 269, 307, 319.

J.E. (Jan Evans) Sacramento, CA. Freelance magazine writer. Inspirational writer. Poet. pp. 111, 150, 242, 256.

F.F. (Faye Field) Longview, TX. Former college English teacher. Inspirational writer, lecturer. Poet. Author of over 200 magazine articles. pp. 15, 114, 196, 219, 266, 302.

A.F. (Anne FitzPatrick) Dewitt, NY. Former psychiatric aide. Inspirational writer. Freelance writer. pp. 18, 83, 294, 373.

A.G. (Arthur Gordon) Savannah, GA. Editorial Director, *Guideposts* magazine. Former staff writer, *Reader's Digest*. Novelist. Latest book: *A Touch of Wonder*. pp. 16, 79, 216, 287.

B.R.G. (Betty R. Graham) Alexandria, VA. Writer/editor, Dept. of the Army. Organist for Woodlawn Baptist Church. Former creative writing teacher. Inspirational writer. pp. 21, 41, 75, 197, 297.

D.H. (Doris Haase) Burbank, CA. Educational secretary. Inspirational writer. pp. 99, 152, 325, 359.

J.L.H. (Janice L. Hansen) Greenville, MI. Inspirational writer. Radio storywriter for "Children's Bible Hour." Sunday-school assignment writer. p. 118.

H.J.H. (H. Jack Haring) Grover's Mill, NJ. Administrative editor, *Guideposts* magazine. pp. 186, 328.

R.H.H. (Rosalind Hoyle Haring) Grover's Mill, NJ. Freelance writer. p. 349.

M.F.H. (Madge Fisher Harrah) Albuquerque, NM. Freelance writer and artist. pp. 29, 238.

B.H. (Beverly Heirich) Maui, HI. Inspirational writer. Former magazine editor and journalist. pp. 71, 248, 309, 363.

M.M.H. (Marilyn Morgan Helleberg) Kearney, NE. Inspirational writer. Prayer retreat leader. Former college English teacher. Latest book: *Beyond TM: A Practical Guide to the Lost Traditions of Christian Meditation*. pp. 14, 19, 32, 45, 56, 69, 76, 88, 100, 136, 153, 172, 184, 217, 238, 243, 250, 267, 292, 301, 334, 362.

J.H. (Jeanne Hill) Akron, OH. Registered nurse. Inspirational writer and speaker. Latest book: *Seven Secrets of Prayer Joy*. p. 174.

M.H. (Marjorie Holmes) McMurray, PA. Contributing editor, *Guideposts* magazine. Inspirational writer. Nationally syndicated columnist. Latest book: *God and Vitamins—How Exercise, Diet, and Faith Can Change Your Life*. pp. 28, 60, 73, 170, 232, 255.

P.B.H. (Phoebe Bell Honig) Pittsfield, MA. Freelance writer. Artist and poet. pp. 51, 144, 162, 201, 234, 264, 271, 290, 324, 342, 358.

C.H. (Charlotte Hutchison) Carlsbad, CA. Freelance inspirational writer. p. 109.

J.J. (Jeff Japinga) Princeton, NJ. Editorial assistant, *Guideposts* magazine. pp. 98, 185, 224, 328, 348, 356.

E.A.J. (Ellen A. Javernick) Loveland, CO. Preschool teacher. Inspirational and children's writer. p. 300.

M.C.J. (Marilyn Connell Jensen) Bronxville, NY. Book editor, *Guideposts* magazine. pp. 169, 296.

E.J. (Eunice Jordan) Marysville, OH. Inspirational writer and poet. p. 298.

S.J. (Sam Justice) Yonkers, NY. College English teacher. Business writer. Latest book: *Dealing With the Financial Press*. p. 304.

S.M.K. (Sue Monk Kidd) Anderson, SC. Contributing editor, *Guideposts* magazine. Inspirational writer and speaker. Former registered nurse. pp. 11, 26, 40, 47, 52, 68, 78, 99, 117, 147, 171, 182, 193, 210, 229, 244, 262, 272, 289, 295, 305, 323, 333, 376.

G.K. (Glenn Kittler) New York, NY. Contributing editor, *Guideposts* magazine. Journalist and inspirational writer. Author of 40 books. pp. 13, 42, 59, 81, 178, 192, 228, 360.

L.A.L. (Lynne A. Laukhuf) Fairfield, CT. Librarian. Inspirational writer. p. 168.

S.L. (Sue Lennon) Bloomfield Hills, MI. Former teacher. Inspirational writer. p. 327.

A.J.L. (Aletha J. Lindstrom) Battle Creek, MI. Inspirational and children's writer. Librarian. Former teacher. Latest book: *Sojourner Truth: Slave, Abolitionist, Worker for Women's Rights*. pp. 27, 46, 156, 164, 279, 308, 343, 352, 374.

D.L. (Daniel Little) Vestal, NY. Wholesale florist. Pastor. Inspirational writer. p. 268.

J.McD. (James McDermott) Brooklyn, NY. Senior editor, *Guideposts* magazine. pp. 23, 75, 111, 120, 167, 213, 237, 254, 290, 318.

M.J.M. (Mary Jane Meyer) Enid, OK. Freelance inspirational writer. Poet. Latest book: *Bits of Faith and Love and Fun*. p. 17.

B.M. (Brian Miller) Mounds, OK. Missionary. Freelance writer. pp. 85, 269, 350, 371.

G.N. (Gertrude Naugler) Olympia, WA. Freelance writer. Newspaper columnist. Latest book: *The World and Julie*. pp. 24, 57, 278.

D.A.P. (Dee Ann Palmer) Redlands, CA. Registered nurse. Freelance writer. p. 62.

J.D.P. (Jeanette Doyle Parr) Decatur, AR. Inspirational writer. pp. 355, 367, 375.

P.R.P. (Patricia R. Patterson) Gainesville, FL. Former newspaperwoman. Inspirational writer. pp. 181, 202.

N.V.P. (Norman Vincent Peale) Pawling, NY. Minister, Marble Collegiate Church. Founder, co-publisher and editor of *Guideposts* magazine. Lecturer and writer. Co-founder of the Institutes of Religion and Health. Founder of the Foundation for Christian Living. Author of 21 inspirational books of which the latest is: *Dynamic Imaging*. pp. 12, 25, 68, 92, 121, 140, 286, 368.

R.S.P. (Ruth Stafford Peale) Pawling, NY. Co-publisher and editor of *Guideposts* magazine. General Secretary and editor-in-chief of the Foundation for Christian Living. Member, Board of Directors of the Institutes of Religion and Health. Nationally syndicated columnist and lecturer. Latest book: *The Adventure of Being a Wife*. p. 175.

E.B.P. (Edward B. Pitoniak) New York, NY. Editorial assistant, *Guideposts* magazine. pp. 20, 132, 163, 214, 227, 257, 276, 293, 338, 354.

M.R. (Marjorie Reidhead) Reston, VA. Schoolteacher. Former missionary. Inspirational writer. p. 322.

F.R. (Fran Roberts) Newton, NJ. Freelance writer and editor. Former newspaperwoman. Author of award-winning column: *Thursday's Child*. p. 280.

G.J.R. (Grady Jim Robinson) St. Louis, MO. Newspaper columnist. Magazine journalist. Banquet speaker. p. 31.

E.V.S. (Eleanor V. Sass) New York, NY. Associate editor, *Guideposts* magazine. pp. 82, 116, 149, 180, 208, 226, 312.

R.S. (Richard Schneider) Rye, NY. Senior editor, *Guideposts* magazine. Latest book: *Crossroads*, with Leon Jaworski. pp. 34, 58, 145, 212, 231, 258, 270, 320, 331, 364, 366.

N.S.S. (Nancy S. Schraffenberger) New York, NY. Associate editor, *Guideposts* magazine. pp. 177, 197, 226, 310, 321.

N.S. (Nita Schuh) Dallas, TX. Captain, U.S. Navy (Retired). Inspirational writer. Latest book: *After Winter, Spring*. pp. 50, 203.

P.V.S. (Penney V. Schwab) Copeland, KS. Inspirational writer. Columnist. Organist. pp. 10, 143, 241.

J.S. (Janet Shaffer) Lynchburg, VA. Freelance writer, photographer, artist. Editor, industrial publication. Latest book: *Peter Francisco: Virginia Giant*. p. 151.

K.B.S. (Kathryn B. Slattery) Minnetonka, MN. Contributing editor, *Guideposts* magazine. Latest book: *A Bright-Shining Place*. p. 151.

G.S. (Gary Sledge) Pleasantville, NY. Director of Research and Development and Planned Giving, Guideposts Outreach Ministries. p. 350.

S.M.S. (Shari Myers Smith) South Salem, NY. Freelance writer. Inspirational writer. p. 91.

P.H.S. (Patricia H. Sprinkle) Chicago, IL. Freelance writer. Latest book: *Hunger: Understanding the Crisis Through Games, Drama and Songs*. pp. 18, 40, 134, 154, 166, 207, 219, 299, 337.

R.R.S. (Rebecca R. Staton) Mattoon, IL. Director of children's day-care center. p. 182.

P.S. (Pat Sullivan) Chicago, IL. Inspirational writer. Speech writer. Newspaper columnist. p. 200.

D.S. (Doris Swehla) Spokane, WA. Freelance writer. Inspirational writer. Newsletter editor. pp. 35, 165, 199, 372.

L.V. (Lael Van Riper) Montrose, CO. Community Outreach worker. Freelance writer. p. 118.

V.V. (Van Varner) New York, NY. Senior Staff editor, *Guideposts* magazine. pp. 13, 36, 44, 49, 131, 204, 306, 335, 341, 351, 357, 363.

S.P.W. (Shirley Pope Waite) Walla, Walla, WA. Freelance inspirational writer and speaker. Community college and inspirational writing instructor. pp. 61, 130, 209, 256, 337.

M.W. (Marilyn Watson) Roswell, NM. Freelance inspirational writer and artist. p. 277.

M.G.W. (Madeline G. Weatherford) Bronx, NY. Executive secretary, *Guideposts* magazine. p. 235.

M.B.W. (Marion Bond West) Lilburn, GA. Inspirational writer and lecturer. Latest book: *Learning to Lean*. pp. 22, 43, 71, 86, 112, 123, 154, 173, 183, 212, 224, 275, 365.

L.E.W. (Lois E. Woods) Sumner, WA. Bookkeeper. Freelance writer. pp. 91, 110, 155, 205.

A NOTE FROM THE EDITORS

This devotional book was prepared by the same editorial staff that creates *Guideposts*, a monthly magazine filled with true stories of people's adventures in faith.

If you have found enjoyment in *Daily Guideposts*, we think you'll find monthly enjoyment — and inspiration — in the exciting and faith-filled stories that appear in our magazine.

Guideposts is not sold on the newsstand. It's available by subscription only. And subscribing is easy. All you have to do is write Guideposts Associates, Inc.; Carmel, New York 10512. A year's subscription costs only $4.95 in the United States, $5.95 in Canada and overseas.

When you subscribe, each month you can count on receiving exciting new evidence of God's presence, His guidance and His limitless love for all of us.